MYSTIC SEAPORT'S

SEAFOOD SECRETS

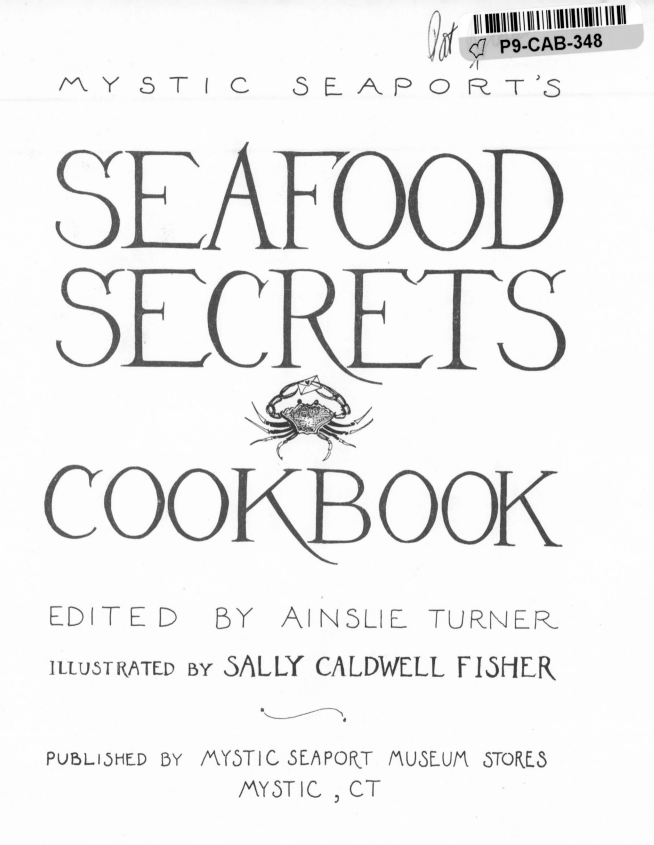

COOKBOOK

EDITED BY AINSLIE TURNER

ILLUSTRATED BY SALLY CALDWELL FISHER

PUBLISHED BY MYSTIC SEAPORT MUSEUM STORES
MYSTIC, CT

Net income earned from *Mystic Seaport's Seafood Secrets Cookbook* will go toward supporting the programs at Mystic Seaport Museum, a non-profit educational institution.

For additional copies of *Mystic Seaport's Seafood Secrets Cookbook*, use the Order Blank in the back of the book or write directly to: Mystic Seaport Museum Stores
                          Bookstore
                          Mystic, CT 06355

                      or for credit card orders:
                      Call Toll Free (800) 331-BOOK
                         in Conn. (203) 572-8551

Suggested retail price: $14.95 + $4.00 for packing and shipping charges. (Connecticut residents add State Sales Tax.)

Mystic Seaport's Seafood Secrets Cookbook may be obtained by organizations for fund-raising projects or by retail outlets at special rates. Write to the above address for all of the details or call the above number.

ISBN 0-939510-08-1

First printing 1990
Second printing 1991

CONTENTS

INTRODUCTION

So many of my special childhood memories are linked to important family get-togethers and cooking traditions. The sounds and smells of someone lovingly preparing a simple dinner, or planning a lavish celebration still stir my heart. And since I was raised in New England, seafood played a large part in these celebrations and everyday cooking experiences.

At our house you did not need a calendar to tell you when Friday rolled around. My father believed that fish "just tended" to be fresher on Friday. And, of course, we all believed him. We never knew what fish he would bring home for dinner on Friday. Sometimes, an end of the week business trip would include Cape Cod, and on those Fridays he'd pull up in the driveway and call out to my mother to "put on the pot." That night we would feast on steamed lobsters, garlic shrimp or a casserole of clams and mussels. Other Fridays had mother laying out bowls of freshly beaten eggs, flour, and bread crumbs ready to dip and sauté thick cod steaks, Boston haddock or juicy Nantucket scallops.

Looking back, I realize our New England family was very lucky to have such a large assortment of fresh seafood readily available. In the 1950s access to fresh fish was limited to coastal towns. In fact it was considered "chic" to serve frozen fish stick nibbles at a cocktail party. Now all America can dine on fresh fish flown in from the coasts as well as our bountiful Great Lakes.. We can even sample exotic varieties of fish, such as mahi-mahi, snapper and squid.

The recent trend to return to more home entertaining is so pleasing, and seafood remains in first place as the entrée of choice. It is exciting for the cook to create that special chowder, a truly delicious casserole, or discover a tasty new shish kabob combination. In today's fish cooking "anything goes."

As we share our "Seafood Secrets" with you keep in mind the three keys to success:

- Be creative with ingredients
- Serve a toast to Neptune
- Always turn with the tide

Ainslie Turner

A few last hints:

The world is indeed your oyster when working with a seafood recipe. With very few exceptions, you can substitute almost any species for another. Keeping textures and different cooking times in mind, experiment with different combinations depending on your inclination or budget. If fresh is not always available, don't pass over the excellent canned and frozen products you can select from your market shelves. Remember to always defrost fish slowly, preferably under refrigeration. The fish has already learned to swim once, don't subject it to the hot water wave.

Finally, a word on cooking products. The recipes have been tested as written, using butter, olive oil or vegetable oil. You may substitute low or no cholesterol spreads if you wish. However, the whipped or diet varieties have different melting and browning qualities. So cut down on your calories somewhere else in the meal. The same holds true for lite mayonnaise products. They work fine when used in a salad or spread, but do not hold up well when heated. You are now on your own — here's to good fishing!

RECIPE CONTRIBUTORS

**A special thank you to all the members of Mystic Seaport
who made this cookbook possible.**

Carol Aageson
Tom Aageson
Carol Akerman
Almar, Ltd.
Donna L. Anderson
Rick Anderson
Mary Lou Andrias
James L. Babcock
Mrs. John K. Baker
Beverly Balch
Mrs. Herbert B. Barlow
Audrey Beaumont
Barbara Bergman
Michael A. Berson
Capt. Robert S. Birge
Ginny Bitting
Barbara Blackwood
Tom Blair
Mrs. E. Jared Bliss, Jr.
Marilyn Bonica
Doug Bonoff
Jeannie MacDonald Booth
Jane Bourn
Helen V. Boyt
Clare R. Bray
Charles Breed
Sheryl Buckley
Janice Bukovac
Eleanor M. Burdick
Mildred H. Burns
Elsie M. Calore
Mr. and Mrs. William Campbell
Melinda Carlisle
Elizabeth M. Carlson
Frank H. Chappell, Jr.
Mrs. Sylvia Chesebrough

Doris Chisholm
Mrs. Frederick S. Claghorn
Jerilynn C. Comstock
Carol Connor
Janet R. Cotton
Mrs. John Coward
Phyllis B. Crosby
Eleanor Crowther
Naomi and Harry Curtis
Sue Curtiss
Robinson Cushman
John Danahey
Mrs. D. Weston Darby, Jr.
Virginia B. Darrow
Janet Dean
Connie Dixon
Ann Douglas
Frederick Field Driftmier
Sheila Drometer
Helen Dudek
Betsy Durham
Susan Durham
Juanita Erickson
Charles Fields
Janice M. Fitton
Tracey Flynn
Dorothy Frew
Raymond Fritz
Helen Garry
Pat Gates
Lawrence E. Gemma
Judy Georg
Jean George
June Getchius
Patricia-ann Goodrich
Nancy N. Gould

Karen Graf
Frances Greenleaf
Jane Grogan
Anne Gunderson
Elizabeth Haigis
Kathleen Hanning
Mrs. D.E. Hanson
Mary B. Harding
Sherry A. Hazelton
Martha B. Healy
Sally Rowe Heckscher
Margaret Henry
Arthur J. Hocking III
Ann Holmes
Ernst Holzborn
Lois M. Hoops
Lyman B. Hoops
Mrs. Ralph M. Howard
Marian Bingham Hubbell
Robert W. Hubner
Mrs. Roger M. Huebsch
Ann Illinger
Mrs. George M. Isdale
Betty Jacobsen
Bonnie James
Livingston S. Jennings
Katherine T. Johnstone
Virginia Crowell Jones
Sharon Kast
Barbara Kerin
Patricia A. Kilcoyne
Mary Ann Kirschberg
Joyce B. Kistler
Nancy Klein
Marilyn Kollmeyer
Ed Kowalewski

John Kramer
Helen Kreidler
Mrs. John A. Kress
Loretta Krupinski
Mrs. Robert V. Krusewski
Thomas Kucharchik, M.D.
Lani Landon
Rosalie B. Lee
Faith Leitner
Lucy Leigh
Benjamin F. Lewis
Benjamin R. Lewis
Joan Klein Lillquist
Patricia Lindholm
Terri A. Livernois
Dorrie Long
Trudy Loy
Patricia Callaway McGrath
Ellen H. McGuire
Mrs. Ronald W. MacDonald
Ellie MacDougall
Diane MacFadyen
Barbara Mahany
Chris B. Mahany
Ruth E. Zientek Mahoney
Mary Martin
Joan Martinson
Jane B. Mason
Martha L. Mason
Lil Maxwell
Jo Merrill
Norma Beardsworth Merrill
Mike Mesnard
Marlee Miksovsky
Luree Miller
Joanne Millovitsch
Lawrence Monteiro
Marge Moore
Elizabeth Ann Morrissey

Mrs. Henry A. Morss, Jr.
Jan Nazzaro
Harry L. Nelson, Jr.
Chris and Greg Norwood
Kerstin E. Ohlén
Carol Ortiz
Gabrielle R. Osborn
Harriet W. Patterson
Irene M. Patterson
Jean Petryshn
Shirley A. Phelps
Susan Pirc
Jo Plant
Theodore Pratt
Phyliss M. Pray
Elaine Potuchek
Mike Pugliese
William J. Raftery
Rosalie Rathbun
Mrs. Michael Reimers
Michael S. Rhoads
Nancy R. Richartz
Gail Rogers
Bridget Rolfe
Rob Roy
Marjorie D. Sabin
David L. Sargent
Robin Schneider
Mr. and Mrs. Peter Schweitzer
Peter W. Schwimer
Anne M. Scott
Jan Scottron
Victor Scottron
Marjorie and Rowland Seckinger
Jeannette A. Semon
Margaret S. Sentz
Mable Seymour
Linda Wright Sheehan
Michael H. Sherwood

Stephen Shilowitz
Susan Skewes
Mrs. Allen Smith
Mrs. Hugh R. Smith
Sally Smith
David C. Snyder
Barbarellen Sottile
Joe Spado
Peggy Squibb
Kathryn Stuart Steel
Jane Steinke
William H. Strutton, M.D.
Teri Summers-Minette
Herman R. Sutherland
Carol H. Sweetman
Sally Swift
Trish Taylor
Marsha Thompson
Frankie Thorington
Alex Turner
Brie Turner
Jennifer Turner
Mrs. Mark Turner
Joseph M. Vrooman
W. Gary Wakeman
Lyn Waldron
Martha Walter
Johnnie Mae Wasserman
Charles Wenderoth
Mrs. Richard L. West
Louise H. White
Mr. and Mrs. Foster B. Whitlock
Mr. and Mrs. James Y. Whittier
Florence B. Wilson
Dede Wirth
Fran Worsley
Anne, Barbara, Dede, Justine,
    Marlene, Mel and Muriel

A special thanks to Dede Wirth for production assistance.

MARTiNi BAiT

Bloody Mary Cup

Serves 8

A New Year's morning wake-up for house guests or Sunday morning cockpit "starter" for a lazy crew.

1 medium onion
2 stalks celery
1 green pepper
1 cucumber, seeded
2 teaspoons Worcestershire sauce
¼ teaspoon salt
1 tablespoon lemon juice, freshly squeezed
1 tablespoon Rose's Lime Juice
4 cups chilled tomato juice
2 4½-ounce cans cocktail shrimp, drained
8 oz. Vodka
Tabasco sauce

1. If you are at home rather than on boat, chop onion, celery, green p and cucumber in the food proces coarse. If you are at sea, just ch

2. Combine vegetables in large bo seasoning, tomato juice, shrimp vodka.

3. Chill for an hour, spoon into stemmed glasses and pass the Tabasco to taste.

Any Seafood Puffs

Makes 3 to 4 dozen

Great to pull out of the freezer for a quick appetizer.

Puffs:
½ cup butter
1 cup water
½ teaspoon salt
1 cup flour
4 eggs

Filling:
1 cup of fish, cooked — shrimp or crab-meat, canned tuna or salmon are great if you have frozen puffs in the freezer
½ cup mayonnaise
¼ cup celery, finely chopped
½ teaspoon curry powder, optional
salt and pepper to taste

1. In a medium saucepan, heat butter and water over high heat. Stir until butter is melted.

2. When mixture begins to boil, add the salt and flour all at once. Lower the heat.

3. Stir mixture vigorously over low heat until completely mixed. The mixture will pull away from the sides and form a small ball.

4. Remove immediately from the heat and add the eggs one at a time. Beat well after each addition until smooth and shiny.

5. Drop by teaspoonful, 3 inches apart onto an ungreased baking sheet. Shape into mounds.

6. Bake at 400° for 50 minutes. Cool on a rack. Either freeze at this point or split and fill with seafood filling mixture or your favorite fish or seafood salad.

Penthouse Caviar Pie

Serves 16

6 eggs, hard-boiled
2 tablespoons mayonnaise
2 tablespoon butter, softened
salt and pepper
½ cup scallions, finely chopped
1 to 1½ cups sour cream
1 2-ounce jar caviar, black or red, drained
⅓ cup parsley, chopped

Must be made ahead.

1. Coarsely chop eggs with a fork and stir in mayonnaise and softened butter. Season to taste with salt and pepper. This should remain lumpy, so if you care to use the food processor, only pulse 2 or 3 times. Spread the mixture on the bottom of a 9-inch quiche pan or similar dish with sides. Sprinkle scallions on top.

2. Gently spread the sour cream over the onions being careful not to disturb them. Spoon the caviar onto the sour cream and spread with a knife to cover evenly. Sprinkle chopped parsley around the edges and chill several hours. Serve with a firm crisp cracker such as melba toast or bagel chips.

Anchovy and Cheese Crostini

Serves 4 to 6

A gourmet cheese melt.

8 thin slices bread
32 anchovy fillets
½ pound Mozzarella cheese
1 teaspoon oregano
½ cup butter

1. Remove the crusts from bread and cut each slice into 4 strips.

2. Place a thin slice of cheese on each piece and top with an anchovy fillet.

3. Sprinkle with oregano and sandwich with another bread finger.

4. In a large pan, melt the butter and fry sandwiches on both sides until golden brown and the cheese is nicely melted. These can be cooked earlier in the day and placed on a baking sheet to reheat at party time.

Clam Puffs à la Trader Vic's

Makes 20 puffs

1 3-ounce package cream cheese
1 7-ounce can minced clams, drained
1 teaspoon onion, minced
dash of Worcestershire sauce
1 egg white, well beaten

1. Blend drained clams with cream cheese, add seasoning and fold in egg white.
2. Drop by teaspoonfuls onto crisp crackers and slip under the broiler. Serve immediately.

Clam Broth Puffs

A double clam treat.

Makes 3 to 4 dozen

Puffs:
1 cup clam broth, liquid drained from canned clams with enough water added to equal 1 cup
½ cup butter
1 cup flour
4 eggs at room temperature

Clam Filling:
3 10½-ounce cans minced clams
6 3-ounce packages chive cream cheese, softened
6 drops hot sauce
½ teaspoon black pepper
1 teaspoon seasoned salt

Puff preparation:
1. Heat the clam liquid in a saucepan. Add butter and bring to a boil.
2. Add the flour all at once and stir vigorously with a wooden spoon over low heat until mixture leaves the sides of the pan and forms a ball.
3. Add eggs, one at a time, beating thoroughly after each addition.
4. Put level teaspoons of batter on ungreased baking sheet 1 inch apart. Bake at 400° for 10 minutes. Reduce heat to 300° without opening the oven door and bake 20 to 25 minutes until puffs are dry and golden.
5. Cool, cut in half and fill with clam mixture, replace tops.
6. Bake in 400° oven for 15 minutes or until hot.

Clam Filling preparation:
1. Drain clams. Add to the softened cream cheese and combine with seasonings.
2. Fill puffs and either bake or freeze.

West Indies Conch Fritters

Makes 2 dozen

Just imagine yourself standing at a beach bar.

6 large conch, cleaned, blanched and finely chopped (about 2 cups)
1 large green pepper, finely chopped
1 small red pepper, finely chopped
1 medium onion, finely chopped
1½ cups flour
1 cup milk
1½ teaspoons baking powder
1 egg, beaten
1 teaspoon thyme
pinch of Cayenne
pinch dry hot red pepper flakes
salt and pepper
oil

Requires some advance preparation.

1. In a large bowl, combine conch meat, peppers, onion and flour. Mix well.
2. Add the milk, baking powder, egg and seasonings. Blend well and let stand for 30 minutes.
3. In a large skillet or wok, heat oil 2 inches deep over medium high heat. Drop mixture by teaspoons and fry until golden brown, turning from side to side.
4. Remove and drain. Keep warm in the oven on a baking sheet while you finish the batch.

Hot Clam and Artichoke Pot

Serves 12

2 8-ounce packages of cream cheese, softened
2 tablespoons milk
2 tablespoons lime juice, freshly squeezed
2 tablespoons horseradish
2 scallions, chopped
2 tablespoons white wine Worcestershire
2 6½-ounce cans of chopped clams, drained
1 8-ounce can sliced water chestnuts, drained
1 13½-ounce can artichoke hearts, drained and cut into bite-size pieces
flat leaf Italian parsley sprigs

1. In a medium-size bowl, cream the cheese with the milk until smooth.
2. Add lime juice, horseradish, green onion and Worcestershire.
3. Fold in clams, water chestnuts and artichoke hearts.
4. Pour into a 2-quart casserole dish.
5. Bake in a 350° oven for 15 minutes or until bubbling.
6. Garnish with parsley and serve with melba toast.

This is equally good served cold to take on a boat or picnic.

Club Clam Puffs

What could be simpler?

1 3-ounce package cream cheese
2 tablespoons heavy cream
1 7-ounce can minced clams, drained
½ teaspoon Worcestershire sauce
½ teaspoon onion, minced
paprika

1. Mix all ingredients and spread on toast rounds or triangles, crusts trimmed.
2. Broil for a few minutes until puffy. Sprinkle with paprika.

Uncle Gary's Crabby Clams

Serves 4

Cover the table with newspapers and dine.

4 dozen fresh little neck, cherrystone or soft clams
4 12-ounce cans beer
8 tablespoons Old Bay Crab Seasoning

1. Rinse clams thoroughly in cold water.
2. Place clams in a 4- to 5-quart pot.
3. Pour beer over clams and sprinkle with the crab seasoning.
4. Cover pot and bring the beer to a gentle boil.
5. As soon as clams begin to open, remove immediately and place in a large bowl. Serve family style with individual butter servers on each plate.

Garlic Butter Sauce:
8 ounces butter
4 tablespoons olive oil
2 garlic cloves, freshly minced

Garlic Butter Sauce preparation:
1. In a small saucepan melt butter on very low heat.
2. Stir in garlic and olive oil to melted butter. Heat for 4 minutes.
3. Remove and place in individual butter servers.

While this recipe is used as an appetizer, quantities can be increased to make this a most pleasing entrée. For those counting calories, you can forego the garlic butter sauce and still find the clams prepared in this manner quite sweet and flavorful.

Maryland Crab Dip

1 pound lump crabmeat
1 cup mayonnaise*
1 8-ounce package cream cheese*
1 medium onion, chopped
2 scallions, finely chopped
1 tablespoon lemon juice
⅛ teaspoon dill
dash hot pepper sauce

***This works successfully with the "lite,"
"lofat" or "no cholesterol" style mayonnaise
or cream cheese.**

1. Blend all ingredients, except crabmeat, together with a whisk until smooth. This can be done in your food processor. Pulse for a few seconds until smooth.
2. Fold in the crab and transfer to an ovenproof serving dish.
3. Bake at 350° for 30 minutes until bubbly. Serve with toast points.

Crab Sauté with Proscuitto

Serves 4 as a first course

2 tablespoons butter
2 tablespoons shallots, minced
½ pound fresh lump crabmeat, cartilage removed
2 teaspoons fresh parsley, chopped
1 tablespoon dry sherry
⅛ teaspoon pepper, freshly ground
8 thin slices of prosciutto
fresh dill or watercress sprigs

1. In a medium skillet melt butter. Add the shallots and sauté for one minute.
2. Stir in the crab and parsely. Pour the sherry into the pan and heat until nicely hot. Season with pepper.
3. Arrange 2 slices of prosciutto on each plate, folding it to one side. Spoon the crab onto the plate, garnish with greens.

Crab or Shrimp Pizza Plate

Serves 6 to 8

1 8-ounce package cream cheese
1 tablespoon chives, chopped
1 6-ounce can crabmeat or tiny shrimp, drained
1 cup cocktail sauce — make your own, see "Good Hot-Hot Sauce" in index, or bottled will do just fine

1. Soften cream cheese at room temperature, stir in chives. Spread on a flat 8- to 10-inch plate.
2. Spread cocktail sauce over cheese to cover.
3. Sprinkle crab or shrimp on sauce and serve with wheat crackers.

   Can be spread with a knife or scooped with a cracker.

Islandia II Crab Puffs

Makes 40 puffs

10 slices white bread
12 ounces crab meat
8 ounces Swiss cheese, shredded
⅓ cup mayonnaise
2 tablespoons sherry
1 tablespoon lemon juice
sea salt to taste
pinch of Cayenne pepper
½ teaspoon dill
½ cup grated Parmesan cheese
paprika

1. Preheat oven to 350°. Remove crusts from bread slices and cut each into quarters. Bake on a cookie sheet for 4 minutes; cool.
2. Mix crabmeat, Swiss cheese, mayonnaise, sherry, lemon juice, salt, pepper and dill. Spoon the mixture on the toasted side of the bread, sprinkle lightly with Parmesan and paprika. (Can be frozen at this point.)
3. To serve, bake for 10 minutes or until light brown. If frozen, bake 20 to 25 minutes.

Sourdough Crab Dip

Makes 2 loaves

2 round loaves sourdough or French bread, unsliced
2 8-ounce packages cream cheese
2 6½-ounce cans crabmeat, cartilage removed
1 teaspoon horseradish
1½ teaspoons lemon juice, freshly squeezed
4 scallions, chopped
⅓ cup pimento stuffed olives, chopped
¾ cup almonds, slivered

Be sure to make ahead and chill thoroughly.

1. Cut the top off the bread and discard. Remove the center of the loaf, leaving ½-inch thick sides and bottom. Cut removed bread into 1-inch cubes.
2. Place the bread shell in a 325° oven for 10 minutes until dried out.
3. Mix the cream cheese with the crabmeat and stir in the remaining ingredients.
4. Place the bread shell on a baking sheet and fill with the crab mixture. Cover completely with aluminum foil and bake for 20 minutes until center is hot.
5. Serve on a large platter and surround with reserved bread cubes for dipping.

Crabmeat and Grapefruit Cocktail   Serves 6 as a first course

A perfect beginning for Sunday Brunch.

3 medium pink grapefruit
8 ounces crabmeat
dash Cayenne pepper
1 ounce rum
¾ cup cooked asparagus or broccoli,
   chopped

1. Cut grapefruits in half and remove the segments with a grapefruit knife. Discard the pith from the skin, scoop shells clean and save. Collect the juice and add to fruit.

2. Mix the crabmeat with the grapefruit, season with Cayenne.

3. Add the rum and asparagus or broccoli and toss. Refrigerate until ready to serve. Fill shells with mixture, arrange on a lettuce leaf and spoon Louis Dressing over top.

Louis Dressing:

1 cup mayonnaise
⅓ cup chili sauce
1 tablespoon onion, grated
1 tablespoon parsley, chopped
1 teaspoon Worcestershire sauce
2 tablespoons lemon juice, freshly squeezed

Requires some advance preparation.

Louis Dressing:

Mix all ingredients, cover and chill. This is excellent on any cold fish or seafood salad.

Oriental Crabmeat Balls   Makes 4 dozen 1-inch balls

A light soy sauce-honey dip goes well with these.

½ pound fresh or frozen crabmeat, drained
   and chopped
1 pound ground lean pork
1 can water chestnuts
1 5-ounce can mushrooms, drained
   and chopped
½ teaspoon salt
1 teaspoon ginger root, freshly minced
1 tablespoon soy sauce
cornstarch
1 egg, beaten with 1 tablespoon water
fat or oil (peanut is best), about 1-inch deep

1. Combine pork, crab, water chestnuts, mushrooms, salt, ginger and soy sauce in a bowl. Mix thoroughly.

2. Shape into 1-inch balls, roll in cornstarch and then in beaten egg.

3. Drop into hot fat and fry slowly until golden brown on both sides. Drain and serve speared with toothpicks.

Divine Deviled Eggs with Crab

Serves 10 to 12

A beautiful companion with a cocktail.

1 dozen medium eggs, hard-boiled
and chilled
8 ounces Alaskan king crab or lump crab,
cartilage removed
1 cup mayonnaise
2 tablespoons lemon juice,
freshly squeezed
½ teaspoon snipped fresh dill
dash black pepper

Requires some advance preparation.

1. Cut cooked eggs in half lengthwise.
Remove yolks and reserve in a covered
container.
2. Combine the mayonnaise with lemon
juice, dill and pepper.
3. Mix with the crabmeat adding the lemon
mayonnaise to hold mixture together.
4. Fill egg halves with crab and chill lightly
covered until ready to serve.
5. Sieve the yolks into a small bowl and
sprinkle a small amount over each egg
to decorate. Arrange with more sprigs
of dill on a platter.

Joanne's Steamed Blue Crabs

Serves 8 to 10

The aroma is divine.

24 to 30 blue shell crabs, prepared
salt
pepper
4 tablespoons olive oil
2 garlic cloves, slivered
1½ cups water

Crab preparation:
Remove top shell, front plate of shell and
bottom flap. Anything inside that is not
white meat should be removed. With a
brush, scrub off remaining shell.

1. Place a layer of crabs in a large pot.
Sprinkle with salt and pepper. Put a sliver
of garlic in each crab.
2. Pour 1 tablespoon olive oil over crabs
and repeat each layer in the same
manner. Pour in the water and cover.
3. Steam for 8 to 10 minutes or until claws
turn red. Serve crabs and broth with rye
bread for dipping.

Can be eaten warm or cold.

Herring Salad with Pickled Red Beets

Serves 6 to 8 as a first course or makes a large platter

Start your holiday buffet off with this first course.

1 16-ounce can sliced beets
white vinegar
sugar
2 herring fillets
1 red onion, sliced
1 large apple, diced
1 cup heavy cream, whipped
parsley sprigs

1. Drain the juice from beets into a measuring cup. Add half the amount of vinegar and the same of sugar. Place liquids and sugar in a saucepan.

2. Boil mixture until sugar is melted. Put beets in a glass jar and pour hot vinegar mixture over the beets. Put in the refrigerator and chill for 2 days (or up to a week.)

3. When ready to serve cut the herring into bite-size pieces and toss with the onion, chopped and apple. Combine the herring with the pickled beets and gently fold in the whipped cream. Garnish with parsley sprigs.

Teri's Pickled Herring

Serves 12

An excellent appetizer for a crowd.

2 pounds salted herring
¾ cup white vinegar
½ cup water
½ cup sugar
2 tablespoons horseradish
1 carrot, thinly sliced
2 small Bermuda onions, thinly sliced
2 teaspoons whole allspice
2 teaspoons whole mustard seed
1 teaspoon crushed hot red pepper
½ teaspoon ground cardamon
3 bay leaves

Must be made ahead.

1. Soak herring in cold water for 12 hours. Discard water.

2. Cook vinegar, water and sugar over medium heat until sugar dissolves. Cool.

3. Mix together horseradish, carrot, onions and spices.

4. In a large glass jar, layer the onion mixture with the herring until all is used—at least 3 times; ending with the onion mixture.

5. Pour vinegar mixture over the layers and tightly secure the lid.

6. Refrigerate at least 2 to 3 days. Serve with the darkest bread that you can buy or bake.

Quick Red and White Herring Salad   Serves 10

A great picnic salad to arrange while the grill is heating.

2 8-ounce jars pickled red beets with onions
1 large dill pickle, chopped
1 apple, chopped
1 jar marinated herring, drained
4 tablespoons mayonnaise or sour cream
1 tablespoon prepared mustard
2 hard-boiled eggs, cut into wedges

1. Drain beets. Combine with pickle, apple and herring. Place on a serving plate.
2. Combine mayonnaise with mustard and stir until smooth. Garnish the herring with egg wedges and pass the mustard sauce with rye bread or crackers.

Inlagd Sill (Pickled Herring)   Serves 10

2 red onions, sliced
4 fillets of herring
½ cup scallions, chopped

Pickling Juice:
1 cup water
1 cup white vinegar
1 teaspoon allspice, crushed from whole allspice
½ cup sugar

Herring fillets should have a little salt left on them. If they are unsalted, sprinkle fillets with a little salt and let stand for a few hours.

Must be made ahead.

1. Cut herring fillets into ½-inch pieces and layer in a glass dish or large jar. Top with some of the red onions, and continue with layers of red onion and herring. The last layer should be herring.
2. Mix water, vinegar, allspice and sugar in a saucepan. Heat and mix until sugar is dissolved.
3. Pour over herring onion mixture in bowl and garnish with scallions. Let stand for several days in the refrigerator to pickle.

Fishers Island Sound Steamed Mussels   Serves 6 to 8

A lighthouse specialty.

4 quarts mussels
¼ cup butter
1 small onion, chopped
1 garlic clove, chopped
½ cup dry white wine

1. In a large pot, melt butter and sauté onion and garlic for 2 minutes until soft and fragrant.
2. Add ½ cup white wine and cover with mussels.
3. Cook over high heat, covered, for 5 minutes. Stir mussels and cook for 5 more minutes until shells have opened. Remove from heat and eat directly from the pot.

Cold Mussels with Tomato-Coriander Sauce

A little Mexican twist here.

Makes one large platter of 25 to 50 mussels, depending on size.

2 pounds mussels, cleaned and debearded
¼ cup dry white wine
1 onion, minced
¼ cup olive oil
2 garlic cloves, minced
1 teaspoon ground cumin
1 pound tomatoes, peeled, seeded and finely chopped (or 1 35-ounce can Italian plum tomatoes, well drained and chopped)
2 4-inch fresh green hot chili peppers, seeded and minced (wear rubber gloves)
2 tablespoons scallions, minced
2 tablespoons minced fresh coriander or 2 teaspoons dried coriander
salt and pepper to taste

Requires some advance preparation.

1. In a heavy stainless steel or enameled kettle, steam the mussels in wine, covered, over high heat for 4 to 6 minutes until shells have opened. Shake the kettle once or twice to distribute mussels. Discard any unopened shells. Reserve liquid.

2. Open mussels and leave the meat in bottom shell. Wrap and chill for at least 2 hours.

3. Strain the reserved liquid through a double thickness of cheesecloth into a small bowl.

4. In a large skillet cook the minced onion in the oil over moderate heat until softened. Add the garlic and continue cooking for another minute.

5. Add the cumin and stir over low heat for one minute. Stir in the tomatoes and ⅓ cup strained mussel liquor. Bring to a boil and simmer stirring occasionally for 10 minutes. Add the chili peppers, scallions, salt and pepper. Let the sauce cool and stir in the coriander.

6. When ready to serve spoon the sauce over the chilled mussels and arrange decoratively on a platter. The completed dish may be prepared a day in advance and kept covered and chilled.

The best mussels are collected on rocky reefs at low tide. They should be under water. Pull off any rocks or weeds stuck to the shells and rinse right there while your sneakers are still wet. Put them in a pot with no water and try to cook within 2 hours after collecting.

Toasted Oysters Aioli

Serves 6

A hot crusty garlic topping.

2 dozen medium oysters
2 teaspoons garlic, finely chopped
I tablespoon parsley, finely chopped
I tablespoon lemon juice, freshly squeezed
I cup mayonnaise
½ cup crushed cracker crumbs
¼ cup Parmesan cheese, grated

1. Open oysters and leave on bottom shell. Discard other shell and gently loosen meat at the muscle.
2. Combine garlic, parsley, lemon juice and mayonnaise.
3. Put a scant teaspoon on each oyster and smooth over with a spoon. Sprinkle with crumbs and cheese.
4. Bake at 450° for 6 to 8 minutes until crumbs are golden. The oysters should remain nice and plump. Let cool for a few minutes before serving.

Oysters Gascogne

Serves 4 to 6

2 dozen raw oysters
3 lemons, cut into wedges
salt, black pepper
10 pork sausages

1. Open oysters and leave in the bottom shell. Arrange on a serving platter over crushed ice.
2. Prick sausages and cook until browned. Cut each into 3 pieces.
3. To serve, have your guests take a chilled oyster, season with salt, pepper and lemon, followed by a hot piece of sausage.

PICKLED OYSTERS

"After taking out the oysters, to each quart of liquor put a teaspoonful of pepper, two blades of mace, three tablespoons of white wine, and four of vinegar, also a tablespoonful of salt. Simmer the oysters in this five minutes, then take them out and put in jars, then boil the pickle, skim it, and pour it over them."

BEECHER'S DOMESTIC RECEIPT BOOK, 1857

Oysters and Steak on a Half Shell

Adjust the amounts of each ingredient to the number in your party.

roast sirloin steak or roast, carved, rare and
   thinly sliced
sour cream
raw oysters, shucked (reserve the deep shell)
salt and pepper
lemon wedges
fresh caviar

Must be made ahead.

1. Cut slices of beef into 3-inch strips.
   Spread each with a little sour cream.
2. Place an oyster on top and sprinkle with
   salt, pepper and lemon juice.
3. Wrap the steak around the oyster and
   place each package back in the shell. Top
   with a little caviar and serve well chilled.

Smoked Oyster Spread

Makes 1 cup

Easy to make — a non-drippy dip.

1 4-ounce can smoked oysters, drained
1 3-ounce package cream cheese
1 large garlic clove, minced
1 tablespoon soy sauce
3 tablespoons parsley, chopped
¼ cup mayonnaise

Must be made ahead.

1. Chop the oysters coarsely and set aside.
2. Combine the cream cheese, garlic, soy
   sauce, parsley and mayonnaise.
3. Gently stir in the oysters and refrigerate
   for at least one hour.

Serve with chunks of dark pumpernickel.

Oyster Wrap-Ups

Makes 2 dozen

2 dozen oysters, shucked and drained;
   reserve 1 cup of liquid
½ cup cocktail sauce
1 tablespoon horseradish
1 tablespoon lemon juice
1 teaspoon vinegar
¼ teaspoon salt
black pepper
12 lean slices bacon, cut in 3-inch strips

1. Mix reserved oyster liquid with cocktail
   sauce, horseradish, lemon juice, vinegar
   and seasonings.
2. Pour mixture over oysters and refrigerate
   several hours to season.
3. Remove oysters from sauce and wrap a
   strip of bacon around each. Secure with
   a toothpick.
4. Broil for 2 to 3 minutes or bake in a
   500° oven until bacon is crisp. Serve
   with melba toasts.

Dilled Smoked Salmon and Potato Cakes   Makes 12 to 14 cakes

¼ pound Nova Scotia salmon, sliced
2 large baking potatoes
2 egg yolks
¼ pound cream cheese
½ cup onion, diced
2 tablespoons butter
½ teaspoon dill
⅛ teaspoon pepper
⅓ cup corn oil
lemon wedges
sour cream

Requires some advance preparation.

1. Bake potatoes in preheated oven at 450° until soft—1 hour.
2. Beat egg yolks in a large mixing bowl.
3. Cut potatoes in half, remove skin and while still hot, mash well and mix with egg yolks.
4. Beat in cream cheese, add dill and black pepper, combining well.
5. In a small pan sauté onions in butter until tender and add to potato mixture.
6. Dice smoked salmon into ⅛-inch cubes and add to other ingredients above. Chill mixture for 1 hour.
7. Shape into cakes 1½-inches in diameter and sauté in oil until nicely browned. Be sure not to crowd pan. Drain and serve with fresh lemon wedges and a little sour cream on top.

Pink Salmon Dip   Makes 1½ cups

1 15½-ounce can salmon, drained and de-boned
⅓ cup country style cottage cheese
3 canned artichoke hearts, rinsed and drained
1 scallion, chopped
6 drops Tabasco
1 teaspoon Dijon mustard
1 tablespoon lemon juice
3 tablespoons dill, chopped
2 tablespoons pimento, drained
1 tablespoon capers, drained

1. Place drained salmon, cottage cheese, artichoke hearts, onion, Tabasco, mustard, and lemon juice in the bowl of a food processor. Blend until smooth.
2. Add dill and capers, pulsate briefly. Add the pimento last, blending so that specks still remain visible. Transfer to a serving bowl.

This improves in flavor the longer it is chilled. Serve with French bread chunks or crackers.

Salmon Party Log

Makes one 8-inch log

1 16-ounce can pink salmon, skin and bones removed
1 8-ounce package cream cheese, softened
1 teaspoon lemon juice
2 teaspoons onion, grated
1 teaspoon prepared horseradish
⅛ teaspoon salt
¼ teaspoon liquid smoke
½ cup pecans, chopped
4 tablespoons parsley, snipped
parsley sprigs

Must be made ahead.

1. In a medium bowl combine cream cheese with salmon, lemon juice, onion, horseradish, salt and liquid smoke. Chill one hour.

2. Shape into a roll on waxed paper or line a fish shaped mold with plastic wrap. Spoon the mixture into the mold and press into corners. Chill for 24 hours.

3. Before serving, place on lettuce leaves and press the pecans and parsley on the surface. Garnish with additional parsley and serve with melba toasts.

Sardines on Toast with Cheese

Makes 2 dozen

A quick emergency snack right from the shelf.

1 4-ounce can sardines, packed in oil
8 slices white bread, crusts trimmed
½ cup chili sauce
¼ cup Parmesan cheese, grated

1. Remove sardines to a dish reserving the oil. Brush the oil over the bread slices. Cut each slice into 3 fingers.

2. Spread a little chili sauce on each piece and top with a strip of sardine. The larger ones will need to be cut lengthwise.

3. Sprinkle with cheese and broil for 2 to 3 minutes until cheese is nicely browned.

Sardine and Apple Salad

Serves 8

A quick inexpensive alternative to herring salad.

2 3¼-ounce cans sardines
1 cup red apple, unpeeled and diced
1 tablespoon lemon juice
½ cup celery, chopped
⅓ cup sour cream

1. Drain sardines and cut into bite-size chunks.

2. Sprinkle apple cubes with lemon juice. Toss with celery, sour cream and sardines until well coated. Serve with pumpernickel toasts.

Beer Marinated Scallops

Serves 12 to 16

2 pounds bay scallops
1 12-ounce can beer
10 small scallions, chopped
1 stalk celery
2 tablespoons parsley, minced
1½ medium lemons, freshly squeezed
¾ cup vegetable oil
¼ teaspoon salt
½ teaspoon black pepper, coarsely cracked

Must be made ahead.

1. Rinse and drain scallops well. Place scallops in a shallow pan.
2. Bring beer to a low boil in a saucepan and pour over scallops. Simmer gently for 2 to 3 minutes. Drain well.
3. Place scallops in a bowl and add scallions, celery, parsley, lemon juice and oil. Mix well and season with salt and pepper.
4. Refrigerate overnight and serve with toothpicks.

This marinade in this dish is wonderful for dipping with French bread.

Scallop Seviche with Dill Sauce

Serves 6 as a first course

Strips of fresh flounder also adapt to this recipe.

1 pound bay or sea scallops
½ cup lime juice
½ cup lemon juice
½ teaspoon salt
black pepper to taste, freshly ground
½ medium onion, thinly sliced
1 garlic clove, minced

1. If scallops are large, cut into bite-size pieces, not too small.
2. Place scallops into glass or ceramic bowl. Rinse with cold water and drain well.
3. Combine lime juice, lemon juice, salt, pepper, garlic and onion.
4. Pour mixture over scallops and stir until well coated.
5. Cover and refrigerate for at least one hour, 6 hours at best. Drain.

Dill Sauce:
6 tablespoons mayonnaise
¾ tablespoon lemon juice
5 to 6 teaspoons fresh dill

Requires some advance preparation.

Dill Sauce preparation:
1. Mix dill into lemon juice to moisten.
2. Gradually stir mixture into mayonnaise until well blended.

To serve either blend the drained scallops with dill sauce and spoon onto individual plates with lettuce leaves and cherry tomatoes.
or
Serve scallops and sauce separately with small forks as an hors d'oeuvre spread at a buffet.

Sesame Scallop Skewers

Serves 8

Try this with a little coconut if you like.

1 pound sea scallops. If large cut into
½-inch pieces
4 tablespoons dry sherry
½ teaspoon salt
12 slices bacon, cut in thirds
2 tablespoons sesame seeds

1. Marinate scallops in the sherry and sugar for 30 minutes.
2. Wrap a piece of bacon around each scallop and secure with a toothpick. Dip in sesame seeds.
3. In a preheated hot oven (475°), bake for 10 to 12 minutes until crisp.

Scallops with Pine Nut and Shallot Butter

Serves 8 as a first course

An elegant appetizer for a special dinner party.

1½ pounds fresh bay scallops
¾ cup butter
4 tablespoons shallots, finely chopped
4 tablespoons pine nuts
1 tablespoon parsley, chopped
½ cup fresh bread crumbs
1 tablespoon lemon juice, freshly squeezed
2 tablespoons Marsala

1. Preheat oven to 500°.
2. Rinse the scallops and pat them dry.
3. Soften butter with a fork and add shallots, pine nuts, parsley, bread crumbs and lemon juice.
4. Divide scallops equally between 8 scallop shells or ramekins.
5. Top the scallops with the pine nut butter, sprinkle with Marsala and place on a baking sheet.
6. Bake 10 minutes until piping hot and bubbling.

Hot Cheesy Shrimp Toasts

Makes 5 to 6 dozen

1 large loaf bread, thinly sliced
½ cup butter, softened
2 6½-ounce cans tiny shrimp, rinsed and drained
1 8-ounce package cream cheese
8 ounces sharp cheddar, grated
1 small onion, chopped

This may be cut in half for a smaller party. They can be prepared ahead and frozen before cutting into quarters. Thaw before baking.

1. Remove the crusts from the bread slices and butter each piece.
2. Mix shrimp, softened cream cheese, grated cheddar and onion to make a paste.
3. Spread paste thinly over buttered bread and cut each into four squares.
4. Bake at 400° for 5 to 10 minutes until slightly browned and crisp on the edges.

Chinese Shrimp Toast

Makes about 16 pieces

1 pound medium shrimp, peeled and
 deveined
1 scallion, minced
1 tablespoon water chestnuts, minced
1 garlic clove, minced
1 teaspoon ginger root, grated
1 tablespoon sherry
1 dash ground pepper
4 slices day old white bread
1 cup peanut or vegetable oil

**For dipping try hot chinese mustard
and/or light soy sauce with ginger slices.**

1. Place half of the shrimp in a bowl and
 set aside.
2. With the remaining half pound, mash and
 dice with a cleaver or wide knife until you
 have a smooth paste.
3. Put paste in another bowl and add
 scallion, water chestnuts, garlic, ginger,
 sherry and pepper.
4. Cut 1-inch circles from the bread (as
 many as the whole shrimps you have
 set aside in step 1).
5. Mound 1 tablespoon of the paste on
 each bread round. Top each with one
 whole shrimp, pressing firmly into
 the paste.
6. Heat oil in a wok or heavy pan over
 medium high heat. Fry shrimp-bread
 pieces 3 or 4 at a time until golden,
 1 to 2 minutes on each side. Drain on
 paper towels.

Fiesta Shrimp Mousse

A hit for a yacht club dance.

Serves 12

3 ¼-ounce packages unflavored gelatin
1 cup cold water
1 8-ounce package cream cheese
1 10-ounce can tomato soup
1 cup mayonnaise
15 drops Tabasco sauce
2 7-ounce cans shrimp, drained
 and chopped
1 cup celery, finely chopped
½ cup green pepper, finely chopped
2 tablespoons onion, grated
1 teaspoon salt
3 teaspoons lemon juice
1 tablespoon Worcestershire sauce

Must be made ahead.

1. Soften gelatin in cold water.
2. Heat soup over medium heat, add the
 cream cheese and warm until the cheese
 is melted and smooth.
3. Add gelatin to the soup mixture and cool
 in the refrigerator for 1 hour until
 mixture begins to thicken.
4. Add all remaining ingredients. Pour into
 a 10-inch oiled decorative mold and
 refrigerate at least 24 hours.
5. When ready to serve, dip mold in hot
 water and turn the mousse onto a serving
 platter surrounded by lettuce leaves.

Christmas Shrimp Appetizer

Serves 8

Pretty red and green holiday colors.

2 pounds medium shrimp
1 red pepper, cut into long strips
1 green pepper, cut into long strips
1 large red onion, thinly sliced
   into rings
¼ cup white rice vinegar
½ cup olive oil
1 8-ounce can ripe olives, sliced
salt
tri-color peppercorns, freshly ground

Must be made ahead.

1. In a large pot of salted boiling water, cook shrimp quickly for 1 to 2 minutes until pink. Remove and drain. Peel and devein.
2. Combine shrimp, peppers and onions and toss. Add the vinegar, olive oil and olives while shrimp are still warm.
3. Season with ground pepper and refrigerate overnight.

Mustard Seed Shrimp

Serves 6 to 8

A different twist to marinated shrimp.

1½ cups mayonnaise
⅓ cup lemon juice, freshly squeezed
¼ cup sugar
½ cup sour cream
1 large red onion, finely chopped
4 tablespoons fresh dill, chopped
   or 2 teaspoons dry dill
1 tablespoon mustard seed
1 tablespoon Worcestershire sauce
2 pounds medium shrimp, cooked
   and peeled

Must be made ahead.

1. In a large bowl, mix mayonnaise, lemon juice, sugar, sour cream, onion and seasonings.
3. Stir in the shrimp, cover and refrigerate overnight.
3. Spoon into a crystal bowl or family heirloom and serve with wooden picks.

Juanita's Shrimp Dip

Serves 8 to 12

1 pound medium shrimp, cooked
   and peeled
1 3½-ounce can tuna, drained
2 teaspoons sugar
½ cup French dressing
12 ounces ketchup
2 tablespoons horseradish
½ cup sweet pickle relish
1 cup black olives, diced

1. Flake tuna in a medium bowl and sprinkle with sugar.
2. Add French dressing, ketchup, horseradish, relish and olives.
3. Mix ingredients well and fold in cooked shrimp.
4. Serve with wooden picks and plenty of cocktail napkins.

Centerpiece Shrimp with Horseradish Sauce   Serves 14 to 16

Put this right in the middle of your buffet table.

1½ pounds medium shrimp, cooked
  and peeled
1 8-ounce can of ripe pitted olives, drained
2 8-ounce cans whole water chestnuts,
  drained
1 medium head of cauliflower, broken into
  bite-size pieces
1 pint cherry tomatoes

Sauce:

2 cups mayonnaise
½ cup horseradish
½ teaspoon salt
2 teaspoons dry mustard
2 teaspoons lemon juice, freshly squeezed

Requires some advance preparation.

1. Combine mayonnaise, horseradish, salt,
   mustard and lemon juice in a medium-
   size bowl and stir until well blended.

2. Toss shrimp, olives, water chestnuts,
   cauliflower and tomatoes together; pour
   horseradish sauce overall and chill for
   2 hours.

3. Serve with toothpicks as an hors d'oeuvre
   or on a bed of bibb lettuce as a
   luncheon entrée.

Bite-Size Spinach and Shrimp Egg Foo Yong   Makes 3 dozen

If made in larger patties, this is a delicious main dish.

½ cup spinach, cooked, chopped and
  well drained
½ cup tiny shrimps, cooked
¼ cup onion, chopped
¼ cup scallions, chopped
¼ cup green pepper, chopped
½ cup bean sprouts
4 eggs
¼ teaspoon salt
dash of pepper

Soy Sauce Dip: Makes 1⅓ cups
2 tablespoons butter
2 tablespoons corn starch
1 cup chicken broth
3 tablespoons soy sauce
2 teaspoons sugar
1 garlic clove, minced
½ teaspoon ginger root, minced

1. Beat the eggs with a fork and combine
   with the remaining ingredients.

2. Drop by teaspoonful on a hot griddle or
   skillet that has been well oiled. Peanut oil
   is excellent because it does not smoke.
   Brown on both sides and remove to a
   warm oven until ready to serve.

Soy Sauce Dip preparation:
1. Stir the cornstarch into the broth until
   well combined. Add the sugar, soy sauce,
   garlic and ginger.

2. Heat the butter in a small saucepan and
   stir in the liquid. Cook, stirring over low
   heat 3 to 4 minutes until thickened. Serve
   sauce with the mini Egg Foo Yongs using
   bamboo skewers for dipping.

Marinated Shrimp and Vegetables   Serves 20 to 25

May be used as a hot-weather entrée.

3 pounds large shrimp, cooked, peeled
  and deveined
2 8½-ounce cans artichoke hearts, drained
  and halved
½ pound fresh mushrooms, halved
1 purple onion, sliced into rings
1 3½-ounce jar non-pareil capers, drained
1 5¾-ounce can pitted black olives, drained
1 pint cherry tomatoes

Marinade:

2 cups vegetable oil
1½ cups vinegar
3 tablespoons Worcestershire sauce
2 tablespoons Tabasco sauce
4 teaspoons sugar
4 teaspoons salt
1 teaspoon black pepper

Must be made ahead.

1. Place shrimp, artichoke hearts, mushrooms, onion slices, capers, olives and tomatoes in a large shallow container.
2. Combine ingredients for marinade and pour over shrimp.
3. Cover tightly and refrigerate for 18 to 24 hours, stirring occasionally.
4. Drain before serving. If desired, spoon shrimp mixture over lettuce.

Sicilian Shrimp   Serves 10 to 12

Toss this with cooked pasta for a summer salad.

3 6-ounce jars marinated artichoke hearts,
  quartered
⅓ cup lemon juice
½ teaspoon basil
½ teaspoon oregano
1 teaspoon garlic, minced
salt and pepper, freshly ground
3 cups cherry tomatoes, halved
1½ pounds medium shrimp, cooked,
  peeled, and deveined
¾ pound raw mushrooms, quartered
olive oil

Must be made ahead.

1. Drain the marinade from the artichoke hearts into a bowl. Add the lemon juice, basil, organo and garlic plus salt and pepper to taste.
2. In a large bowl combine artichoke hearts, tomatoes, mushrooms and shrimp. Pour dressing over all and toss well. Drizzle with additional olive oil if needed.
3. Place in a serving dish lined with grape or lettuce leaves and serve chilled.

Bay Street Shrimp Toasts

Makes 3 dozen

From a commodore's kitchen.

1 pound small shrimp, peeled
1 teaspoon salt
1 tablespoon sherry
1 scallion, chopped
1 egg, beaten
4 water chestnuts, finely chopped
1 tablespoon cornstarch
12 slices white bread, not thin sliced
peanut oil

1. With a large knife, mince the shrimp. Mix with salt, sherry, scallion, egg, water chestnuts and cornstarch. Let mixture stand for 15 minutes.
2. Trim crusts from bread. Cut each slice into 4 triangles.
3. Spread 1 teaspoon of shrimp mixture evenly over bread.
4. Heat oil in wok or frying pan until hot. Add bread, shrimp side down and fry until golden brown. Drain on paper towels.

Serve with plum sauce and/or hot mustard for dipping. These may be frozen cooked or uncooked — reheat briefly to serve.

Beer Batter Shrimp with Sweet and Sour Dip

Makes 3 dozen

A perfect start to a Chinese meal.

2 pounds large shrimp, peeled and deveined
1 cup flour
½ teaspoon sugar
½ teaspoon salt
1 teaspoon baking powder
dash pepper
dash nutmeg
1 egg, beaten
1 cup beer
oil

Sauce:
2 tablespoons brown sugar
2 tablespoons soy sauce
2 tablespoons cornstarch
¼ cup vinegar
¼ cup cold water
1 cup red bell pepper, finely chopped

1. In a medium bowl, combine dry ingredients.
2. Whisk in the beaten egg and stir until well blended. Add the beer.
3. With a small knife, butterfly the shrimp by making a lengthwise cut down the back of each shrimp. Do not cut through.
4. Heat ½ inch of oil in a wok or heavy pan. Dip shrimps in batter and fry for 2 minutes until golden. Drain on paper towels and transfer to a hot platter.

Sauce preparation:
1. Combine the brown sugar, soy sauce, cornstarch, vinegar and water in a saucepan.
2. Bring to a boil. stirring constantly. Simmer for 15 minutes on low heat. Add bell pepper and serve with shrimp.

Swedish Pickled Shrimp

Serves 6

Try this for a festive buffet.

2 to 2½ pounds shrimp, shells intact
½ cup celery tops
¼ cup mixed pickling spices
1 tablespoon salt
2 cups onions, thinly sliced
8 bay leaves
1½ cups vegetable oil
¾ cup white vinegar
3 tablespoons capers with juice
2½ teaspoons celery seed
1½ teaspoon salt
3 drops hot pepper sauce

Must be made ahead.

1. In a large pan, cover shrimp with boiling water. Add celery tops, pickling spices and 1 tablespoon salt.
2. Cover and simmer for 5 minutes.
3. Drain shrimp. Peel and devein under cold water, making sure to rinse off pickling spices.
4. In a shallow dish, layer shrimp, onion and bay leaves. Combine remaining ingredients and pour over shrimp.
5. Cover, chill for at least 24 hours. Spoon the marinade over the shrimps occasionally while they are being refrigerated.

Cockpit Shrimp Platter

Serves 10

Elegance at sea.

1 8-ounce package cream cheese
½ pound small shrimp (a few extra for garnish) cooked, peeled and chunked
½ cup Major Grey's chutney
1 tablespoon almonds, slivered

1. Spread cream cheese evenly over a medium plate.
2. Scatter shrimp on top of cream cheese.
3. Spread chutney over all and sprinkle with almonds.

Perfect Cocktail Shrimp — (per 1 pound shrimp). Peel and devein shrimp before cooking (it is much easier). Place a 1½ quart saucepan of water on high heat. Add a dash of salt, and any seasonings you might like, bay leaf and pickling spice are especially subtle. Bring water to a rapid boil. Drop in the shrimp and stir for 30 seconds until the shrimp have turned pink and curled. Do not boil. Remove immediately and plunge into cold water, drain and refrigerate.

Swordfish and Chili Seviche

Serves 6 to 8

1 pound swordfish, skinned and cut into
  ½-inch pieces
½ cup lime juice, freshly squeezed
½ teaspoon oregano
1 tablespoon olive oil
1 cup tomatoes, peeled, seeded and cut
  into ¼-inch cubes
½ cup scallions, finely chopped
1 4-ounce can green chilies, drained
  and diced
2 teaspoons parsley, finely chopped
½ cup avocado, diced
¼ cup celery, diced
¼ cup ketchup
black pepper, freshly ground, to taste
paprika

Requires some advance preparation.

1. Place fish cubes in a ceramic bowl. Add the lime juice and olive oil. Sprinkle with oregano and toss.

2. Cover and refrigerate for 12 hours, stirring occasionally.

3. An hour before serving, stir in the remaining ingredients and chill. Serve in a glass serving bowl or on lettuce cups as a first course. Garnish with lime slices dipped in paprika.

4 Star ★★★★ Shrimp Remoulade

Serves 10

2 pounds large shrimp, peeled, deveined
  and cooked
1¼ cup mayonnaise
⅓ cup chili sauce
1 teaspoon onion, grated
1 tablespoon parsley, chopped
1 tablespoon Worcestershire sauce
1 teaspoon horseradish
1 tablespoon sweet pickle relish
1 teaspoon Dijon mustard
2 teaspoons capers, rinsed
1 small jar lumpfish caviar (red or black)

Must be made ahead.

1. In a large bowl, combine all of the ingrdients except the shrimp and caviar.

2. Add the shrimp. Carefully fold in caviar and chill for a few hours or overnight. Put in a beautiful bowl, this deserves it. Serve with seafood forks or on small individual plates if it is a more formal affair.

PUT ON THE POT

Fish Stock

Makes 3 to 4 cups

**Use this where called for in recipes or as a base
for your own chowders and sauces.**

1 cup onion, sliced
½ cup celery, sliced
½ cup carrot, sliced
2 pounds fish bones and trimmings
   (use a non-oily variety)
1 cup white wine or vermouth
1 teaspoon salt
½ teaspoon white pepper
¼ teaspoon thyme
1 bay leaf
3 parsley sprigs

1. Put all the ingredients in a large pot or kettle. Add 4 cups of water and bring to a boil. Reduce heat and skim.
2. Simmer partially covered for 30 minutes. Strain through a fine sieve and discard bones.

Duck Island Blackfish Chowder

Serves 6

1 pound Blackfish fillets or steaks cut
   ¾-inch thick. Any other non-oily white
   fish can be substituted
4 strips bacon, chopped
½ cup onion, chopped
½ cup green pepper, chopped
1 cup water
1 cup chopped loose pack frozen broccoli
   or 10-ounce package, thawed
1 large potato, peeled and diced
1 large carrot, peeled and diced
1 tablespoon chicken bouillon granules
1 teaspoon Worcestershire sauce
¼ teaspoon black pepper
1 cup light cream
2 tablespoons flour
1 cup milk

1. Remove skin and bones from fish. Cut into ¾-inch pieces.
2. Sauté bacon in pot, reserve 1 tablespoon of drippings and cook the onion and green pepper in the same pan until tender.
3. Stir in the water, broccoli, potatoes, carrots, bouillon, Worcestershire sauce and pepper. Bring to a boil, reduce heat and cover.
4. Simmer for 5 to 10 minutes until potatoes and carrots are almost tender.
5. Combine cream and flour and whisk into the above mixture. Stir in the milk and add the fish.
6. Bring almost to a boil, reduce heat and simmer gently for 5 minutes until fish is done. DO NOT BOIL.
7. Stir in the bacon and serve. If made ahead, refrigerate and when ready to serve, reheat very slowly.

Bouba

Serves 6

A quick French-Canadian fish chowder.

6 bass fillets, about 2 pounds
6 medium potatoes, sliced
4 medium onions, sliced in ¼-inch pieces
4 tablespoons butter
black pepper, freshly ground
salt
5 to 6 cups water
parsley and paprika to garnish

1. Cover the bottom of a heavy pot with potatoes, onion, butter, salt and pepper. Add enough water to cover. Bring to a boil, reduce heat and cook for 15 minutes.
2. Add the bass fillets, cover and simmer for a half hour. The traditional way to serve this is to strain broth into cups and serve fish and vegetables in a soup plate. Garnish with paprika and parsley.

Corny Clam Chowder

Serves 6

Makes a good, thick, tasty chowder in only 20 minutes.

2 cups water
2 large potatoes, diced
1 large onion, diced
2 large celery stalks, diced
2 tablespoons fresh parsley, chopped
1 16-ounce can creamed corn
1 12-ounce can evaporated milk
1 10-ounce can chopped clams, double this amount if serving as your main course
2 tablespoons butter
salt and pepper to taste

1. In a saucepot cook the potatoes, onion and celery in 2 cups of water for 10 minutes until fork tender. DO NOT DRAIN.
2. Remove from the heat and add corn, evaporated milk and clams with the broth from the can.
3. Gently stir in the parsley, butter and salt and pepper. Heat slowly and do not allow to boil.

As with so many chowders this is better the next day if you can resist it. Freezes well also.

New England style clam chowder did orignate there, but takes several forms. The typical chowder is made with milk, but Rhode Island style consists of clear broth and other ingredients. Some purists have been known to add milk or cream to the Rhode Island chowder before serving. "Back Bay" or Boston style is made with soft shell clams rather then quahogs. It is strictly heresay that an occasional New Englander would ever put a tomato in his chowder — a habit strictly reserved for those in Manhattan.

29

Chowder Master's Clam Chowder   Serves 6 to 8

As traditional a chowder recipe and technique as you could find for a creamy New England chowder . . . with a bit of sage advice for the pot.

¼ pound lean salt pork, with lots of stripes
1 quart and 1 pint chowder clams
4 medium potatoes, peeled and diced
1 medium onion, chopped

Hot cream or milk may be added to the serving bowls according to individual preference — it is not added to the chowder itself.

1. Prepare clams, reserving liquid. An old-fashioned food grinder is great if available. More modern equipment will work, but overprocessing will produce granulated clams in the bottom of the chowder. Cutting up the clams with kitchen shears is not a pleasant job but the tougher parts and the softer parts can be cut into proportionate pieces that will cook evenly. By whatever method, aim for small but recognizable pieces of clam in the chowder.

2. Slice the salt pork into thin strips, trimming away the rind. If you plan to keep the pieces of pork in the chowder when served, cube them instead.

3. In a heavy kettle melt the fat from the pork over medium-low heat until pork is lightly browned. Add onion, chopped and cook until soft and opaque.

4. When pork and onions are ready, add potatoes and water to cover. Cook until potatoes are tender but not soft. Discard pork if you do not want to include it in final chowder.

5. Add one cup of water, the chopped clams and liquor. Return to simmer and cook gently for about 3 minutes. DO NOT STIR. The layer of potatoes protects the clams from the heat and the short cooking time keeps them tender. After the 3 minutes stir and taste, adding more water if the flavor is too strong. It is easier to dilute a strong chowder than to retrieve a watery one, so be careful.

Bratten's Clam Chowder

Serves 4

A pan of homemade corn muffins makes this a meal.

2 6½-ounce cans chopped clams
1¾ cups potatoes, diced
1½ cups onion, chopped
1½ cups celery, chopped
4 cups half-and-half or 1 cup cream,
   3 cups milk
¾ cup butter
¾ cup flour

Garnish:
Bowls of fresh tomatoes, green peppers,
canned corn

1. Drain the chopped clams and reserve juice.

2. Put potatoes, onions and celery in a medium saucepot. Add the clam liquid and enough water to cover. Simmer for 10 minutes until tender.

3. Melt butter in another pan and whisk in the flour, over medium heat. Slowly add the cream or milk, stirring constantly until thickened.

4. Pour the sauce over the vegetables and gently fold in the clams. Heat until bubbly. Ladle into bowls and have guests garnish with chopped vegetables.

So-Healthy Clam Chowder

Serves 10

A family pleaser, akin to a minestrone.

1 tablespoon olive oil
1 medium onion, quartered
1 celery stalk
2 carrots
2 garlic cloves
4 cups V-8 vegetable juice
1 cup clam juice
1 cup dry vermouth
1 bay leaf
2 cups canned chick peas, rinsed
   and drained
1 16-ounce can "no salt added" kernel
   corn, drained
1 pound fresh clams, minced
4 tablespoons fresh parsely, chopped
ground black pepper

1. With the sharp metal blade of the food processor running, drop in the onion and garlic. Pulse the machine several times until mixture is finely chopped.

2. Remove metal blade and replace with 2 mm. slicing disk. Process carrot and celery into work bowl with onion and garlic.

3. Heat olive oil in a medium-large stockpot. Sauté onion, garlic, carrot and celery mixture for 5 minutes.

4. Add the V-8, clam juice, vermouth and bay leaf. Cover and simmer for 10 minutes.

5. Add the chick peas, corn, parsley and clams. Simmer for 5 minutes until clams are cooked and vegetables heated through. Grind in black pepper to taste and serve hot.

Newport Clam Chowder

Serves 8

They never add cream to a chowder in Newport.

24 chowder clams (large quahogs)
¼ pound bacon or salt pork, diced
2 medium onions, finely chopped
3 cups potatoes, diced
1 teaspoon salt
½ teaspoon organo
¼ teaspoon basil
6 cups water
black pepper, freshly ground

1. Shuck clams and coarsely chop or grind, reserving all liquids.
2. In a large kettle, sauté onion with bacon or salt pork until golden. Remove any excess fat.
3. Add the potatoes, salt, basil, oregano and water to the pot. Simmer for 10 minutes and add the chopped clams and cook for 5 more minutes. Adjust seasoning with additional salt and pepper.

If you are not serving this the same day it must be cooled completely before refrigerating.

New England Nuance

Serves 10

This recipe is as flexible as you want to make it.

12 large quahogs, shucked and chopped
butter and salt pork (enough to suit your taste)
2 onions, chopped
8 potatoes, cubed
2 cups clam juice
2 cups water
4 cups milk
2 cups cream
2 tablespoons bread crumbs
½ cup whole wheat flour
2 bay leaves
½ cup celery leaves, chopped
¾ cup mushrooms, sliced

1. Cook potatoes in boiling salted water for 10 minutes. Drain and set aside.
2. Melt butter in large pot and add cubed salt pork, and sliced onions. Sauté for 5 minutes until nicely browned.
3. Add the clam juice, water, milk and cream. Bring mixture to a simmer and stir in potatoes, bread crumbs, flour, bay leaves, celery, mushrooms and chopped clams. Simmer for 30 minutes on low to medium heat.
4. To serve, ladle into soup bowls and gently pour 1 tablespoon melted butter on top. Garnish with celery leaves or parsley sprigs.

Especially good with crisp pumpernickel crackers.

Coney Island Belly Wash

Serves 10 to 12

a.k.a Manhattan Clam Chowder.

4 dozen quahogs, medium to large
½ pound bacon
2 ounces olive oil
6 medium onions, chopped
8 potatoes, peeled and cubed
6 large celery stalks, chopped
2 10¾-ounce cans tomato soup
2 14½-ounce cans stewed tomatoes
1 teaspoon sage
1 teaspoon thyme
salt and pepper
2 bottles light beer

1. Scrub clams, open and place in a bowl with the juice. Allow to settle.
2. Remove clams with a slotted spoon and place in a wooden chopping bowl. Discard any sediment in the broth.
3. Cut bacon into small pieces. Add the olive oil to a large chowder pot.
4. Sauté the bacon for 3 minutes and add the onions. Continue cooking until bacon is crisp and onions limp.
5. Add 2 quarts of water. Bring to a boil and stir in the potatoes, celery, sage and thyme.
6. To the pot, add tomato soup and stewed tomatoes. Season to taste with salt and pepper.
7. Chop the clams finely, add with juice to the pot. Simmer over medium-low heat for 2 to 3 hours, stirring occasionally.
8. Finally, add the beer. Chowder will develop more flavor the second day. Be sure to cool before refrigeration.

Morrisey Manhattan Clam Chowder

Serves 8

Try this with fresh peeled summer tomatoes.

12 large quahogs, chowder clams
3 stalks celery, tops included, chopped
1 large carrot, chopped
3 potatoes, diced
2 tablespoons butter
1 tablespoon parsley, chopped
½ teaspoon thyme
1 bay leaf
salt and pepper
1 14-ounce can tomatoes

1. Place clams in a large pot. Add enough water to cover. Steam over high heat for 5 to 7 minutes until clams open. Reserve clam broth and coarsely chop clams. Set aside.
2. Melt butter in pan. Add the chopped vegetables and sauté for 5 minutes. Add the seasonings and salt and pepper to taste.
3. Return the clams and broth to pot, add the tomatoes. Simmer for a half hour before serving.

Galilee Quahog Chowder

Serves 12

This calls for cold beer, garlic bread and a green salad.

2 pints Rhode Island quahogs, shucked,
   drained and chopped
1 pound salt pork, diced
3 medium onions, diced
2 large garlic cloves, minced
ground black pepper
½ teaspoon thyme
10 medium potatoes, diced
8 cups whole milk

1. In a large heavy pot, cook salt pork until fat is rendered and chunks are lightly browned. Remove from pan.
2. In the remaining fat in pot, sauté the onions and garlic until tender.
3. Add the chopped quahogs, cover and simmer gently for 15 minutes. The recipe may stop here and the mixture chilled or frozen for later use. If serving on the same day proceed.
4. To the quahog, onion and garlic, add diced potatoes, water to cover, thyme and pepper to taste. Cook for 10 minutes until the potatoes are tender. DO NOT DRAIN. Add the warm milk and heat over low heat until steaming.

Auntie Bea's Quahog Chowder

Serves 6 to 8

1 quart quahogs, out of the shell, chopped
4 medium potatoes, cubed
1 large onion, finely chopped
1-inch cube of salt pork
1 quart milk, hot

If you make this a day ahead and slowly reheat it, you will like it even better.

1. Remove rind from the salt pork, if you wish, and mince. In a medium-size saucepot, sauté the pork and onions until soft.
2. Add the potatoes and enough water to cover. Simmer for 10 minutes until potatoes are slightly soft.
3. Add the quahogs and bring to a slow boil. Add the milk and cook, stirring occasionally for 10 minutes.
   DO NOT LET THIS BOIL.
4. Serve with chowder crackers or milk biscuits.

Sherried Cream of Crab Soup   Serves 6

The unusual use of hard-boiled eggs as a thickening ingredient, adds a lovely subtle taste to this soup.

2 tablespoons unsalted butter
2 tablespoons flour
2 hard-boiled eggs, chopped
1 lemon or lime, freshly squeezed and rind grated
3 cups fish stock
2 cups milk
1 cup light cream
salt
black pepper, freshly ground
dash Angostura bitters
¼ cup dry sherry

1. Melt butter in a saucepan and add flour. Cook for 2 minutes, stirring constantly.

2. Remove pan from the heat and add eggs, mashing them to a smooth paste.

3. Add the juice and rind of lemon or lime, fish stock, milk and cream. Whisk over medium heat and simmer slowly for 5 minutes.

4. Add the crabmeat, seasonings to taste and sherry. Reheat, stirring gently, for 5 more minutes.

V.I.P. Quick Crab Bisque   Serves 4

If you have some crabmeat on hand in the freezer, this is a snap.

1 10¾-ounce can cream of tomato soup
1 10½-ounce can beef consommé
1 10½-ounce can split pea soup, no ham
1 cup light cream
½ cup dry sherry
8 ounces crabmeat
fresh toasted croutons

1. Mix the soups together in a saucepan. Do not dilute.

2. Add the cream and whisk until blended

3. Stir in the crabmeat and heat until steaming. DO NOT BOIL.

4. Add the sherry, and ladle into serving bowls, top with croutons.

Grouper Chowder

Serves 6

1½ pounds grouper (or any other white fish)
1 to 1½ pounds fish parts
   (bones, fins, heads, scaled skin, tails, etc.)
1½ cups evaporated milk
5 peppercorns
2 bay leaves
4 strips bacon
1 cup water
1 green pepper, diced
1½ medium onion, diced
½ cup celery stalks and leaves, chopped
3 tablespoons vegetable oil
2 tomatoes, diced
2 potatoes, diced
½ teaspoon thyme
½ teaspoon marjoram
½ teaspoon seasoned salt
1 teaspoon Worcestershire sauce
3 ounces sherry

1. Combine fish parts with evaporated milk, peppercorns, bay leaves, and water. Simmer 10 to 15 minutes. Strain liquid and discard bones.

2. In a heavy pot, fry the bacon, peppers, onion, celery and tomatoes until vegetables are well cooked and golden. Add marjoram and thyme.

3. Boil diced potatoes in salted water for 20 minutes and drain.

4. To the pot with bacon mixture, add the reserved strained fish liquid and potatoes.

5. Add grouper cut into bite-size pieces. Simmer for 10 minutes, add seasoned salt, sherry and Worcestershire sauce and cook for 10 minutes more.

6. Serve with plain crisp crackers.

Mediterranean Mackerel Soup

Serves 4 to 6

1 whole mackerel, about 1 pound
2 cups water
2 tablespoons olive oil
1 cup onion, chopped
1 carrot, chopped
1 garlic clove, crushed
1 16-ounce can stewed tomatoes, chopped, with juice
½ pound potatoes, peeled and cubed
½ cup corn, fresh or frozen
½ teaspoon black pepper
1 teaspoon Worcestershire sauce
1 teaspoon basil
1 teaspoon sugar
salt to taste

1. Cut fish into 3 or 4 pieces. Place in pan with 2 cups water and poach for 20 minutes, until fish flakes easily. Remove fish and separate flesh in pieces from head, skin and bones. Reserve fish pieces and return bones to the pot. Cook for 20 minutes and strain stock.

2. In a 3-quart soup pot, heat the olive oil. Add the onions, garlic and carrots and cook until translucent.

3. Add the fish stock, tomatoes, potatoes, corn and seasonings. Simmer for 10 minutes until potatoes are cooked.

4. Return the reserved fish to the pot and simmer for another 10 minutes, stirring occasionally. Serve steaming hot.

Lite Mussel and Dill Chowder   Serves 4

A low calorie adaptation of a South Pacific favorite.

1 cup dry white wine
5 dozen mussels, scrubbed and debearded
2 tablespoons vegetable oil (safflower, if watching cholesterol)
2 medium onions, finely diced
2 tablespoons flour
2 cups fish stock
2 cups potatoes, diced
1 large carrot, finely diced
1 bay leaf
¼ teaspoon thyme
4 tablespoons dill
2 cups low fat or skim milk
salt and pepper.

1. Pour the wine into a large pot (non-reactive, not aluminum). Bring to a simmer over medium heat. Add mussels and cover. Steam mussels, about 2 minutes until opened, shaking pot from side to side.

2. Transfer opened mussels to a bowl and discard any that remain closed. When cool, remove mussel meats from shells, reserving wine mixture. Strain juice through cheesecloth to remove any shell or sand.

3. Rinse the pot and add oil. Heat over medium heat and add the diced onions. Cook, stirring for 4 minutes.

4. Whisk in the flour and slowly add the reserved wine and juices. Pour in the fish stock and combine well. Bring to a boil and reduce heat to a simmer. Cook for 5 minutes until liquid is thickened.

5. Add the potatoes, carrots, bay leaf, thyme, dill, salt and pepper. Stir well and simmer, partially covered, for 15 minutes until vegetables are fork tender. Discard bay leaf.

6. When ready to serve add the milk and mussel meats. Cook over low heat until bubbly — 3 to 4 minutes. Adjust seasonings at this time if you wish.

When purchasing fresh shellfish, clams, oysters or mussels, always discard any with gaping shells that do not close when handled as they are dead and not useable.

Marvelous Mussels in Broth

Serves 4 mussel lovers

3 pounds mussels, washed and debearded
3 tablespoons olive oil
1 large onion, chopped
1 celery stalk, chopped
3 garlic cloves, minced
1 carrot, grated
⅔ cup dry sherry
1 teaspoon red pepper flakes
1 teaspoon fresh ginger, grated
1 teaspoon basil
2 tablespoons Worcestershire sauce
1 lime, freshly squeezed

1. In a large pot, sauté onion, celery and garlic with the olive oil until lightly browned.
2. Stir in the carrot, sherry, red pepper, ginger, basil and Worcestershire sauce.
3. Add the mussels to the pot, squeeze the lime over and cover. Steam for 7 minutes until mussels open.

The mussels can be eaten with the seasoned broth or you can coarsely chop the meat and turn into a creamy chowder by adding half and half. Either way, this IS marvelous.

Minnesota Salmon Chowder

Serves 6

1 pound salmon steak, poached
½ cup wild rice*
2 tablespoons butter or olive oil
½ cup fennel bulb or celery, chopped
1 garlic clove, crushed
½ cup fresh or frozen green peas
1 quart fish stock
¼ teaspoon dill
½ teaspoon Worcestershire sauce
salt and pepper to taste
parsley, chopped

*As wild rice usually contains some grit, it should be well rinsed.

1. In a large soup pot, sauté onions, fennel/celery and garlic in butter or olive oil until translucent.
2. Combine all ingredients, except the salmon and simmer for 10 minutes.
3. Flake and de-bone the salmon steak and add to the pot with the cooked wild rice.
4. Simmer slowly for 10 minutes and season to taste. Ladle into bowls and sprinkle with parsley.

Wild Rice preparation:

1. Bring wild rice to a boil in 2 cups of water for 2 minutes. Let stand for 1 hour, drain and rinse again.
2. Then cook at a simmer in 2 cups water for 45 minutes until rice "flowers" or opens up. Drain again before adding to the soup stock.

Salmon and Cheese Chowder   Serves 4

Toasted French bread croutons are divine with this creamy soup.

½ cup celery, chopped
½ cup carrot, chopped
2 tablespoons butter or margarine
¼ cup flour
¼ teaspoon paprika
⅛ teaspoon pepper
2 cups chicken broth
2 cups milk
1 15½-ounce can salmon, drained, flaked, skin and bones removed
½ cup American or cheddar cheese, shredded
2 tablespoons parsley, snipped

1. In a 3-quart saucepan, cook celery and carrot in butter for 4 to 5 minutes. They should be tender but not brown.
2. Stir in flour, paprika, pepper and butter. Add chicken broth and mix all at once.
3. Cook and stir over medium heat until mixture is thick and bubbly.
4. Add the salmon, cheese and parsley. Cook and stir until cheese is melted.

Scallop Dragger's Stew   Serves 10

A milky Maine-type dish called the "King" of chowders in Southwest Harbor.

1½ pounds sea scallops
¼ cup salt pork, finely chopped
½ cup onion, chopped
1 garlic clove, minced
2 cups potatoes, cubed
6 tablespoons butter
2 cups light cream
4 cups milk
½ teaspoon oregano
salt and pepper

Must be made ahead.

1. In a cast iron Dutch oven or large heavy pot, sauté the salt pork until light brown.
2. To the drippings, add onion and garlic. Sauté until translucent and season with salt and pepper.
3. Add the potatoes, barely cover with water and simmer for 10 minutes until potatoes are done but still slightly firm.
4. Stir the scallops into mixture in pot and cook over low heat until scallops are barely done. Be careful not to overcook scallops.
5. Remove from heat and stir in butter until it has melted. Add cream, milk and oregano. Season to taste and let sit at least two hours before reheating and serving.

Curried Scallop and Green Pea Soup   Serves 6

4 tablespoons butter
1 tablespoon oil
1 medium onion, minced
2 garlic cloves, minced
1 cup peas, shelled
¼ teaspoon salt
3 tablespoons curry powder
2 tablespoons flour
2 cups chicken broth
¾ cup light cream
½ pound scallops

This can be served hot or chilled. Garnish with fresh mint if your garden is still flowering.

1. Combine 2 tablespoons butter and oil in a saucepan and sauté onion and garlic for 5 minutes until transparent.

2. Add peas, salt and curry powder to the pan and simmer until peas are soft. Remove from heat.

3. Whisk flour into the chicken broth in a small dish, and slowly add to the hot broth.

4. Reheat to a slow simmer until thickened, stirring constantly.

5. Cool for 15 minutes. At this time place remaining 2 tablespoons butter in a medium pan and sauté scallops for 3 minutes until plump.

6. Purée soup in the food processor until smooth. Return to the pan, add cream and sautéed scallops. Keep warm until ready to serve.

Chilled Russian Chlodnik   Serves 10

Your guests will wonder at this marvelous combination.

¾ pound medium shrimp, cooked and peeled
2 medium cucumbers, peeled, seeded and diced (1½ cups)
½ teaspoon salt
dash of white pepper
2 cups sour cream
5 cups buttermilk
½ cup sauerkraut juice
2 garlic cloves, chopped
½ cup scallions, chopped
3 tablespoons fresh dill (2 tablespoons dry)
1 teaspoon fennel seed
2 hard-boiled eggs, finely chopped for garnish

Must be made ahead.

1. Marinate cucumber in salt for a half hour to draw off the moisture, drain.

2. Combine sour cream, buttermilk, sauerkraut juice, garlic and pepper. Whisk until smooth.

3. Put remaining ingredients in a large bowl and stir in sour cream mixture.

4. Chill and garnish each serving with chopped egg.

Shrimp and Cheddar Chowder   Serves 8

Almost like a shrimp rarebit.

4 large onions, sliced
¼ cup butter
1 cup boiling water
6 medium potatoes, peeled and cubed
1 teaspoon salt
¼ teaspoon seasoned pepper
1½ quarts milk
2 cups sharp cheddar cheese, grated
2 pounds raw large shrimp, shelled and deveined
3 tablespoons parsley, snipped

1. In a Dutch oven, sauté the onion slices in hot butter until tender. Add boiling water, potatoes, salt and seasoned pepper. Simmer, covered for 20 minutes or until potatoes are tender. DO NOT DRAIN.

2. Meanwhile, heat milk until hot and stir in the cheese. Stir until melted.

3. Add shrimp to the potatoes and cook for 3 minutes until they turn pink. Add hot milk and cheese mixture and combine well. Heat but do not boil. Sprinkle with snipped parsley.

Shrimp and Crab Callaloo   Serves 12

Start your Cajun dinner with a bowl of this.

1 pound medium shrimp, peeled and deveined
1 pound crab, cartilage removed
2 bags fresh spinach, rinsed and chopped
2 large onions, sliced
6 slices bacon, chopped
1½ quarts stock, fish or chicken
2 tomatoes, chopped
½ teaspoon nutmeg
salt and pepper
Tabasco sauce

1. Sauté bacon and sliced onion in a large pot for 5 minutes, stirring occasionally.

2. Add stock, spinach, tomatoes and seasonings. Bring to a boil, reduce heat and cook for 15 minutes.

3. Add the shellfish and cook gently for 6 to 8 minutes until shrimp are pink. When ready to serve, readjust seasonings and add a few dashes of Tabasco to your taste.

Hearty Squid Stew

Serves 6

Pass the Tabasco sauce for a little additional fire.

1½ pounds cleaned squid, cut into
    1-inch rings
4 large potatoes peeled and diced
2 cups white wine
1 quart fish stock
1 pound tomatoes, chopped fresh or canned
1 6-ounce can tomato paste
1 onion, chopped
3 garlic cloves, minced
2 tablespoons olive oil
2 tablespoons Worcestershire sauce
pinch ground allspice
pinch ground cumin
⅛ teaspoon Cayenne pepper
salt to taste

1. Sauté onion and garlic in olive oil until limp.
2. Add all of the vegetables, liquids and seasonings to the pot and simmer for one hour.
3. Add squid and simmer 1 to 2 hours, stirring occasionally.
4. Serve with crusty bread and a salad.

Chilled Seafood Gazpacho

Serves 8 to 10

Spoon this into a stemmed wine glass for a special occasion.

1½ cups seafood, chopped; shrimp, clams,
    flaked fish or crabmeat. If nothing fresh
    is available a small can of shrimp, crab
    and salmon, drained, make a nice
    combination.
2 celery, stalks
1 medium onion
1 pepper, seeded
1 cucumber, peeled and seeded
1 28-ounce can Italian tomatoes
½ cup parsley sprigs
2 cups tomato juice
1 cup dry white wine
2 tablespoons lemon juice
1 teaspoon salt
¼ teaspoon black pepper
4 drops Tabasco sauce
½ cup sour cream
lemon slices

Must be made ahead.

1. In the bowl of the food processor, chop the celery, onion, pepper and cucumber until coarse.
2. Add the tomatoes and parsley. Pulse for 10 seconds, on and off being sure not to purée. The mixture should remain chunky.
3. Transfer to a large bowl and add tomato juice, white wine, lemon juice, seasonings and chopped seafood. Combine well and chill. Serve, garnished with a lemon slice and dollop of sour cream.

Olympian Fish Chowder Serves 4 to 6

Fit for the gods . . . created by the captain of the "Olympian."

1 to 1½ pounds fish fillets, cod, haddock or any firm fish, cut across in 1-inch slices
4 potatoes, cut in 1-inch cubes
3 medium onions, chopped
1 16-ounce can plum tomatoes
⅓ pound bacon, chopped
2 tablespoons butter
2 cups milk, room temperature
1 8-ounce can evaporated milk
2 tablespoons Worcestershire sauce
1 teaspoon salt
½ teaspoon black pepper

1. Put tomatoes in bottom of pressure cooker*. Do not drain.
2. Layer onions, potatoes, bacon and fish in the pot. Sprinkle with salt and pepper.
3. Cook for 10 minutes until pressure is up. Reduce pressure at once and add butter and Worcestershire sauce.
4. Stir gently once to combine and add the milk. Reheat if necessary but do not allow to boil. Serve with fresh hot cornbread and coleslaw for a hearty meal.

*Without Presssure Cooker:
1. Follow the same procedure except cook bacon and onions separately until onions are transparent.
2. Transfer to a large covered pot and cook until potatoes and fish are done.

Down East Fish 'n Vegetable Chowder Serves 6

A real favorite with the younger members of the family.

3 strips bacon, diced
3 medium onions, thinly sliced
1 garlic clove, minced
1 cup celery, thinly sliced
3 large potatoes, diced
2 cups water
1½ teaspoons salt
1 bay leaf
½ teaspoon thyme leaves
1 pound fresh fish fillets (cod, perch or flounder) cut in chunks
1 10-ounce package frozen mixed vegetables or peas and carrots, thawed
2 cups light cream
½ cup milk

1. Cook bacon in Dutch oven or large saucepan over medium heat; remove bacon bits and reserve.
2. Sauté onions, garlic and celery in bacon drippings, stirring often, until onions are light yellow, about 15 minutes.
3. Add potatoes, 1 cup water, salt, bay leaf and thyme. Simmer covered about 20 minutes, or until potatoes are almost tender.
4. Add fish, frozen vegetables and remaining 1 cup water. Simmer covered 10 to 12 minutes longer, or until fish is cooked.
5. Add cream and milk; heat to just boiling. Serve with reserved bacon bits.

Mr. Josep Fish Soup

Serves 2 or 3

½ large white onion, sliced
⅓ large red pepper, cut in thin strips
1 large carrot, sliced
4 to 5 small boiling potatoes, cubed
3 large garlic cloves, coarsely chopped
1½ quarts fish stock (if nothing else is available, use fish stock cubes to make this)
1½ teaspoons curry powder
1 teaspoon chili powder
½ teaspoon cracked black pepper
¼ teaspoon Cayenne pepper
1 pound fresh fish, in big bite-size chunks cut from boneless fillets. Use a good firm fish with a nice flavor, such as cod or hake. You do not want a fish that will fall apart in cooking or while eating with chopsticks.

1. Put all ingredients except fish in a large pot. Boil for about 20 minutes. Then add fish.

2. Cook until done, about 15 minutes depending on the size of the chunks. The fish will usually float up to the surface when it is cooked.

3. You may wish to add pieces of cabbage or seaweed.

This is spicy hot soup. If that doesn't result, use more of the spices. You could also add Tabasco or ground ginger, but they aren't necessary.

Although this recipe was developed after a trip to Korea, it is not intended as authentically Korean at all; it merely reflects new ideas gained from experiencing the Korean cuisine. The recipe will serve two hungry diners, or three if accompanied by bread and perhaps a salad.

Ruth's Mid-East Fish and Vegetable Stew   Serves 4

From a generous member who spent 2 years in Kartoum, Sudan and sailed the Nile river often.

½ pound Nile perch, tilefish or other firm
   fillets, cubed
1 16-ounce can stewed tomatoes
1 cup vegetable juice
1 cup water
1 cup onion, thinly sliced
1 cup pepper, cubed
1 garlic clove, minced
1 small baby eggplant, cubed
1 small yellow squash, cubed
1 small zucchini, cubed
handful of beans or peas — whatever
   else you may have fresh in the garden
   or refrigerator
¼ teaspoon each; basil, thyme, oregano
½ cup chicken broth (optional, depending
   on the moisture in the vegetables)
½ cup white wine
½ cup mushrooms, sliced
salt and coarsely ground pepper

1. Bring on the pot and combine all ingredients except fish and mushrooms. Cover and simmer for 20 to 25 minutes.
2. Add the cubed fish and mushrooms. Simmer for 5 minutes until fish is lightly cooked. Serve immediately.

Hock's Seafood Soup

Serves 6 to 8

A fragrant dinner soup, serve with hot herb bread.

16 cherrystone clams
¾ pound medium shrimp, peeled
1½ pounds firm white fish fillets, cod,
   halibut or a non-oily type, cut into
   1-inch pieces
3 tablespoons olive oil
2 onions, finely chopped
2 garlic cloves, minced
1 large green pepper, chopped
1 10½-ounce can tomato purée
3 8-ounce bottles clam juice
1 cup red or dry white wine
2 13-ounce cans chicken broth
3 bay leaves
1 lemon, thinly sliced
2 large carrots, thinly sliced
½ teaspoon each; basil, thyme, crushed red
   pepper flakes and coriander seed,
   crushed
parsley sprigs for garnish

1. Heat olive oil in a 5-quart kettle on
   medium heat.
2. Sauté onion, garlic and green pepper
   until soft.
3. Stir in the tomato purée, clam juice, wine,
   chicken broth, bay leaves, lemon slices,
   carrots and seasonings. Simmer
   uncovered for 10 minutes.
4. Add the clams and simmer until clams
   begin to open — about 7 minutes.
5. Combine the shrimp and cubed fish with
   the clams and vegetables. Stir gently and
   simmer for 7 more minutes, until shrimp
   have turned pink and clams are fully
   opened.

**Garnish with parsley sprigs and serve with small
forks to help with the clams.**

Bayou Seafood Gumbo I

Serves 8 to 10

**Prepare this in a big copper kettle
and place it right on the table.**

1 pound medium shrimp, peeled and
   deveined
1 pound clams, shucked
½ pound crabmeat
½ pound firm fish fillets, bass, halibut, cod
2 strips bacon
2 onions, chopped
2 garlic cloves, crushed
1 green pepper, chopped
2 16-ounce cans whole tomatoes
1 cup water
1 bay leaf
1 pound okra, cut in ½-inch pieces or
   1 box frozen okra
salt, black pepper or Cayenne to taste

1. In a large pot sauté bacon until crisp.
   Remove and crumble.
2. Add the onions, garlic and green pepper
   and fry for 5 minutes until soft.
3. Add the tomatoes, water, bay leaf, okra,
   salt and pepper. Cook over medium heat
   for 15 minutes.
4. Add the shrimp, clams, crabmeat and
   fish. Simmer for 1 hour. Serve in large
   bowls over white rice.

Pilgrim Stew

Serves 6

¼ cup olive oil
1 stalk celery, chopped
1 medium onion, chopped
1 garlic clove, chopped
1 leek, chopped
½ teaspoon thyme
½ bay leaf
2 cups tomatoes, quartered
3 cups bottled clam juice
1 cup dry white wine
salt and pepper to taste
2 tablespoons parsley, chopped
2 small lobster, or three culls, boiled and broken into parts
12 mussels, with shells scraped clean and boiled
12 extra large shrimp, boiled and cleaned
24 small scallops
1 pound codfish, cut into small pieces

1. In a large pot, heat the oil, and then add the celery, onion, garlic, leek, thyme, and bay leaf. Simmer slowly for 15 minutes.

2. In a second pot, boil the lobsters for about six minutes, adding the shrimp for the last two minutes. Then, break off the lobster claws, and split and clean the tail meat. Shell and devein the shrimp. Place the mussels in the remaining hot water and boil until they open — about 10 minutes.

3. In the first pot, add the tomatoes, clam juice, dry white wine, salt, pepper and parsley. Simmer for 15 minutes.

4. Add the raw scallops and codfish pieces to the first pot, stir them under and cook for 10 minutes. Then add the shrimp and lobster parts, and continue cooking for another 10 minutes. Finally, place the cooked and opened mussels around the top of the stew and serve.

Above is one of my favorite recipes, and I should probably give you a bit of explanation. Every year, at the time of the Thanksgiving holiday, my wife and I enjoy reading William Bradford's journals about the Pilgrims and their experiences at Plymouth Plantation. Although it has become the custom to celebrate Thanksgiving with a turkey dinner, our Pilgrim forbearers also ate a great deal of seafood which was somewhat easier to obtain. So my recipe for "Pilgrim Stew" is based on what I imagined they were able to collect for their stewpot in those early years.

R.S. — Stonington, CT

Winter Harbor Fish Chowder   Serves 8

As with most chowders, even better the next day.

4 slices bacon or ¼-pound salt pork, diced
1 large onion, sliced
3 potatoes, peeled and diced
3 to 4 cups boiling water, depending on
   your kettle
1½ pounds haddock or cod
3 6-ounce cans evaporated milk
salt and pepper
8 pats of butter

1. Fry bacon in a large kettle. When crisp, remove and drain.

2. Add onion to pan and sauté until transparent.

3. Pour off any extra fat, leaving 3 table-spoons. Spread potatoes evenly over the onions.

4. Add enough boiling water to barely cover the potatoes, top with fish, skin side up. It should not be immersed in water.

5. Cover and simmer for 15 minutes until potatoes are tender. Remove skin from the fish and break it up gently.

6. Over low heat, stir in evaporated milk, salt and pepper. Serve with a pat of butter and crisp bacon or salt pork bits.

Gram Kezer's Oven Fish Chowder   Serves 8

This recipe comes from Gram Kezer who lives on Plum Island, Massachusetts. She made this as her great granddaughter's first bowl of chowder, and it is still a family favorite.

1½ pounds whitefish (ocean cat or wolf fish
   are favorites). Haddock, cod or hake may
   be substituted.
4 medium potatoes, peeled and diced
1 large onion, chopped
leaves from 4 celery stalks
   (about ½ cup), chopped
1 teaspoon dill
1 garlic clove, finely minced
½ teaspoon salt
½ teaspoon black pepper
½ cup dry vermouth
2 cups boiling water
2 tablespoons butter
1 cup half-and-half cream

1. Place all ingredients except cream in a large 4-quart casserole dish. Stir to combine.

2. Cover and bake in a 350° oven for one hour. Remove from oven and gently stir in the half-and-half. Cover again and let stand for 10 minutes.

May be rewarmed but do not boil.

Caldeirada . . . Portuguese Fish Soup   Serves 8

Serve over a white or brown rice pilaf and sprinkle with a few peas.

1 pound haddock
2 cups onion, chopped
1 tablespoon olive oil
1 tablespoon butter
1 garlic clove, minced
1 large green pepper, chopped
1 large carrot, chopped
4 medium tomatoes, chopped
2 cups beef stock, canned
½ cup dry white wine
½ teaspoon sugar
½ teaspoon basil
1 teaspoon paprika
black pepper to taste
1 pound medium shrimp, peeled
   and deveined

1. Cut haddock into ¾-inch chunks and set aside.

2. In a large pot, melt the butter, add the olive oil and sauté the onions until soft.

3. Add the garlic, peppers, carrot and tomatoes and stir together.

4. Add beef stock, wine, sugar basil and paprika.

5. Bring to a boil, reduce heat and simmer for 15 minutes. Add the cut up fish and cook over medium heat for 4 minutes.

6. Add the shrimp and cook until the shrimp are pink, 1 to 2 minutes, depending on the size of the shrimp.

Northwest Cioppino

Serves 6 to 8

From a faithful Seaport sailor.

¼ cup olive oil
1 cup onion, diced
1 cup celery, diced
3 garlic cloves, minced
¾ cup green pepper, julienne sliced
1 cup carrot, sliced
1 29-ounce can stewed tomatoes
1 15-ounce can tomato sauce
1 cup white wine
3 tablespoons parsley, minced
2 teaspoons salt
½ teaspoon black pepper
1 teaspoon basil
½ teaspoon thyme
1 pound red snapper
1 pound cod
1 pound halibut
8 ounces lump crabmeat, cartilage removed
1½ to 2 dozen hard shell clams, washed.

1. Add olive oil to a large saucepan and sauté onion, garlic, celery, green pepper and carrots for 5 minutes. Stir in the tomatoes, tomato sauce, white wine, parsley and seasonings. Cover and simmer for 30 minutes.

2. Cut snapper and cod into 2-inch pieces and halibut into 1-inch pieces. In a large kettle place the cut up fish, crabmeat and clams. Pour the hot sauce overall and stir gently. Cover and simmer for 15 to 20 minutes until clams open and fish flakes at the touch of a fork. Sprinkle with parsley.

Bombay Curried Fish Soup

Serves 4

The hotter the curry powder, the better the soup.

½ cup leek, rinsed and thinly sliced
1 carrot, chopped
½ cup onion, minced
2 tablespoons butter
1 tablespoon curry powder
½ cup tomato, chopped
2 cups fish stock
½ teaspoon malt vinegar
½ teaspoon light brown sugar
1 cup light cream
1 medium potato, diced
½ pound scrod fillet with or without the
   skin, cut into 1-inch cubes
fresh parsley
salt and ground black pepper

1. Melt butter in a medium-size soup pot and sauté leek, carrot and onion until softened.
2. Add curry powder and tomato, cook for 5 minutes.
3. Stir in fish stock, vinegar, brown sugar, and bring to a boil.
4. Reduce heat, cover and simmer broth for 15 minutes over medium heat.
5. Add potato and cream, again simmer for 15 minutes until potato is tender.
6. Uncover, drop in fish and let it poach for 5 minutes.
7. Add salt and pepper to taste. Ladle into bowls and sprinkle with parsley.

V.I.P. Shellfish Chowder

Serves 4

Rich, creamy and slightly sinful.

¼ pound shrimp, peeled and deveined
1 cup light cream
12 mussels or cherrystone clams, well rinsed
¼ cup bacon or salt pork, minced
1 tablespoon butter
¼ cup onion, chopped
¼ cup celery, chopped
⅛ teaspoon thyme
2 cups milk
1 large potato, finely diced
½ pound scallops
Cayenne pepper
parsley, chopped

1. In a small bowl, soak the shrimp in the cream for 30 minutes.
2. Steam the mussels or clams in a small amount of water until the shells open, remove the meats and set aside.
3. Place the bacon and butter in a medium saucepan. Add the onion, celery and thyme and cook until vegetables are soft. Add the milk and potatoes, reduce heat and simmer for 10 minutes.
4. Add the shrimp/cream mixture, mussels or clams, and scallops. Bring to a gentle boil, reduce heat and simmer for 5 minutes until shrimp and scallops are just cooked. Season to taste with Cayenne and garnish with parsley.

Iberian Seafood Chowder

Serves 10 to 12

2 pounds fresh haddock or cod, cut into
   bite-size pieces
1 pint fresh clams, diced (or 2 8-ounce cans)
1 pint fresh oysters (or 2 small cans)
1 pint fresh mussels
1 cup bacon or salt pork, diced
2 8-ounce cans of corn niblets, drained
2 cups pimento-stuffed olives, sliced
2 cups celery, diced
4 medium potatoes, cubed
2 cups carrots, diced
1 medium size zucchini, cubed
2 cups onions, chopped
6 cups milk
1 teaspoon dill
¼ teaspoon pepper
4 tablespoons flour
Worcestershire sauce, salt, and
   Tabasco sauce to taste

**Any other seafood may be added or substituted,
fresh or canned.**

1. In a large chowder pot render bacon and/or salt pork. Pour off a little of the grease, and add the celery, onions and the 4 tablespoons flour. Let simmer for about 10 minutes, stirring occasionally.

2. In a separate kettle, start cooking the carrots. Boil for 3 minutes, and then add the potatoes. Boil for 5 more minutes and add the zucchini and cook for 3 more minutes. Drain, saving 2 cups of the liquid for the chowder.

3. In the same kettle used for the vegetables or in another kettle, bring 4 cups of water to a rapid boil. Into the boiling water add the haddock or cod, AND THEN IMMEDIATELY TURN OFF THE HEAT. Leave the fish in the slowly cooling water for just a very few minutes. DO NOT OVERCOOK THE FISH!

4. Put the cooked fish with its juice into the chowder pot along with all the other ingredients, EXCEPT THE MILK. Add the 2 cups of broth from the cooked vegetables. Bring all of the mixture to a rapid boil, and immediately lower the heat and add the 6 cups of milk and the seasonings to taste. DO NOT LET BOIL AGAIN AFTER MILK IS ADDED. Keep warm until served, or let cool and refrigerate for use later.

**Our yankee forefathers were forced to eat fish more often than
they preferred, and many old recipes try to mask the flavor of
the fish with strong indgredients such as anchovies, vinegar,
pickled vegetables and lemon peel.**

Narragansett Bay Seafood Chowder   Serves 6

With lobster and scallops, rich and warming.

1 medium onion, chopped
1 tablespoon butter or margarine
2 cups water or fish stock
2 cups potatoes, diced
¾ cup lobster meat, cooked
¾ cup bay scallops
½ pound haddock or flounder fillets
2 cups light cream
pinch nutmeg
salt and pepper
parsley, chopped
paprika

1. Melt butter in medium saucepot. Sauté onion for 5 minutes.
2. Add the water, potatoes and seafood. Simmer over low heat for 15 minutes until potatoes are tender.
3. Stir in the cream and seasonings.
4. Reheat, being careful not to boil. Ladle into wide-rimmed bowls and sprinkle with parsley and paprika.

If you wish to prepare this the day ahead, follow steps 1 and 2. Refrigerate when ready to serve, reheat seafood mixture slowly. Stir in cream and seasonings.

THE MAIN CATCH

Wok Fried Sea Bass

Ch'ao-yü-pien

1 pound Sea Bass fillets (yellow pike or any
other firm fish will do)
2 tablespoons cornstarch
1 egg white
1 tablespoon Chinese rice wine or dry sherry
2 teaspoons salt
4 tablespoons peanut oil
1 teaspoon finely chopped fresh ginger
1 scallion, including green top,
finely chopped

Serves 4 to 6 if served
as part of a Chinese meal

1. Wash fish fillets under cold water and pat
dry. Cut into 1½-inch squares, ½-inch thick.

2. Place the 2 tablespoons cornstarch in a
small bowl, add the fish pieces and toss
until each piece is well coated.

3. Combine the egg white, wine and salt.
Dip the pieces of fish into the mixture.

4. Set a 12-inch wok or 10-inch heavy skillet
over high heat for 30 seconds.

5. Pour in the 4 tablespoons oil, swirl it
around the pan and reduce heat to
medium.

6. Add the ginger and scallions, stir around
for a few seconds and add the pieces
of fish.

7. Stir fry gently for 1 to 2 minutes until
fish is firm and white. Transfer the entire
contents of the pan to a heated platter
and serve at once.

Portuguese Baked Bluefish

Serves 4

1½ pounds bluefish fillets
4 tablespoons butter
1 tablespoon prepared brown mustard
1 tablespoon ketchup
1 tablespoon Worcestershire sauce
2 tablespoons brown sugar

1. Pat the bluefish fillets dry, don't ever
rinse them. Place on a lightly buttered
brown paper bag on a baking sheet.

2. Melt the butter in a saucepan and add
the mustard, ketchup and Worcestershire
sauce. Spread the mixture on top of the
fillets and sprinkle with brown sugar.
Bake at 350° for 15 to 20 minutes until
fish is white and flaky.

Lil's Baked Bluefish with Crust on Top   Serves 6

A secret from one of our talented local female artists.

Pastry:

1½ cups sifted flour
1 teaspoon sugar
1 teaspoon salt
½ cup corn oil
2 tablespoons cold milk

Bluefish:

1 5- to 6-pound bluefish, cleaned with head
  and tail still on
*stuffing, your favorite
1 cherry tomato
a bunch of nasturtiums with leaves

***Try stuffing for Cranberry Stuffed Fish or
Louisiana Rice Stuffed Catfish (See index). Both
offer a nice combination with the bluefish.**

Pastry preparation:

1. Combine flour, sugar and salt in a
   mixing bowl.
2. In a small cup, whip oil and milk with a
   fork. Pour all at once into dry ingredients
   and mix with a fork until dough forms a
   ball. Chill for 2 hours.

Bluefish preparation:

1. Stuff fish and place on a well-greased
   baking sheet. Bake at 350° for 20 minutes
   and remove from the oven.
2. Roll out crust into a long shape to
   resemble the size of the fish. Cover the
   fish and tuck the edges snugly around
   edges of fish.
3. Using a small knife make half-moon slits
   over the body to represent scales. Cut a
   circle out where the eye is. Turn oven up
   to 450° and bake fish for 20 minutes.
   Let cool 5 minutes before removing from
   the pan.
4. Serve the bluefish on a fish platter, put a
   cherry tomato in the eye and make a
   necklace of nasturtiums. Forget the usual
   parsley and add more flowers and leaves
   around the platter.

**Bluefish fillets are large, oily, juicy and have a stronger fish taste,
and are higher in calories than white fish.**

Bookstore Bluefish

Serves 4

A mystical secret revealed.

1½ pounds bluefish fillets
1 onion, finely chopped
½ medium green pepper, chopped
1 garlic clove, minced
2 tablespoons olive oil
2 14-ounce cans stewed tomatoes
2 tablespoons tomato paste
1 tablespoon parsley, chopped
1 teaspoon oregano
salt and pepper

1. Sauté onion, green pepper and garlic in olive oil until tender. Add stewed tomatoes, tomato paste, parsley, oregano, salt and pepper to taste. Simmer for 5 minutes.

2. Place bluefish fillets in a buttered casserole dish. Pour sauce over fish and bake at 350° for 20 minutes.

3. Serve with hot buttered rice.

Louisiana Rice-Stuffed Catfish

Serves 6

An early morning of fishing produces an elegant dinner.

6 pan dressed catfish, ¾- to 1-pound each
1 teaspoon salt
2 tablespoons oil
1 cup celery and leaves, chopped
¼ cup onion, chopped
¾ cup water
2 tablespoons lemon juice
¼ cup orange juice
1 tablespoon orange rind, grated
¾ teaspoon salt
1 cup cooked white or wild rice
½ cup toasted pecans
2 tablespoons butter, melted
2 tablespoons orange juice

1. Clean, rinse and pat fish dry. Sprinkle inside and out with salt.

2. Sauté celery and onion in oil until tender. Add water, lemon juice, orange juice, rind and salt; bring to a boil. Add cooked rice and stir to moisten. Cover and remove from heat. let stand 5 minutes and add nuts, mixing thoroughly.

3. Stuff fish loosely with the rice and secure opening with small skewers or toothpicks. Place fish in a well-greased 14x11x1-inch baking dish. Combine melted butter with 2 tablespoons remaining orange juice and brush the fish with the mixture. Bake in a 350° oven for 25 to 35 minutes, basting occasionally with orange butter. Remove skewers before serving.

Fried Catfish with Hanning Hushpuppies

3 pounds freshwater catfish fillets
1 to 1½ cups cornmeal, the stone-ground
   Rhode Island meal is best
vegetable oil

Hanning Hushpuppies:

1 cup cornmeal
½ cup flour
1 tablespoon baking powder
½ teaspoon salt
½ teaspoon black pepper
½ teaspoon red pepper
1 tablespoon sugar
1 small onion, minced
1 egg, well beaten
½ cup buttermilk

1. Dip the catfish in the cornmeal and coat thoroughly. In a large heavy pan, heat enough oil to cover fish and deep fry for 3 to 4 minutes, depending on thickness of fillets.

2. Drain the fish on paper towels. Keep warm in a low oven while making hushpuppies.

Hushpuppy preparation:

1. Combine the dry ingredients in a mixing bowl. Add the onion, egg and moisten with buttermilk.

2. Drop by tablespoons into the hot oil and cook until golden brown, turning as they cook. Drain on paper towels before serving.

Freshwater catfish are usually farmed and scientifically fed to give a light sweet fish taste. It is firm enough for barbecue and contains more oil than other white fish. Saltwater catfish or wolf fish is similar in texture but is not as sweet.

Hot Cherrystones Tetrazzini   Serves 4

This can also be baked in a large decorative casserole dish and served family style.

32 cherrystone clams, freshly opened
¼ cup butter
1 small onion, minced
1 small green pepper, minced
¼ cup flour
1 cup milk
4 tablespoons dry white wine
½ teaspoon oregano
1 tablespoon parsley, chopped
salt and pepper
½ pound thin spaghetti
½ cup shredded Gruyère cheese
¼ cup Parmesan cheese, freshly grated
paprika

1. Open the clams over a bowl, reserving all of the juices.

2. Melt butter in a saucepan and add onions and green pepper. Sauté for 3 minutes until just opaque.

3. Stir the flour into the butter and vegetable mixture. Slowly add the milk, stirring constantly over medium heat. Add the white wine, reserved clam juice, oregano, parsley and salt and pepper to taste. Cook until thickened. Remove from heat and fold in the cherrystones.

4. Cook the spaghetti until tender and drain. Divide spaghetti among 4 large individual casseroles. Move spaghetti to sides of dishes forming a well in the center of each. Spoon clam mixture into the center of each dish. Sprinkle with Gruyère, Parmesan and paprika. Bake in 375° oven for 15 to 20 minutes until top is lightly browned.

Hard-shell clams in the shell are sold in the following sizes:
- **Littlenecks — mainly served raw on the half shell.**
- **Cherrystones — generally used whole on the halfshell.**
- **Quahog or Chowder — usually chopped and used in chowder or other cooked dishes.**

Clams and Hen in a Pot

Serves 2

A surprise dinner for two, you will have fun eating this.

1 46-ounce can chicken broth
1½ pounds littleneck clams (about 18),
   scrubbed
1 game hen
⅓ cup dry sherry
⅓ cup white turnip, julienned
1 leek, quartered
1 cup whole mushrooms
2 large tomatoes, peeled and chopped
½ cup peas
½ package fresh spinach, rinsed
salt and pepper
⅓ cup scallions, chopped

1. Place the clams in a medium saucepan with ½ inch of water. Cover and steam until shells open, set aside.

2. In a medium saucepot, place the chicken broth, game hen and sherry. Cover and simmer for 45 minutes.

3. Add the turnip and leek, cook for 10 minutes. Stir in the mushrooms, tomatoes, peas and spinach and simmer for 5 minutes, seasoning with salt and pepper. Drop the clams in the pot to warm.

4. To serve, remove the game hen to a platter and split. Place each half in a large soup bowl, surrounded with the vegetables and clams, pour the hot broth on top. Sprinkle with the scallions.

Calico Crab Cakes

Serves 4

If you really want to indulge, serve these with homemade French fried potatoes.

1 pound crabmeat, cartilage removed
½ cup green pepper, diced
½ cup red pepper, diced
1 tablespoon butter
⅓ cup tartar sauce
2 teaspoons Worcestershire sauce
2 teaspoons parsley, minced
1 egg
4 saltine crackers, crumbled
salt and pepper
⅓ cup butter
½ cup vegetable oil

1. Sauté green and red peppers in butter until tender. Cool.

2. In a mixing bowl gently combine remaining ingredients being careful not to overwork. You want the crab chunks to have some texture. If the mixture seems too moist, crumble in another cracker or two.

3. Mold the mixture into patties 2½-inches wide and ½-inch thick. These may be refrigerated if you prefer to prepare them ahead.

4. In a large skillet heat butter and oil over medium heat. Fry cakes on each side until golden. Remove from pan and drain. Serve immediately with additional tartar sauce.

Blue Claw Crabcakes Dijonaise   Serves 4

Special thanks to a great Nantucket chef.

½ pound blue crabmeat (or lump crabmeat)
8 slices good quality firm white bread,
   trimmed and diced
3 eggs, beaten
4 scallions, chopped
3 celery stalks, diced
¼ cup parsley, chopped
1 tablespoon Dijon mustard
½ teaspoon salt
½ teaspoon pepper
¼ cup heavy cream
3 tablespoons butter
parsley, chopped, for garnish

Dijonaise Sauce:

⅓ cup white wine or vermouth
3 shallots, finely chopped
1¾ cups heavy cream
2 tablespoons Dijon mustard
1 teaspoon lemon juice, freshly squeezed
pinch of black pepper
2 tablespoons unsalted butter

1. Mix all ingredients, except the butter, together in a large bowl being careful not to overmix or break up the crab lumps. Set aside for 15 minutes so that bread can absorb the moisture.
2. Form the crab mixture into 8 cakes, ½ inch thick. Melt the butter in a heavy skillet and sauté the cakes over medium heat until both sides are golden and firm.

Dijonaise Sauce preparation:

1. In a 1-quart saucepan bring wine and shallots to a boil and reduce over medium heat until almost dry.
2. Add heavy cream and mustard, reduce by one half.
3. Add lemon juice, pepper and whisk in butter. Immediately remove from heat when butter is melted.
4. Pour sauce on 4 hot plates and place cooked crabcakes on top. Sprinkle sauce with chopped parsley for garnish.

Sippican Harbor Crab Supreme   Serves 8 to 10

Perfect for those "no time to cook" days.

1½ pounds crabmeat
1 8-ounce can water chestnuts, drained
   and sliced
2 cups celery, chopped
1 12-ounce can cream of mushroom soup
2 cups mayonnaise
3 cups herb stuffing mix
¼ pound butter, melted

1. Mix crabmeat, water chestnuts, celery, mushroom soup and mayonnaise in a large bowl. Spread in a large 12x10x1½-inch buttered casserole dish.
2. Melt the butter in a saucepan and add the stuffing mix. Combine until crumbs are well coated with butter and spread mixture on top of the crab. Bake for 30 minutes at 350°.

Crabmeat Stroganoff

Serves 4 to 6

1 pound crabmeat, cartilage removed
3 tablespoons butter
1 cup mushrooms, sliced
½ cup onion, finely chopped
½ cup dry white wine
2 teaspoons dill
1 tablespoon parsley, chopped
½ teaspoon garlic powder
1 teaspoon grated lemon peel
black pepper
2 cups sour cream
8 ounces spinach noodles, cooked
   according to package directions
paprika

1. Sauté mushrooms and onions in the butter in a large skillet until lightly browned.
2. Add white wine, dill, parsley, garlic powder and lemon peel. Cook for 3 to 4 minutes and gently stir in crabmeat.
3. Simmer over medium heat for several minutes and fold in sour cream. Cool until bubbling and serve immediately over green buttered noodles. Sprinkle with paprika.

Crab Mushroom Florentine

Serves 4

A real time saver–this dish goes together quickly and tastes like a million.

1 10-ounce package fresh spinach
2 tablespoons butter
½ pound mushrooms, sliced
8 ounces crabmeat, flaked
1 cup sour cream
1 cup cheddar cheese, grated
1 8-ounce can tomato sauce
2 tablespoons onion, minced
½ teaspoon salt
¼ teaspoon black pepper
¼ teaspoon nutmeg

1. Wash and stem the spinach. Place in a pot with 2 tablespoons of water and cover. Steam for 3 minutes, drain and chop. Spread in a buttered 2-quart baking dish.
2. Sauté the mushrooms in the butter until soft. Cover the spinach with mushrooms, pouring pan juices and butter overall.
3. Combine the remaining ingredients, gently folding in the crabmeat so as not to break it up too much. Pour sauce mixture into the pan over the mushrooms and bake at 350° for 25 to 30 minutes.

Great served over rice or noodles.

Crunchy Crabmeat Casserole

Serves 4 large appetites,
6 small appetites

1 pound crabmeat or any cooked seafood
1 cup celery, chopped
½ cup onion, chopped
1 cup peas, frozen or freshly cooked
2 tablespoons parsley, chopped
1 cup mayonnaise
1 cup milk
1½ cups herb stuffing mix plus
  ½ cup reserved and crushed
1 tablespoon butter

1. Toss the crabmeat, celery, onion, peas and parsley in a mixing bowl.
2. Fold in the mayonnaise, milk and 1½ cups stuffing mix. Combine well and spoon into a well-buttered 2-quart casserole dish. Spread the ½ cup crushed stuffing on top and dot with butter.
3. Bake uncovered in a 350° oven for 30 minutes until browned. If you prepare this ahead of time and refrigerate, allow an extra 10 minutes of cooking time.

Water Street Crab Casserole

Serves 6

Herald the return of great company casseroles.

3 cups lump crabmeat, cartilage removed. Reserve a few nice pieces to top the casserole. Cooked shrimp, peeled and deveined may also be used
4 tablespoons butter
4 tablespoons flour
1 cup milk
1 cup chicken stock
½ teaspoon curry powder
½ teaspoon dry mustard
½ teaspoon paprika
¼ teaspoon basil
2 tablespoons parsley, minced
1 8-ounce can sliced mushrooms, drained, or equal amounts of fresh, briefly sautéed in butter
2 tablespoons lemon juice, freshly squeezed
⅔ cup light cream
salt and pepper
¼ teaspoon grated lemon peel
½ cup fresh bread crumbs, buttered

1. Melt butter in a medium saucepan and stir in flour. Whisk in the milk and chicken stock gradually, stirring constantly over medium heat until thickened.
2. Add the curry powder, paprika, mustard, basil, parsley, mushrooms, lemon juice and cream. Season to taste with salt and pepper and simmer for 2 to 3 minutes.
3. Place the crabmeat in a 2-quart casserole and lightly toss with lemon peel. Pour in the sauce and fold gently into the crabmeat. Arrange reserved leg meat on top and sprinkle with buttered crumbs. Bake in 350° oven for 20 minutes until bubbly and brown.

Crabmeat Seviche

Serves 2 to 4

1½ pounds fresh crabmeat
2 medium tomatoes
1 small onion
1 small green pepper
1 small hot jalapeño pepper
3 limes, freshly squeezed
1 lemon, freshly squeezed
½ teaspoon black pepper, freshly ground
1 garlic clove, minced
¼ teaspoon Cayenne pepper
tomato slices
lemon slices
lime slices
lettuce

Must be made ahead.

1. Finely dice tomatoes, onions and peppers.
2. Place crabmeat in a medium bowl, add diced vegetables, lemon and lime juice, black pepper and garlic. Toss well and refrigerate at least 2 hours.
3. To serve, spoon salad onto a bed of garden lettuce and garnish with slices of tomato, lemon and lime.

Noank Deviled Crab Casserole

Serves 6

This has been served many times, both ashore and afloat.

1½ pounds fresh crabmeat or 3 7-ounce cans crabmeat, rinsed and picked over well
1 green pepper
¾ pound mushrooms
6 sweet gherkins
3 small white onions
2 tablespoons parsley, chopped
6 tablespoons butter
5 tablespoons flour
1½ cups milk
½ cup light cream
½ cup dry sherry
½ teaspoon salt
black pepper, freshly ground
dash of Cayenne
¾ cup dry fresh bread crumbs

1. Chop the pepper, mushrooms, gherkins and onions. Mix with the parsley and crabmeat.
2. In a saucepan melt the butter. Add the flour and stir with a whisk until blended. Meanwhile, bring the milk and cream to a boil. Pour all at once into the butter-flour mixture and stir rapidly until the sauce is smooth and thickens. Stir in the sherry.
3. Fold the crabmeat and vegetable mixture into the hot sauce and season with salt, pepper and Cayenne. Pour into a buttered 2-quart casserole and sprinkle with bread crumbs. Dot with additional butter and bake for 30 minutes at 350°.

Chesapeake Crab Imperial

Serves 4

1 pound fresh crabmeat, cartilage removed
1 tablespoon butter
1 tablespoon flour
½ cup milk
1 tablespoon onion, chopped
2 teaspoons Worcestershire sauce
2 cups fresh bread crumbs, it need not be
  all white bread
½ cup mayonnaise
½ lemon, freshly squeezed
½ teaspoon salt
¼ teaspoon Old Bay Seasoning
black pepper
2 tablespoons butter
paprika

1. In a medium saucepan, melt 1 tablespoon butter and mix in the flour. Slowly add the milk, stirring constantly. Cook over medium heat until sauce is smooth and thick. Mix in the onion and Worcestershire sauce, remove from heat and cool.

2. Gently fold in the bread crumbs, mayonnaise, lemon juice, salt, pepper and Old Bay Seasoning.

3. In another pan, melt the remaining butter and cook for 2 to 3 minutes until slightly browned. Add the crabmeat and toss lightly.

4. Combine the crabmeat with the sauce mixture and pour into a 1-quart casserole. Sprinkle with paprika and bake at 450° for 10 to 15 minutes until hot and lightly browned on top.

Over a period of 10 years cruising the Chesapeake Bay for 2 months each summer, we have learned to catch blue crabs the fun way. All you need is a salted eel or chicken necks for bait, lots of string, weights, a wire mesh dipping net and a pound of patience. A dozen blue crabs measuring 6-inches from point to point will yield a good pound of meat.

Savannah Crabmeat Hash

Serves 4

A Sunday standby with buttered biscuits.

1 pound crabmeat, cartilage removed
4 strips bacon, chopped
1 large onion, chopped
2 cups boiled potatoes, cubed
2 tablespoons parsley, chopped
1 tablespoon lemon juice, freshly squeezed
4 tablespoons cream
salt and Cayenne pepper
4 eggs
hot pepper sauce

1. In a large heavy skillet, cook the bacon until crisp. Remove from the pan. There should be about 2 tablespoons of dripping in the pan. If not, add a little olive oil. Add the onions and potatoes to the skillet and fry for 10 minutes, stirring frequently until brown and crispy.

2. Add the crabmeat, cooked bacon, parsley, lemon juice, and cream. Combine well and season with salt and Cayenne. Continue to cook without stirring until bottom is crisp and golden brown.

3. Turn onto a platter and top with poached or fried eggs. Pass the hot pepper sauce to taste.

Crab Stuffed Chicken Breasts

Serves 6

Light and easy, try serving with lemon rice.

6 chicken breasts, skinned and boned
4 tablespoons butter
½ cup onion, chopped
½ cup celery, chopped
¼ cup dry white wine
2 6-ounce cans crabmeat, cartilage removed, rinsed and drained
½ cup herb stuffing mix or cracker crumbs
½ cup flour
salt and pepper
melted butter

1. Pound chicken breasts until uniform in size.

2. In a medium frying pan, melt the butter and sauté onion and celery until tender. Add the wine, crabmeat and crumbs, tossing lightly.

3. Place stuffing down the center of the chicken breasts and roll up. Tie each breast with string.

4. Roll each piece in a mixture of the flour, salt and pepper. Place in a 9x12-inch baking dish and drizzle with extra melted butter. Bake for 45 minutes in a 325° oven.

Mother's Deviled Crabs

Serves 12

12 hardshell blue crabs
2 tablespoons vinegar
4 tablespoons butter
1 onion, finely minced
1 tablespoon parsley, chopped
1 teaspoon prepared mustard
2 teaspoons lemon juice, freshly squeezed
2 tablespoons flour
1 teaspoon salt
⅛ teaspoon Cayenne pepper
1 cup milk
1 extra large egg (or 2 small)
½ cup bread or cracker crumbs
2 tablespoons butter, melted

If you do not have access to fresh crabs, substitute 2⅔ cups lump crabmeat and bake in individual ramekins.

1. In a large pot, boil crabs for 20 to 25 minutes, adding 2 tablespoons of vinegar to the water. Pick meat from shells, reserving the 12 large back shells.

2. Melt 4 tablespoons of butter in a saucepan and add the onion. Cook for 5 minutes until opaque. Do not brown.

3. Stir in the parsley, mustard, lemon juice, flour, salt and pepper. Whisk in the milk and simmer until thickened. Gently fold in the crabmeat and remove from the stove. Beat in the egg.

4. Fill the shells with the mixture. Mix the crumbs with the melted butter and sprinkle on each crab. Bake at 400° for 10 minutes until nicely browned.

One of my happy childhood memories is of crabbing on the Chesapeake Bay at our summer cottage. My mother, a native of New Orleans, sometimes used the catch in a crab gumbo, usually the crabs were dumped in a pot for a crab boil. Picking the crabmeat was a messy job (our cat hovered over looking for tidbits), but when mother made Deviled Crabs, everyone was ecstatic.

— J.M.

Cod Ratatouille with Feta Cheese Serves 6 to 8

You will love a big basket of toasted Pita bread with this.

3 pounds cod fillets, or any nice
  thick flaky fish
2 tablespoons olive oil
3 garlic cloves, minced
2 small onions, sliced
1 large green pepper, cut into strips
1 medium eggplant, peeled and cubed
2 small zucchini, chopped
1 cup mushrooms, sliced
6 tomatoes, peeled and chopped
½ cup white wine
1 teaspoon basil
½ teaspoon oregano
pinch of salt, sugar and pepper
6 ounces Feta cheese

1. In a large saucepan sauté the garlic and onion for 2 minutes. Add the peppers, eggplant, zucchini, mushrooms and tomatoes. Continue to cook stirring occasionally for 5 minutes.

2. Add the wine and seasonings to the pan and simmer, covered, for 5 minutes. The vegetables should still be firm and crisp.

3. Place the fish fillets in a buttered, 3-quart casserole dish, in one layer. Top with the vegetable mixture and cover with aluminum foil. Bake for 15 minutes in a 350° oven. Uncover, crumble cheese on top and bake for 10 minutes until cheese has melted.

Cod Alla Rosa   Serves 6

A Christmas Eve tradition handed down from mother to mother.

2 pounds dry codfish
¼ cup dried Italian black olives
1 small onion
2 tablespoons olive oil
1 16-ounce can tomato sauce
¼ tablespoon dry hot red pepper flakes

Dry cod has to be soaked in water for 2 or 3 days. Change water several times making sure all of the salt is out of the fish before you continue.

1. Chop onion and sauté in oil for 2 minutes until tender. Add tomato sauce and bring to a simmer.

2. Cut fish into large chunks, add to the sauce along with the black olives and hot pepper flakes. Cook over medium heat for 20 minutes until fish flakes with a fork.

Fillets of Flounder Preziosa

Serves 4

1 pound flounder fillets
2 tablespoons butter
1 small onion, chopped
1 19-ounce can tomatoes, drained and diced
½ pound mushrooms, sliced
½ teaspoon salt
½ teaspoon basil
1 tablespoon parsley, chopped
dash of Cayenne pepper
1 dozen small oysters, shucked
½ cup fresh bread crumbs
½ cup butter, melted

1. In a medium saucepan, sauté onions in 2 tablespoons butter until translucent, 2 to 3 minutes.
2. Add the tomatoes and mushrooms and simmer over medium heat for 5 minutes. Season with salt, pepper, parsley and basil. Cook for 15 minutes until sauce has thickened.
3. Transfer half of the tomato vegetable mixture to a 2-quart baking dish. Layer the fish fillets in the pan and cover with remaining sauce.
4. Put the oysters on top and sprinkle with bread crumbs. Pour the melted butter evenly overall and bake in a 400° oven for 30 minutes. Serve with risotto or buttered orzo.

Frew's Flounder Bake

Serves 6

A quick and easy to prepare fish florentine.

6 to 8 large flounder fillets, about 2 pounds
3 8-ounce packages spinach, cooked, chopped and well drained
2 cups sour cream
½ cup scallions, chopped
1 lemon, freshly squeezed
1 teaspoon salt
2 tablespoons flour
½ cup cheddar cheese, grated
bread crumbs, buttered
paprika

1. In a medium mixing bowl, combine spinach, sour cream, scallions, lemon juice, salt and flour. Spread half of mixture in a buttered 2-quart baking dish.
2. Cover with the fish slices and spread remaining sour cream mixture over fish. Sprinkle with cheddar cheese, buttered crumbs and a dusting of paprika. Bake at 350° for 25 minutes until bubbling hot.

Tomato Herb Flounder

Serves 4

A heart smart way to also prepare scrod, snapper or grouper.

1½ pounds flounder fillets
2 medium tomatoes, diced
8 scallions including tops, sliced
4 tablespoons fresh parsley, chopped
1 teaspoon oregano
1 teaspoon basil
1 teaspoon tarragon
¼ teaspoon salt
⅛ teaspoon black pepper
1 lemon, freshly squeezed
¼ cup olive oil
½ cup lowfat Mozzarella cheese, grated

1. Fold each piece of flounder in half, end to end, and layer in a baking dish.
2. Combine remaining ingredients, except cheese, in a mixing bowl, stirring thoroughly. Spread over the flounder. Sprinkle with cheese and bake at 375° for 20 to 30 minutes, depending on thickness of the fish.

Muffin-Pan Turbans of Flounder

Serves 6 to 8

A particularly pretty presentation you can sauce as you wish.

1½ pounds flounder fillets
2 tablespoons butter
1 cup mushrooms, chopped
1 tablespoon lemon, freshly squeezed
1 cup fresh bread crumbs
1 tablespoon parsley, chopped
½ teaspoon salt
⅛ teaspoon black pepper
⅛ teaspoon celery salt
pinch Cayenne, nutmeg
2 tablespoons butter, melted
½ cup chicken stock

1. Cut the flounder fillets in half, lengthwise. Line well-buttered muffin pan with the strips, white side of the flounder facing out.
2. Melt the 2 tablespoons butter in a skillet and sauté the mushrooms for 2 to 3 minutes. Add the lemon juice, bread crumbs, parsley and seasonings. Pour the additional 2 tablespoons melted butter and chicken stock overall. Combine well.
3. Fill each muffin cup with the stuffing and cover pan with aluminum foil. Bake for 20 minutes in a 375° oven. To unmold, run a sharp knife around the outside of each portion. Serve with your choice of:
   - Hollandaise sauce
   - Brown Caper Butter
   - Spiced Parsley Sauce
   (See index)

Elegant Stuffed Fluke with Dill Butter   Serves 3 to 4

Serve with sautéed mushrooms and fresh green beans.

2 large fillets of fluke, about ¾ pound
  each. Flounder can be used if you can
  find it this large, if not, you can use
  4 pieces of flounder and increase
  amounts of stuffing and butter
2 tablespoons onion, grated
⅔ cup butter
1 tablespoon parsley, chopped
1 cup herb stuffing crumbs
1 teaspoon grated lemon peel
1 tablespoon lemon juice, freshly squeezed
black pepper
½ teaspoon dill
lemon slices

1. Melt ⅓ cup butter in a saucepan and sauté onion briefly until soft. Add the parsley, crumbs, lemon peel and lemon juice. Season with black pepper.

2. Place one fish fillet on a baking sheet. Mound the mixture on the fish fillet and top with second piece of fish.

3. Melt the remaining ⅓ cup of butter and add the dill. Pour the dill butter over the fish and bake at 350° for 20 to 30 minutes. Remove pan from oven and spoon pan juices overall. Return to oven for 5 more minutes. Slip onto a platter and garnish with additional dill and lemon slices.

Grouper Mattie en Papier   Serves 2

Cheers to Mangrove Matties.

6 ounces fillets of grouper (or any white
  fish), cleaned
6 ounces bay scallops
4 ounces medium or small shrimp, peeled
1 teaspoon butter
4 ounces crabmeat
2 scallions, chopped
1 shallot, chopped fine
½ lemon
1 bay leaf
6 ounces heavy cream
6 ounces fish stock (water may be
  substituted)
1 ounce brandy
1½ ounces white wine
4 tablespoons butter
4 tablespoons flour
salt and white pepper to taste

1. Melt 1 teaspoon of butter in large saucepan. Add shrimp and scallops and sauté until shrimp are evenly colored pink. Remove from pan and reserve on side. Replace pan to heat and add shallots and sauté until golden brown. Add brandy and allow to flame.

2. Add white wine and juice from the lemon and let reduce by half the volume. Add heavy cream, fish stock, bay leaf and bring to slow simmer.

3. In separate pan prepare a roux. Melt remaining butter and add the flour. The consistency should resemble wet sand. Slowly cook until it reaches a blond color, about 10 minutes. Stirring occasionally, combine the roux with heavy cream and fish stock. Bring back to a simmer and cook for 20 minutes, stirring occasionally.

4. Add shrimp, scallops, scallions, crabmeat and simmer for an additional 10 minutes. Adjust flavor with salt and white pepper. Remove from heat and cool. This sauce can be made 24 hours in advance of serving.

5. Make bag. Fold sheet of parchment paper in half lengthwise, and then open. Place a large spoonful of seafood sauce on half the paper. Place grouper fillet on sauce. Add another large spoonful of sauce on top of the fish. Fold the paper closed. Starting at one of the sealed corners, fold the excess paper at a 45° angle. Continue folding at angles until reaching the other sealed corner. Fold excess paper under. Bag should now resemble a round sealed packet.

6. Lightly oil the outside of paper bag, and place on a sheetpan in a preheated oven (375°) for 20 minutes. Bag will take on a ballooned appearance and should be served straight out of the oven, paper and all. BON APPETIT!!

Kastaway Ginger Mahi-Mahi

Serves 2

From a memorable charter in the Bahamas.

2 8-ounce mahi-mahi fish fillets
4 tablespoons butter
4 tablespoons soy sauce
1 teaspoon ginger, minced
1 garlic clove, minced
1 tablespoon dry sherry

1. In a large frying pan, melt the butter and add soy sauce. Cook until mixture bubbles. Add minced ginger and garlic. Stir well and add the sherry.

2. Put the mahi-mahi fillets in the pan and sauté over medium heat for 5 minutes on each side depending on size of fillets. Remove to a plate and pour sauce over top.

For a variation, add green pepper, chopped and onions to the butter and soy sauce mixture.

Heart Healthy But Delish Fish   Serves 4

**For those of us who must stay on a low saturated fat diet,
but who crave a white sauce with our fish.**

4 8-ounce salmon or halibut steaks
1 cup nonfat yogurt
2½ cups orange juice, freshly squeezed
2½ cups diet ginger ale

1. Boil 2 cups of orange juice with 2 cups of diet ginger ale. Reserve ½ cup of each for sauce. Do not leave your post: make this sacrifice so that you can be sure that the release of CO_2 from the ginger ale does not make the pot boil over.

2. Add the fish, reduce heat and gently poach for 10 to 15 minutes.

3. While fish is poaching, make sauce from 1 cup yogurt and remaining ½ cup of orange juice. Slowly whisk in the remaining ginger ale, tasting to sweeten as you wish.

4. Drain fish, remove to a hot platter and pour sauce overall. Garnish with watercress sprigs.

Halibut Jardiniere   Serves 4

A meal in one with richly seasoned broth and vegetables.

1½ pounds skinned and boned halibut,
  or other firm fleshed fish,
  cut into 3-inch pieces
2 tablespoons olive oil
2 garlic cloves, minced
1 cup leeks, cleaned and chopped
2 cups water
½ cup white wine
2 cups escarole leaves, torn into pieces
2 carrots, cut into strips
1 celery stalk, sliced
2 large potatoes, peeled and sliced
1 zucchini, sliced
1 tomato, cubed
1 bay leaf
½ teaspoon tarragon
salt and black pepper
fresh parsley

1. Heat the olive oil in a large soup pot. Add the leeks and garlic, sauté, stirring occasionally until vegetables are softened but not brown, about 3 minutes.

2. Add water, wine, escarole, carrots, celery, and potatoes. Heat to boiling, reduce heat and simmer for 10 minutes.

3. Put the zucchini and tomato in the pot and add the seasonings. Place the halibut on top of the vegetables, spooning some hot broth over the fish. Cover and simmer for 5 minutes until fish is opaque.

4. To serve, ladle vegetables and pieces of fish into large soup plates and garnish with parsley. Serve with hot crusty sourdough bread.

Cold Mackerel in White Wine   Serves 6

A Fourth of July family favorite.

6 mackerel, cleaned, split and boned
4 medium onions, thinly sliced
2 celery stalks, thinly sliced
4 carrots, thinly sliced
½ teaspoon thyme
¼ teaspoon black peppercorns
2 bay leaves
1½ cups white wine
⅓ cup olive oil
parsley, freshly chopped
lemon slices
lettuce

Must be made ahead.

1. Arrange mackerel in a flat 12x8-inch ovenproof dish.
2. In a saucepan bring the onions, carrots, celery, thyme, peppercorns, bay leaves, and white wine to boil. Cook over medium heat for 5 minutes.
3. Pour the hot wine and vegetable mixture over the fish, drizzle with olive oil, cover and bake at 350° for 15 minutes. Cool and refrigerate in the same dish, overnight. Serve chilled on a bed of garden lettuce surrounded by the vegetables. Sprinkle with parsley and garnish with lemon slices.

Monkfish Medallions   Serves 2

Don't pass this strange looking fish up. It is distinctively sweet and has the texture of fresh crab.

4 pieces of monkfish, (¾- to 1-pound)
black pepper, freshly ground
4 tablespoons butter
¾ cup mushrooms, quartered
2 scallions, chopped
1 tablespoon shallots, chopped
2 tablespoons dry sherry
1 tablespoon parsley, chopped
buttered toast

1. Generously season the fish with black pepper. Melt 2 tablespoons of the butter in a medium frying pan and add the fish. Cook over medium heat for 4 minutes until lightly browned.
2. Add the remaining 2 tablespoons butter to the pan along with the mushrooms, scallions and shallots. Stir vegetables around and cover the pan. Cook for 3 minutes.
3. Turn the fish and add the sherry and parsley. Spoon the juices over the fish and cook for 3 more minutes. Serve medallions on buttered toast with the mushrooms on top.

Mussel Timbale Mélanie   Serves 4

As prepared at a favorite restaurant in Riec-sur-Belon, France.

4 quarts mussels
¾ cup butter
½ cup carrot, finely chopped
2 medium onions, finely chopped
½ cup celery, finely chopped
½ cup dry white wine
2 tablespoons tomato paste
I cup fish stock or clam juice
4 garlic cloves, chopped
I bay leaf
¼ teaspoon thyme
3 sprigs parsley
½ cup flour
salt
white pepper, freshly ground
pinch each; ground clove, nutmeg
and ginger
I cup port wine
2 tablespoons cognac
½ pound fillet of sole, cut into thin strips
4 tablespoons heavy cream
rice pilaf

1. Scrub the mussels thoroughly and trim off the beards. Place in a large, heavy saucepot with a tablespoon of water and cook, covered, over high heat until the shells open, 6 or 7 minutes. Discard any mussels that do not open. Remove the mussels from their shells, and set aside. Strain and reserve the liquid in the pan.

2. Heat 4 tablespoons of the butter in a heavy saucepan and add the carrots, onions, and celery and sauté for 5 minutes. Stir occasionally so as not to brown the vegetables.

3. Add the white wine, tomato paste, fish stock, garlic, bay leaf, thyme, parsley and the liquid from the mussels. Cover and cook over low heat for 1½ hours. Strain through a sieve, pressing some of the vegetables through. Set aside.

4. Heat the remaining 8 tablespoons of butter in a saucepan, add the flour and cook, stirring with a wooden spoon for 2 minutes. Be careful not to let the mixture brown. Add the reserved sauce, the seasonings, port wine and cognac. Simmer gently for 45 minutes. Add the sole, cook for 5 more minutes, do not stir around as fish will break up. Add the cream and mussels, heat until bubbly.

5. Butter a ring mold and press hot rice pilaf in firmly. Unmold onto a hot serving platter and fill center with parsley sprigs. Serve the mussels spooned over the hot rice.

Oyster and Egg Cocottes

Serves 6

Prepare these in muffin pans if you are having a crowd for brunch.

4 strips bacon
6 large eggs
18 oysters, shucked
3 thin slices Gruyère, halved
2 tablespoons butter
1 cup heavy cream
salt
pepper, freshly cracked
parsley sprigs
6 slices buttered toast, crusts trimmed

1. Cut the bacon into a fine dice and sauté until crisp. Remove from pan and drain.

2. Butter 6 small ovenproof baking cups (sides and bottoms). Sprinkle bacon into the cups.

3. Put a piece of Gruyère in each cup and cover with a spoonful of cream.

4. Break a fresh egg into each cup. Pour another spoonful of cream on top of the egg and carefully put 3 oysters into each dish.

5. Season with salt and pepper and bake in a 350° oven for 6 to 8 minutes until eggs are set and oysters wrinkled.

6. Run a sharp knife around each cup and serve each egg on a piece of hot buttered toast. Garnish with parsley.

TO MAKE A SALAD WITH FRESH SALMON

"Take some cooked Salmon, and mince it small with apples and onions, put to it oil, vinegar and pepper, and serve it up, garnishing your dish with slices of lemon and capers.

THE LADY'S COMPANION, 1753

Biscuit Crust Oyster Pie   Serves 4

Serve in big wedges, spooning the juices over the crust.

Dough:

1⅛ cups Bisquick baking mix
⅓ cup milk

Dough preparation:

1. Mix ingredients together until dough forms, beat for 30 seconds. If mixture is too sticky gradually add enough baking mix to make dough easy to handle. Knead for 10 turns on a well dusted surface (use the baking mix).
2. Roll dough ½-inch thick to size that will cover pie plate. Invert pan onto the dough and cut a circle around the edge. Set aside while preparing pie.

Filling:

½ pound bacon, cut into ½-inch pieces
⅔ cup onion, finely chopped
1 pint freshly shucked oysters, drained
   (2 dozen medium oysters)
1½ tablespoons parsley, minced
¾ teaspoon salt
⅛ teaspoon black pepper
Cayenne pepper
2 tablespoons lemon juice, freshly squeezed
2 tablespoons melted butter

Filling preparation:

1. In a heavy skillet fry the bacon and onions until bacon is crisp and onions are soft, then drain.
2. Place the oysters on the bottom of a buttered 9-inch pie pan. Cover with the bacon and onions. Sprinkle with parsley, salt, pepper, Cayenne, lemon juice and butter. Cover with the Biscuit dough and make several slits in the top. Bake for 15 minutes in a 450° oven until browned.

After shucking fresh clams, and especially oysters, examine for bits of shell, paying particular attention to the muscle where the pieces of shell often hide.

Taylor-Made Salmon

Serves 8

The vegetable topping keeps the fish beautifully moist and tender.

8 salmon steaks, 1½-inches thick
2 10-ounce bags spinach leaves
4 garlic cloves, minced
2 tablespoons olive oil
3 cucumbers, seeds removed and thinly sliced
3 tomatoes, sliced
⅓ cup Parmesan cheese, grated
salt and pepper
1 lemon

1. Arrange the salmon in an ovenproof broiling dish. Squeeze the lemon over the fish and season with salt and pepper. Let sit for 10 minutes.

2. Wash and drain spinach. In a large pot, sauté spinach and garlic in olive oil for 2 to 3 minutes until spinach just begins to wilt. Cover and set aside.

3. Broil salmon for 5 minutes, turn and baste with pan juices. Cook for 5 more minutes.

4. Cover fish with cucumber slices and tomatoes. Sprinkle with a pinch more salt and pepper. Broil for 3 minutes until tomatoes are soft.

5. Return spinach to stove and re-sauté just to heat. Sprinkle with Parmesan. Serve each salmon steak on a bed of hot spinach and pour the pan juices overall.

Hot Salmon Salad

Serves 6

A perfect ladies luncheon for your garden club or bridge group.

2 cups cooked salmon
2 cups celery, chopped
1 8-ounce can water chestnuts, drained and sliced
1 small onion, minced
½ teaspoon salt
½ teaspoon dill
1 lemon, freshly squeezed and rind grated
½ cup sharp cheddar cheese, grated
1 cup mayonnaise
½ cup almonds, sliced
1 cup crushed potato chips

1. Mix celery, water chestnuts, onion, salt, dill, lemon juice and rind. Add the cheese and mayonnaise, combining well.

2. Gently fold in the cooked salmon and pour into a well-buttered 2-quart casserole. Sprinkle with almonds and potato chips and bake for 15 minutes in a 450° oven until browned.

Three Way Salmon Loaf

2 cups flaked salmon (canned works fine)
1 teaspoon lemon juice, freshly squeezed
season to taste with your choice of:
    ½ teaspoon dry English mustard,
    2 tablespoons minced onion,
    1 teaspoon dill, or
    1 tablespoon parsley
salt, pepper, paprika
Worcestershire sauce
2 eggs
½ cup light cream
1 cup dry bread crumbs
2 tablespoons butter

1. In a medium mixing bowl combine the salmon and lemon juice. Toss with your choice of seasoning combinations, salt, pepper, a few shakes of paprika and Worcestershire sauce.

2. In another bowl beat the eggs until foamy, add the cream and bread crumbs. Gently stir into salmon mixture. It should be moist so add a little more cream if needed. Pour into a well-buttered loaf pan and dot with butter. Bake at 350° for 30 minutes.

3. Serve with a plain white sauce, an egg dill sauce or parsley butter.

This mixture can also be formed into Salmon Croquettes or cakes. Use a little less cream, shape and roll in additional bread crumbs. Beat an egg with a little water, dip cakes in egg wash briefly and coat again with crumbs. Pan fry or deep fry and serve with a sauce as above.

Whole Roast Salmon with Parsley Dill Sauce   Serves 6
Surround the fish with fresh peas and boiled new potatoes.

1 6-pound salmon, cleaned with head and tail still on
¼ cup olive oil
a handful of fresh herbs, stems on, such as dill, parsley or fennel
2 cups white wine
2 onions, thinly sliced
2 lemons, thinly sliced
1 tablespoon black peppercorns

Requires some advance preparation.

1. Rinse the salmon inside and out and pat dry. Rub it all over with the olive oil and place in a roasting pan, making sure the bottom is well oiled so the fish will not stick.

2. Stuff the cavity with the herbs, one sliced onion and one sliced lemon. Arrange the other onion and lemon on top.

3. Pour the wine over the fish and sprinkle the peppercorns in the pan. Measure the thickness of the fish at its thickest part and bake at 400° for 8 to 10 minutes per inch, basting occasionally with the pan juices. Transfer to a large oval platter, garnish with more herbs and serve with sauce.

Parsley Dill Sauce:

1½ cups mayonnaise
1 tablespoon lemon juice, freshly squeezed
3 tablespoons fresh parsley, chopped
3 tablespoons fresh dill, chopped
2 sweet gherkins, minced
½ teaspoon white pepper

Parsley Dill Sauce preparation:

1. Combine all of the ingredients and mix well.
2. Cover and refrigerate several hours until ready to use. Pass in a sauceboat when serving the roast salmon.

Scallop-Stuffed Acorn Squash

Serves 6

1½ pounds scallops
3 medium acorn squash
4 tablespoons butter, melted
salt
black pepper
2 tablespoons onion, grated
1 tablespoon prepared horseradish
2 tablespoons flour
¼ teaspoon salt
¾ cup milk
1 4-ounce can mushrooms, chopped
½ cup fresh bread crumbs
butter to moisten

1. Cut squash in half and remove seeds. Brush the center with 2 tablespoons of the melted butter and sprinkle with salt and pepper.
2. Place squash in a 3-quart casserole with ½-inch of water. Cover with foil and bake in a 350° oven until tender (or follow your microwave directions for cooking squash — it is quicker!).
3. Add remaining 2 tablespoons butter to saucepan. Add the scallops, onion, horse-radish and mushrooms. Sauté for 3 or 4 minutes, stirring occasionally. Blend in the flour and ¼ teaspoon of salt.
4. Gradually add the milk and simmer for 3 minutes, stirring constantly until sauce thickens.
5. Fill the squash halves with the scallop mixture, top with crumbs and dot with butter. At this point they may be refrigerated up to 8 hours.
6. Bake at 350° for 20 minutes or until heated through and browned on top.

Doug's Scallop and Scrod Bake   Serves 8

Drizzle a bit of olive oil over hot fresh pasta and serve alongside.

2 pounds scrod
1 pound scallops
2 lemons
⅓ cup olive oil
2 green peppers, cut into 1-inch strips
12 ounces mushrooms, thinly sliced
2 garlic cloves, minced
2 large tomatoes, sliced
½ teaspoon oregano
black pepper
1 cup fresh bread crumbs
2 tablespoons butter

1. Cut the fish into serving size pieces and place in a shallow pan in one layer. Add the scallops and squeeze one lemon overall.

2. In a large frying pan, sauté the green peppers, mushrooms and garlic in the olive oil for 3 minutes. Add the scallops and continue cooking until nicely browned.

3. Drain the scallop mixture and spoon into a 9x12-inch baking dish. Add the sliced tomatoes and layer the fish on top. Season with oregano, pepper and the juice of the other lemon.

4. Sprinkle the bread crumbs over the fish and dot with butter. Cover and bake in a 375° oven for 15 minutes until fish flakes with a fork. Let rest for several minutes before serving.

Scallop Sauté Doria   Serves 4

Try this when the summer produce is at its peak.

1 large tomato, peeled, seeded and chopped
1 cucumber, peeled
1 tablespoon shallots, chopped
3 tablespoons butter
1½ pounds scallops
2 tablespoons tomato purée
1 cup heavy cream
1 tablespoon fresh basil, chopped
black pepper, freshly ground
2 tablespoons fresh lemon juice
French bread

1. Cut cucumber in half lengthwise. Scrape out the seeds with a teaspoon and slice into ⅛-inch pieces.

2. Heat the butter in a large saucepan. Add the shallots and sauté until transparent, not quite a minute. Add the scallops and cook over high heat for ½ minute.

3. Add the tomatoes and cucumbers, sauté, stirring for 1 minute.

4. Stir in the tomato purée, cream, basil and black pepper to taste. Reduce sauce over high heat for 3 minutes until thickened. Stir in lemon juice and serve over toasted slices of French bread.

Saffron Scallops under Puff Pastry

Serves 4 as a first course
or luncheon dish

1 pound scallops
4 shallots, finely chopped
4 pinches saffron
1 teaspoon parsley, chopped
2 cups heavy cream
salt and white pepper
2 medium tomatoes, peeled, seeded and cut
    in small pieces
puff pastry (homemade or defrosted frozen),
    four 5-inch squares
1 egg, beaten
1 tablespoon milk

Requires some advance preparation.

1. Combine shallots, saffron, parsley and cream in a small saucepan. Simmer gently for 30 minutes until reduced by two-thirds.

2. Divide scallops into four scallop shells or small baking dishes and top with tomatoes. Pour the sauce over the scallops.

3. Add milk to beaten egg and brush on underside of pastry squares. Put over scallops and press tightly around the edges. Refrigerate for at least an hour.

4. When ready to bake, brush tops with egg glaze and bake in a 450° oven for 15 to 20 minutes until golden brown.

Moroccan Scallops

Serves 4

Somewhat like a curry — tangy and sweet.

1½ pounds scallops
2 tablespoons olive oil
1 medium onion, chopped
1 cup mushrooms, sliced
1 garlic clove, minced
1 16-ounce can tomatoes, crushed
½ cup raisins
½ cup almonds, slivered
2 tablespoons brown sugar
2 teaspoons cinnamon
1 teaspoon allspice
½ teaspoon ground cloves
¼ cup dry sherry
¼ teaspoon salt
Cayenne pepper
parsley, chopped

1. In a large skillet, sauté the scallops in the olive oil for 3 to 4 minutes. Remove from the pan. Add the onion, mushrooms and garlic and cook until tender-crisp, about 3 more minutes.

2. Add the tomatoes, raisins, almonds, brown sugar, cinnamon, allspice, cloves and sherry. Season with salt and Cayenne to taste. Simmer for 30 minutes to reduce the sauce and stir in the scallops. Heat gently for 5 minutes and spoon over hot rice, garnishing generously with chopped parsley.

Candlelight Scallops

Serves 2

Make this earlier in the day and reheat gently for a special occasion dinner.

1 pound scallops
4 scallions, finely chopped
1 tablespoon lemon juice, freshly squeezed
½ cup dry white wine or vermouth
½ cup water
1 bay leaf
2 parsley sprigs
salt and pepper
2 tablespoons butter
2 tablespoons flour
1 tomato, peeled, seeded and chopped
1 egg yolk
¼ cup whipping cream
1 tablespoon parsley, finely chopped

1. Place the scallops, scallions, lemon juice, wine, water, bay leaf and parsley sprigs in a 1-quart saucepan. Season with salt and pepper. Cover and simmer over low heat for 5 minutes until scallops are white and opaque.

2. Drain the scallops and reserve the liquid. Discard the bay leaf and parsley sprigs.

3. In the same saucepan, heat the butter and add the flour. Stir in the reserved poaching liquid and whisk until smooth and thickened.

4. Beat the egg yolk lightly with a fork in a small bowl and add the cream. Add mixture to the cooked sauce and simmer gently. Add the tomato and scallops and cook for several minutes until bubbly.

Serve over hot rice and garnish with additional parsley.

Stuffed Scallop Casserole

Serves 4

This has much the taste and texture of rich baked stuffed shrimp; in fact, substitute shrimp or crabmeat if you wish.

½ pound scallops
8 tablespoons butter, melted
1 cup light cream
8 slices white bread plus 2 heels, cubed
1 8-ounce can chopped mushrooms,
    2 tablespoons liquid reserved
salt and pepper
3 large slices Muenster cheese, cut into
    2-inch strips

1. Place one third of the bread crumbs in the bottom of a buttered 2-quart casserole.

2. Top with half the scallops, a few mushrooms and sprinke with salt and pepper. Pour over some of the melted butter and cream.

3. Repeat 2 or 3 times depending on depth of casserole dish, ending with crumbs, cream, butter and 2 tablespoons reserved mushroom juice for moisture.

4. Top off with sliced Muenster and bake at 350° for 35 to 45 minutes.

Scallop Sauté Piccata

Serves 4

You need nothing more with this than a chilled vegetable antipasto.

1½ pounds scallops
3 tablespoons butter
2 garlic cloves, minced
½ teaspoon paprika
½ teaspoon salt
⅛ teaspoon pepper, freshly ground
2 tablespoons lemon juice, freshly squeezed
3 tablespoons dry vermouth
2 tablespoons parsley, chopped

1. Heat the butter in a large heavy skillet. Add the garlic, sprinkle with paprika, salt and pepper, blending well.

2. Increase heat. Pat the scallops dry and add enough to cover the bottom of the pan without crowding. You want them to brown, not steam. Cook until tender, 3 to 4 minutes, stirring occasionally.

3. Remove scallops from pan with a slotted spoon and keep warm in the oven. Repeat cooking the remaining scallops in the same manner, remove also.

4. Lower the heat under the pan and add the lemon juice, wine and chopped parsley. Heat until bubbling and pour over the scallops.

Serve over slices of buttered crusty bread or with white rice.

Scallops in Chili Cream

Serves 4

Easily put together at the last minute, just warm the scallops slowly.

1½ pounds scallops
3 tablespoons butter
1 green pepper, cut into thin strips
1 small onion, diced
1 tomato, seeded and chopped
1 tablespoon parsley, chopped
1 teaspoon chili powder
1 cup heavy cream
2 tablespoons chili sauce
salt and pepper
4 crisp corn tortillas
1 cup white rice, cooked
parsley sprigs

1. Melt butter in a saucepan. Add the green pepper and onion. Sauté slowly until vegetables are tender, but not brown.

2. Add the tomato, parsley and chili powder, combining well. Stir in the scallops and cook over medium-high heat for 3 minutes. Add the cream, bring to a boil and simmer for 2 to 3 minutes until sauce has thickened. Stir in the chili sauce and season with salt and pepper.

3. Place a hot tortilla on each plate and top with rice. Make a well in the center and spoon scallop mixture over the rice.

Garnish with parsley sprigs and serve with a platter of sliced avocado, tomatoes, cucumbers and black olives.

Coquilles St. Jacques Martini   Serves 2

No gin taste at all, just a subtle sweetness — superb.

1 pound fresh scallops
½ cup flour
salt and pepper
4 tablespoons butter
1 small carrot, cut into very thin
　julienne strips
½ cup zucchini, shredded
½ cup heavy cream
4 tablespoons gin
sprinkling of lemon juice
parsley, chopped

1. Combine the flour with salt and pepper. Add the scallops and toss in the flour to coat well.

2. Heat the butter in a large skillet and add the scallops. Cook on one side until lightly browned, stir and add the carrots. Sauté for another minute until scallops are just slightly firm.

3. Pour the gin over the scallops, tip the pan and ignite. When the flames subside, add the zucchini, cream and lemon juice. Turn heat to high and cook for one minute to reduce the cream.

Serve in hot puff pastry, over buttered toast points or rice.

Coquilles St. Jacques Parisienne   Serves 6

Not as difficult to prepare as you may have thought.

1½ pounds scallops
1 pound mushrooms, sliced
5 tablespoons butter
1 lemon
1 cup dry white wine
1 bay leaf
¼ teaspoon thyme
½ teaspoon salt
⅛ teaspoon pepper
4 tablespoons flour
1 cup milk or cream
¾ cup bread crumbs, buttered
½ cup tiny cooked shrimp (optional)
6 tablespoons grated Gruyère cheese

1. Melt 2 tablespoons butter in a sauté pan and cook mushrooms for 3 to 4 minutes over medium heat until golden brown. Squeeze the lemon over mushrooms and toss.

2. In a large saucepan combine wine, bay leaf, thyme, salt and pepper. Bring to a boil. Add scallops and reduce heat. Simmer for 4 to 5 minutes until scallops are slightly firm. Drain and reserve 1 cup of the poaching liquid.

3. Melt the remaining 3 tablespoons of butter and add the flour, combining well. Slowly whisk in the reserved scallop broth and milk or cream. Cook until thickened. Remove from heat and fold in the cooked mushrooms and scallops.

4. Spoon into 6 large scallop shells and sprinkle with buttered crumbs. Top with tiny shrimp and I tablespoon Gruyère per shell. Run under a hot broiler to brown or bake in a 400° oven for 10 minutes.

Scallops and Shrimp Gruyère

Serves 8

I pound scallops
I pound large shrimp, cooked and cleaned
8 tablespoons butter
7 tablespoons flour
3 cups milk
12 ounces Gruyère cheese,
  cut into small pieces
¼ teaspoon garlic powder
¼ teaspoon dry mustard
2 teaspoons tomato paste
3 teaspoons lemon, freshly sqeezed
½ teaspoon salt
¼ teaspoon white pepper
½ pound mushrooms, sliced
¼ cup green pepper, chopped
paprika
16 patty shells

1. Melt 6 tablespoons butter in a medium saucepan. Stir in the flour and combine well. Add the milk and cook over medium heat, whisking constantly until sauce is thick. Stir in the cheese and simmer until melted. Add the garlic powder, dry mustard, tomato paste, 2 teaspoons lemon juice, and salt and pepper.

2. Place the scallops in a saucepan, add the remaining teaspoon lemon juice. Cover with water and poach for 5 minutes. Remove scallops with a slotted spoon and reserve ½ cup poaching liquid, adding it to the cheese sauce.

3. Melt remaining 2 tablespoons butter in a sauté pan and cook the mushroom until tender. Add the mushrooms, poached scallops and shrimp to the cheese sauce. Simmer for 10 minutes and spoon into a large serving dish. Sprinkle with green pepper and paprika.

4. Ladle into hot patty shells, 2 per person and serve with fresh asparagus spears.

This sauce freezes very well and if you want to save some time, cook the patty shells ahead and crisp them for a few minutes in a hot oven at the last minute.

85

Surf and Feather

Serves 8

The creamy shrimp and olive sauce can also be used to top baked fish.

2 cups sour cream
1 teaspoon tarragon
1 teaspoon thyme
¼ teaspoon salt
1 teaspoon paprika
1 garlic clove, minced
4 large chicken breasts, halved
1½ cup cracker crumbs
1 cup large shrimp, cooked
½ cup pitted ripe olives, quartered
buttered noodles

1. Combine the sour cream with herbs and seasonings in a mixing bowl.
2. Dip the chicken into sour cream mixture and then into crumbs.
3. Place chicken in a well-greased 13x9x2-inch baking dish and bake uncovered for 40 minutes.
4. To the remaining sour cream mixture, add shrimp and olives; spoon around chicken. Bake for 10 minutes more. Serve with buttered noodles.

Shrimp and Crabmeat Gratineé

Serves 6

A special occasion dinner that can be prepared ahead.

1 pound medium shrimp, peeled and deveined
2 7½-ounce cans king crab, rinsed and cartilage removed
1 9-ounce package artichoke hearts, frozen
4 tablespoons butter
½ pound mushrooms, sliced
1 garlic clove, minced
2 tablespoons shallots, chopped
¼ cup flour
1 tablespoon dill, freshly chopped
pepper to taste
¾ cup milk
⅔ cup sherry or dry white wine
8 ounces sharp cheddar, grated
¼ cup Parmesan cheese, grated

1. Cook the shrimp in a pan of boiling salted water for 2 to 3 minutes until shrimp are pink, drain. Cook artichoke hearts according to package directions. Cut in half and set aside with the shrimp.
2. Melt 2 tablespoons of the butter in a medium saucepan and sauté the mushrooms for 3 minutes until just tender. Remove mushrooms from the pan and add the remaining 2 tablespoons of butter, garlic and shallots. Sauté gently for 5 minutes and remove pan from the heat.
3. Whisk in the flour, pepper and dill. Add the milk and cook, stirring constantly until sauce thickens. Add the sherry and half of the grated cheddar cheese.
4. Gently fold the flaked crab, shrimp, artichoke hearts, mushrooms and remaining cheddar cheese into the sauce. Pour into a buttered 2-quart casserole and sprinkle with Parmesan cheese and dot with additional butter. Bake for 30 minutes at 375° until golden brown.

Rama's Nasik Goreng

Serves 4 to 6

A traditional mid-Eastern dish.

1 pound medium shrimp, peeled and
deveined
1 cup rice
2 cups water
4 slices bacon
2 medium onions, chopped
½ pound ground beef
⅓ cup celery leaves, freshly chopped
2 tablespoons soy sauce
1 teaspoon curry powder
¼ teaspoon dry mustard

1. Cook rice in boiling water in a covered
2-quart saucepan for 20 minutes until fluffy.

2. While rice cooks, fry the bacon in a large
skillet until crisp. Drain and crumble.

3. In the same pan, cook ground beef and
onions in a small amount of bacon fat
for 5 minutes until nicely browned.

4. Stir in the celery, soy sauce, curry
powder, mustard and shrimp. Cook for
3 to 4 minutes, stirring occasionally until
shrimp are pink. Add the hot cooked rice
and gently stir until coated. Sprinkle with
crumbled bacon and serve.

Commodore's Sweet and Sour Shrimp

Serves 4

Batter-fried shrimp — a delicious Chinese recipe.

1 pound medium shrimp,
peeled and deveined
¼ cup cornstarch
⅓ cup flour
¼ cup water
1 egg
1 teaspoon salt
peanut oil

1. Mix the cornstarch, flour, water, egg and
salt together in a medium bowl. Add the
shrimp and coat well with the batter.

2. Heat ¼-inch of oil in a wok or heavy
skillet. Drop shrimp, one by one, into the
hot oil and fry until crisp and lightly
browned. Drain on paper towels and
keep warm.

Sauce:

2 tablespoons peanut oil
1 green pepper, cubed
1 carrot, finely diced
1 garlic clove, minced
4 tablespoons sugar
4 tablespoons white vinegar
2 tablespoons ketchup
1 tablespoon soy sauce
½ cup chicken broth
1 tablespoon cornstarch dissolved in
2 tablespoons water

Sauce preparation:

1. Heat oil in a large saucepan. Sauté green
pepper, carrot and garlic for 2 minutes.

2. Add the sugar, vinegar, ketchup, soy
sauce and chicken broth. Mix well and
bring to a boil. Stir in the dissolved
cornstarch and cook until sauce has
thickened. Pour sauce over hot shrimp
and serve with rice.

Baked Spiced Shrimp

Lots of wonderful sauce for dipping.

Serves 8 to 10 as an appetizer
and 6 to 8 as an entrée

3 pounds large shrimp, peeled and deveined
1 cup butter
½ cup olive oil
½ teaspoon oregano
1 tablespoon coarse black pepper
    (or to taste)
¾ teaspoon salt
½ teaspoon paprika
1 tablespoon parsley, chopped
¾ teaspoon basil
2 garlic cloves, minced
1 lemon, freshly squeezed

1. Put the shrimp in a large baking pan, keeping them in one layer.
2. Melt the butter and add the remaining ingredients. Pour mixture over the shrimp and bake for 8 minutes in a 450° oven. Remove from oven and place pan under the broiler for 5 more minutes to brown.

Serve with lots of crusty French bread.

Shrimp Galley West

Serves 6

Passed along from a favorite mother-in-law whose family dates back to the days of the great whaling masters from old New Bedford.

1 ham slice, 10 to 12-ounces
2 large onions, chopped
1 green pepper, chopped
1 red pepper, chopped
1 28-ounce can plum tomatoes
¾ cup rice
1 to 1½ pounds medium shrimp, cooked and peeled. The amount depends on the size of the appetites
½ pint sour cream
salt, pepper, Tabasco sauce and paprika

1. In a medium pan, fry the ham slice in a little butter until nicely browned. Cut into strips and return to the pan.
2. Add the onions, peppers, tomatoes and rice. Bring to a boil and let simmer for 45 minutes.
3. Stir in the shrimp and cook for 5 minutes. Add the sour cream, salt, pepper and Tabasco to taste. Cook for a few minutes to blend the seasonings but do not allow it to boil. Serve hot and sprinkle with paprika.

If freezing a casserole, remember that it reduces the strength of the flavors. Always over-season slightly.

Shrimp and Wild Rice Casserole Serves 6

A nice color and texture combination — dinner guests will want the recipe.

½ cup green pepper, diced
¼ teaspoon curry powder
2 10-ounce cans cream of mushroom soup, diluted with equal amounts of milk
1 cup cheddar cheese, grated
2 pounds medium shrimp, cooked and peeled
2 tablespoons lemon juice, freshly squeezed
1 teaspoon Worcestershire sauce
1 teaspoon dry mustard
½ teaspoon black pepper
¼ teaspoon onion salt
4 cups wild rice, cooked
paprika

1. Sauté green pepper in the butter, along with the curry powder. When tender, remove from stove.

2. In a large saucepot, prepare the mushroom soup with the milk and heat until bubbling. Add the green peppers and ½ cup cheddar cheese and stir until cheese has melted.

3. Add the cooked shrimp, lemon juice, Worcestershire sauce and seasonings. Mix in the wild rice and combine well.

4. Turn the mixture into a large, 4-quart, buttered casserole and sprinkle with remaining ½ cup cheese and paprika. Bake in a 350° oven for 40 minutes.

Saucy Shrimp Supreme

Serves 4 to 6

2 pounds medium shrimp, peeled and cooked
4 tablespoons butter
4 tablespoons flour
1½ cups milk
2 tablespoons Worcestershire sauce
⅔ cup ketchup
salt and pepper to taste
cooked white rice

1. Cut the cooked shrimp in half along the backside so that you retain the shape.

2. Melt the butter in a saucepan and stir in the flour. Cook over low heat for 1 minute and slowly add the milk, stirring until thickened. DO NOT BOIL.

3. To the cream sauce, add the Worcestershire sauce, ketchup and season with salt and pepper. Stir in the cooked shrimp and when very hot, serve over mounds of white rice.

This freezes well and can also be served as an appetizer, either hot or cold with crackers or bread cubes for dipping.

Shore-Style Shrimp Atheneum

Serves 4

1 pound medium shrimp, peeled
  and deveined
1 onion, chopped
1 green pepper, chopped
2 large garlic cloves, minced
1 tablespoon olive oil
4 cups plum tomatoes, coarsely chopped
  with the liquid
4 tablespoons parsley, freshly chopped
4 tablespoons sherry
¼ pound Feta cheese, crumbled
salt and pepper
parsley sprigs

1. In a medium saucepan, sauté the onion, green pepper and garlic in the olive oil until translucent.
2. Add the tomatoes and their liquid and simmer gently for 15 minutes. Add the parsley, sherry, oregano, salt, pepper and half of the Feta cheese.
3. Return the pan to a simmer and add the shrimp. Cook for 4 to 5 minutes until shrimp are pink, being careful not to overcook.
4. Serve steaming hot in shallow soup plates, crumble rest of Feta on top and garnish with parsley sprigs.

You will need lots of crusty bread to soak up the heavenly juices.

Sour Cream Shrimp Curry

Serves 6

If planning to prepare this on your boat, take the sour cream container with curry, ginger, lemon juice, salt and pepper already stirred in. Carry the shrimp and chopped vegetables along in plastic bags and have minimal galley clean-up time.

3 cups cooked medium shrimp, whole or
  sliced lengthwise
6 tablespoons butter
½ cup onion, chopped
½ cup green pepper, chopped
2 garlic cloves, minced
2 cups sour cream
2 teaspoons curry powder
2 teaspoons lemon juice, freshly squeezed
½ teaspoon ginger
¾ teaspoon salt
dash of pepper

1. Melt the butter in a saucepan and add onion, green pepper and garlic. Sauté for 2 minutes until tender-crisp.
2. Stir in the sour cream, curry powder, lemon juice, ginger, salt and pepper to taste. Add the shrimp and heat over a low heat, stirring gently until nice and hot, but not boiling. Serve over white rice or toast points.

Pacific Shrimp with Rosemary   Serves 6

**If you have never experimented with rosemary and seafood together,
you are in for a surprise.**

1½ pounds medium shrimp,
   peeled and deveined
⅓ cup olive oil
6 garlic cloves, finely chopped
½ cup scallions, chopped
1 medium red pepper, cut into thin strips
1 14-ounce can artichoke hearts, quartered
2 tablespoons parsley, chopped
2 teaspoons rosemary, crushed
½ cup dry white wine
½ teaspoon salt
black pepper, freshly ground
2 tablespoons butter

1. Heat the olive oil in a heavy skillet and add the garlic, scallions and red pepper. Stirring frequently, sauté for 2 minutes.
2. Add the shrimp to the pan and sauté for 2 more minutes. Gently stir in the artichoke hearts and add the parsley, rosemary, white wine, salt and black pepper to taste.
3. Increase the heat for one minute to blend the seasonings. Swirl in the butter and serve over hot rice or fresh pasta.

Tijuana Shrimp Pizza — OLÉ!   Serves 4

Make a few of these for a different after-movie or pool party treat.

1 12-inch pizza crust, a prepared crust,
   frozen or refrigerated is fine
1 8-ounce can tomato sauce
½ cup chunky salsa
1 cup small shrimp, cooked
         or
2 4½-ounce cans cocktail shrimp, drained
1 4-ounce can green chilies, chopped and
   drained
1½ cups shredded Monterey Jack cheese
1 cup lettuce, shredded
2 medium tomatoes, chopped
¼ cup black olives, chopped
sour cream

1. Place the crust on a pizza pan or large baking sheet.
2. Mix tomato sauce and salsa. Spread over the crust.
3. Cover crust with shrimp, chilies and sprinkle evenly with shredded cheese. Bake in 425° oven for 20 to 25 minutes until cheese is melted.
4. Remove pie from oven, top with lettuce, tomato and chopped olives. Pass the cold Mexican beer and sour cream.

Sherried Shrimp and Artichokes   Serves 4

1 14-ounce can artichoke hearts, drained
   and quartered
¾ pound medium shrimp, cooked
6 tablespoons butter
¼ pound mushrooms, sliced
3 tablespoons flour
1½ cups milk
¼ cup dry sherry
1 tablespoon Worcestershire sauce
salt and pepper
¼ cup Parmesan cheese, grated
paprika

1. Arrange artichoke hearts in a buttered
   2-quart baking dish. Cover with the
   cooked shrimp.

2. In a small saucepan, melt 3 tablespoons
   butter. Sauté the mushrooms for 3 minutes
   and spread over the shrimp.

3. Melt remaining 3 tablespoons of butter
   in the pan. Add the flour and mix well.
   Whisk in the milk, sherry and
   Worcestershire. Cook until thickened.
   Season to taste with salt and pepper.

4. Pour the sauce evenly over the
   mushrooms and sprinkle with Parmesan
   cheese and paprika. Bake in a 375° oven
   for 30 to 40 minutes.

**Complete the dinner with wild rice and a tossed
green salad.**

Grilled Cajun Shrimp and Vegetables   Serves 6

If you are ambitious, this can be done on skewers for a dazzling presentation.

2 pounds medium shrimp, peeled, deveined,
   tail left on
3 medium zucchini or yellow squash, sliced
1 pint cherry tomatoes
2 tablespoons cajun spice
2 tablespoons minced dry garlic
2 large lemons, freshly squeezed
½ cup vermouth
¾ cup olive oil

Requires some advance preparation.

1. Arrange shrimp and vegetables in a single
   layer in a baking dish.

2. In a small bowl, combine remaining
   ingredients and mix well. Pour over the
   shrimp and let marinate for at least
   30 minutes; even better, prepare the
   night before.

3. Grill under a preheated broiler for 4 to 6
   minutes, check and turn shrimp and
   vegetables over. Cook for 4 to 6 minutes
   more until shrimp are pink.

Serve over pasta, orzo or rice.

**When tossing or stirring cooked rice, use a fork rather than a
spoon to avoid crushing the grains.**

Beach House Shrimp Creole   Serves 4

A quick rainy day dish put-together by an old, beloved family friend.

1 pound medium shrimp, peeled and
  cooked
6 tablespoons butter
1 medium onion, finely chopped
1 large green pepper, cut into strips
1 16-ounce can stewed tomatoes
3 ounces tomato paste
2 bay leaves
salt, pepper, and Tabasco sauce to taste

1. Melt 3 tablespoons of butter in a medium saucepan. Cook the onion and green pepper until tender.

2. Add the tomatoes with their juice and the tomato paste. Crush the tomatoes, add the bay leaves, seasonings, and remaining 3 tablespoons of butter. Simmer for 10 minutes until sauce is smooth and creamy.

3. Just before serving add the shrimp and cook for a minute or two, just to heat through. Spoon over rice or pasta.

The sauce may be made well in advance and reheated before adding the shrimp.

Dave's Fon Sz Ha Mai

This brings back memories of many a Chinese feast.

2 4-ounce packages Chinese cellophane
  noodles (Fon Sz)
1 pound small-medium shrimp, peeled
2 eggs, slightly beaten
3 scallions, cut into 2-inch lengths and
  shredded
3 cups lettuce, shredded
2 slices fresh ginger, shredded
2 garlic cloves, minced
1 teaspoon sugar
3 tablespoons soy sauce
2 tablespoons water
5 tablespoons peanut or vegetable oil
pinch of salt

1. Soak noodles for 15 minutes in cold water, drain, dry and cut into 2-inch lengths.

2. Heat wok over medium-high heat. Add 1 tablespoon of oil and a pinch of salt.

3. Turn heat to medium, add eggs and scramble. Shred eggs with fork, remove from wok and set aside.

4. Add 2 tablespoons oil to wok and fry ginger and garlic until light brown. Stir in shrimp and stir fry for 2 minutes.

5. Over high heat with remaining 2 table-spoons of oil, cook the noodles, scallions, and shrimp, stirring constantly for 3 minutes.

6. Return the egg to the wok, add the shredded lettuce, soy sauce, sugar and water. Mix well for 1 minute and turn off the heat. There should be no gravy in this dish and the noodles should be dry but soft.

Greek Shrimp Salad

Serves 4

1 pound large shrimp, cooked and peeled
6 ounces Feta cheese, crumbled
12 cherry tomatoes, halved
6 scallions, chopped
1 hard-boiled egg yolk, mashed
¼ cup olive oil
1 tablespoon rice wine vinegar
1 tablespoon lemon juice
1 teaspoon dill
black pepper
Boston or romaine lettuce leaves

Requires some advance preparation.

1. Gently toss shrimp, Feta, tomatoes and scallions in a bowl.
2. Shake remaining ingredients in a jar until well combined. Chill salad and dressing until serving time.
3. Pour dressing over salad and toss with love. Serve over lettuce leaves.

When serving this on a boat, do steps 1 and 2 at home and add the dressing at the last minute afloat.

Shrimp Salad Veronique

Serves 8

Exquisite tastes and textures.

2 cups medium shrimp, peeled and cooked
2 celery stalks with leaves, chopped
1 apple, chopped
1 pound seedless green grapes, stemmed
8 small clusters grapes for garnish
⅓ cup almonds, toasted
lettuce leaves

Dressing:
1 cup mayonnaise
½ cup plain yogurt
2 teaspoons curry powder
½ cup fruit chutney, chopped
2 tablespoons lime juice, freshly squeezed

Requires some advance preparation.

1. Prepare dressing by combining all ingredients and mixing well.
2. Put shrimp, celery, apple and stemmed grapes in a large bowl. Pour dressing over and toss. Refrigerate for several hours.
3. When ready to serve, spoon the salad over lettuce greens and sprinkle with toasted almonds. Place a small cluster of chilled grapes on each plate.

Bahama Mama Shrimp Flambé   Serves 4

1½ pounds large shrimp,
    peeled and deveined
⅛ teaspoon black pepper, coarsely ground
4 tablespoons butter
⅓ cup scallions, minced
1 small green pepper, cut into thin strips
½ cup heavy cream
2 teaspoons Dijon mustard
½ cup shredded coconut
1 small tomato, peeled and diced
2 tablespoons rum
cooked rice

1. Melt the butter in a large heavy skillet. Add the scallions and green pepper, sauté for 2 minutes.

2. Season the shrimp with the black pepper and add them to the pan. Cook for 2 to 3 minutes until pink.

3. Meanwhile, combine the cream, mustard, coconut and tomato in a small bowl. Pour the cream mixture over the shrimp and cook over medium heat for 2 minutes.

4. In a small saucepan, heat the rum until warm. Ignite, and spoon flaming rum over the shrimp. Stir until flames subside and spoon over rice.

Florida Shrimp Bake   Serves 2

A garlic lover's Nirvana . . . . never enough.

¾ pound medium shrimp, peeled
    and deveined
6 tablespoons butter
1 tablespoon lemon juice, freshly sqeezed
3 garlic cloves, minced
1 teaspoon Worcestershire sauce
½ teaspoon hot red pepper flakes
¼ teaspoon salt
⅓ cup cracker crumbs

1. Arrange shrimp in one layer in a shallow baking dish.

2. In a small saucepan, melt the butter and add the lemon juice, garlic, Worcestershire sauce, red pepper and salt. Pour mixture evenly over the shrimp, reserving 2 tablespoons.

3. Add the remaining butter to the cracker crumbs and mix well. Sprinkle crumbs over the shrimp and bake in a 450° oven for 8 to 10 minutes until browned.

South of the Border Shrimp
Serves 2

Straight from Maine with a touch of Tijuana.

1 pound medium shrimp, peeled
and deveined
3 tablespoons butter
1 teaspoon chili powder
1 teaspoon garlic, minced
1 teaspoon black pepper, freshly ground
⅛ teaspoon Cayenne pepper
2 teaspoons Worcestershire sauce
2 tablespoons dry red wine
¼ teaspoon salt

Requires some advance preparation.

1. In a small saucepan, melt the butter. Add the chili powder, garlic, two peppers, Worcestershire sauce, red wine and salt. Bring to a slow boil, remove from heat and cool.

2. Arrange shrimp in a baking dish just large enough to hold them in one layer. Pour sauce over shrimp and marinate, refrigerated for several hours.

3. Bake the shrimp in a preheated 400° oven for 8 to 10 minutes until shrimp are just firm.

Serve with lots of crusty bread to dip in the spicy sauce.

Captain Bob's Baked Stuffed Shrimp
Serves 4 to 6

20 to 26 extra large shrimp
24 buttery crackers, crushed
⅓ cup seasoned bread crumbs
6 ounces tiny salad shrimp, chopped
½ cup walnuts, finely chopped
⅛ teaspoon garlic powder
¼ cup Parmesan cheese, grated
6 ounces butter, melted

1. Split shrimp down backside with a sharp knife and devein. Break shell slightly so shrimp will lie flat.

2. Combine crackers, bread crumbs, tiny shrimp, walnuts, garlic powder and Parmesan cheese. Toss mixture with a fork. Add the hot melted butter and combine well.

3. Spread shrimp out on a baking sheet and stuff each cavity with the crumbs. Bake at 325° for 12 to 15 minutes depending on how large the shrimp are. Serve with lemon butter if you wish, but they do not need additional butter.

Shrimp and Avocado Remoulade Serves 4

**Remember this for a hot summer evening,
you can prepare everything the night before.**

1 pound medium shrimp, cooked, peeled
and deveined
4 large garden lettuce leaves; red leaf,
Boston or romaine
1 cup lettuce, chopped
2 ripe avocados, sliced

Remoulade Sauce:

1 bunch scallions
2 small celery stalks
½ cup parsley, loosely packed
3 tablespoons Dijon or Creole mustard
5 teaspoon paprika
1¼ teaspoon salt
½ teaspoon pepper, freshly ground
¼ teaspoon Cayenne pepper
6 tablespoons white wine vinegar
5 teaspoons lemon juice, freshly squeezed
½ teaspoon basil
½ teaspoon tarragon
¾ cup olive oil
lemon slices

Requires some advance preparation.

1. Coarsely chop the scallions, celery and
parsley. Place in a bowl of a food
processor and pulse on and off for
1 minute until finely puréed. Remove
mixture to a stainless steel or glass bowl.

2. Add the mustard, paprika, salt, pepper,
vinegar, lemon juice, basil and tarragon,
combining well. Gradually whisk in the
olive oil, mixing well between each
addition. Cover and refrigerate for at
least 3 hours.

3. To serve, place a lettuce leaf on each
chilled plate. Top each with some
chopped lettuce and fan the sliced
avocado around the edge. Arrange the
shrimp in the center. Whisk the
remoulade sauce to re-combine and
spoon over the shrimp. Garnish with
lemon slices.

Baked Snapper with Orange Rice Stuffing   Serves 6

1 3- to 4-pound snapper, whole and
   dressed
1 cup celery, chopped
½ cup onion, chopped
4 tablespoons butter
½ cup water
½ cup orange juice
2 tablespoons lemon juice
½ teaspoon salt
⅛ teaspoon black pepper
1 cup rice, cooked
½ cup mandarin oranges
melted butter
orange slices
parsley sprigs

1. In a medium saucepan melt the butter
   and sauté onions and celery until tender,
   about 3 minutes. Transfer to a mixing
   bowl.
2. Add the water, orange juice, lemon juice,
   salt, pepper and rice. Combine well and
   add the orange pieces.
3. Pat the fish dry and sprinkle inside and
   out with additional salt and pepper. Stuff
   the fish loosely with the dressing and
   secure the opening with skewers or
   toothpicks.
4. Place the fish in a well-buttered baking
   dish, brush with melted butter and lightly
   cover with foil. Bake at 350° for
   30 minutes, remove foil and baste again.
   Cook for 15 minutes, uncovered, until the
   fish around the backbone flakes nicely.
   Place on a platter surrounded by orange
   slices and fresh parsley.

Baked Snapper Harry Gory   Serves 4

Foil baking keeps the fish particularly moist.

3 pounds whole red snapper or bass
3 tablespoons vegetable oil
3 whole scallions, sliced
2 slices fresh ginger, grated
2 tablespoons salted black beans, minced
   (may be obtained from an Oriental
   specialty market)
1 large lemon, freshly squeezed
1 tablespoon soy sauce
scallion strips
hot steamed rice

1. Rinse fish inside and out with cold water,
   pat dry and place on a large platter.
2. In a small bowl mix together oil,
   scallions, ginger, black beans, lemon
   juice and soy sauce. Coat fish with
   mixture inside and out.
3. Place whole fish on a large sheet of
   heavy duty aluminum foil or into an oven
   brown-in-bag. Pour remaining sauce over
   fish and crimp foil to form an envelope.
   Place in shallow roasting pan.
4. Make a few slits in the top and bake at
   400° for 45 minutes. Open foil or bag,
   remove fish and pour hot juices over top.
   Serve on a platter surrounded by steamed
   rice and scallion strips.

Vegetable Stuffed Sole with Vermouth Sauce Serves 6

Makes an eye appealing and low-calorie dinner.

2 pounds sole fillets
½ teaspoon dill
¼ teaspoon salt
¼ teaspoon black pepper
2 medium carrots, cut into thin strips
1 large green pepper, cut into thin strips
½ cup vermouth or dry white wine
2 tablespoons butter
2 tablespoons flour
1 cup milk
½ teaspoon paprika
1 tablespoon parsley, freshly chopped
additional salt and pepper to taste
parsley or dill sprigs

1. Mix dill, salt and pepper. Place sole fillets on a work space and sprinkle with the seasoning mixture.

2. Divide the carrot and pepper strips among the fillets and roll each piece of fish into a bundle. Place seam side down in an ungreased 9x13-inch baking dish. Pour ¼ cup wine over the fish, cover with foil and bake for 20 to 25 minutes at 325° until fish flakes easily with a fork.

3. Meanwhile, melt butter in a 1½-quart saucepan. Add the flour and cook for one minute, stirring constantly. Remove pan from the heat.

4. Whisk in the milk and remaining ¼ cup wine, return to the heat. Add the paprika and chopped parsley and season to taste with salt and pepper. Cook over low heat for 3 minutes until thick and creamy.

5. Arrange the fish on a serving platter and add any remaining pan juices to the sauce. Pour the hot sauce over the fish rolls and garnish with additional parsley or fresh dill sprigs.

To clean fresh ginger, scrub it with a brush then slice or chop it. Put it in a screw-top jar and cover with sherry or vodka. It will keep for months in the refrigerator.

Salt Acres Sole

A lemon butter with fresh chopped herbs can also be poured on top if you prefer.

8 large pieces sole or flounder
4 tablespoons butter
1 small green pepper, diced
1 garlic clove, minced
2 cups white bread crumbs,
  coarsely crumbled
2 tablespoons parsley, freshly chopped
1 pound medium shrimp, cooked and cut
  into small pieces. Reserve 8 whole shrimp
  to garnish each fish roll
salt and Cayenne pepper
2 tablespoons butter, melted
parsley sprigs

1. Melt butter in a medium saucepan and sauté green pepper and garlic for 2 minutes. Add the bread crumbs, parsley and chopped shrimp. Toss well to combine and season with salt and Cayenne.

2. Lay fish fillets out on the counter and divide the stuffing between the pieces. Roll up fish, starting at the small end and secure with a toothpick. Place seam side down in a buttered shallow baking dish. Brush the fillets with melted butter and bake for 15 to 20 minutes in a 325° oven.

3. Transfer the fish rolls to a heated platter. Remove the toothpicks and spoon Hollandaise over each fillet. Garnish each with a whole shrimp and parsley sprigs.

Hollandaise Sauce:

½ cup butter
2 egg yolks
1 tablespoon lemon juice, freshly squeezed
⅛ cup hot water
½ teaspoon salt
dash Cayenne pepper

Hollandaise Sauce preparation:

1. In a double boiler melt the butter over simmering, not boiling, water.
2. Add the egg yolks and beat with a wire whisk until thickened.
3. Add the lemon juice and water, continue mixing until creamy. Taste and adjust seasoning with a little more lemon juice, salt and Cayenne. Cover and remove from heat if not ready to serve immediately.

To reheat, warm again over gently simmering water, stirring constantly.

Sole is a type of flounder (flatfish). There are many varieties such as gray, lemon, sand dab and black back. Some varieties are not as white as others. Turbot is also a flatfish with a sweet delicate flavor. Given a choice, one might choose turbot over sole.

Elegant Soused Sole

Serves 4 to 6

A Saturday night party dish that can be baked at the last minute.

1¼ to 1½ pounds sole fillets, pick the
    largest ones at the market
1½ cups white wine
1 8-ounce bottle clam juice
2 bay leaves
2 tablespoons parsley, snipped
6 tablespoons butter, mixed with ¼
    teaspoon each: basil, thyme, rosemary
    and garlic powder
8 ounces mushrooms, sliced
4 tablespoons flour
3 tablespoons brandy
1 8-ounce can water chestnuts, sliced
2 7-ounce cans crabmeat, rinsed
    and cartilage removed
⅓ cup sherry
½ cup cream
1 cup Gruyère cheese, grated
salt and pepper

1. In a medium saucepan, heat the 1½ cups white wine over medium heat for 8 minutes. Add the clam juice, bay leaves and parsley. Simmer for 10 minutes and remove bay leaves.

2. In a second pan, melt the butter-herb mixture. Add the mushrooms and sauté for 3 minutes until slightly soft. Remove from pan, leaving as much butter and juice in the pan as possible. Stir in the flour and remove from the heat.

3. Gradually add in the wine mixture and brandy, stirring over medium heat until thickened and smooth. Stir in the water chestnuts, cooked mushrooms, crabmeat, sherry, cream and ½ cup Gruyère. Season to taste with salt and pepper.

4. Spread half of the mixture in the bottom of a shallow baking dish. Arrange flounder fillets over sauce and cover with remaining mixture. Sprinkle the other ½ cup cheese on top and bake uncovered at 375° for 20 to 25 minutes.

Simply Sherried Sole

Serves 4

A family standby for generations — especially quick and easy.

1½ to 2 pounds fillet of sole
salt and pepper
4 tablespoons bread crumbs
3 tablespoons butter
4 tablespoons Parmesan cheese, grated
pinch of nutmeg
2 tablespoons milk
2 tablespoons sherry
½ cup chicken broth

1. Lay fillets evenly across a flat baking dish, overlapping slightly. Sprinkle with salt and pepper, cover well with bread crumbs and dot with butter. Shake nutmeg over lightly, then cover with Parmesan cheese

2. Combine milk, sherry and chicken broth. Pour around edge of the dish. Bake 20 minutes in a 350° oven.

Sweet and Sour Squid

Serves 4 "squid lovers

You will need toasted garlic bread, and lots of it.

2 pounds squid
1 cup celery, chopped
1 cup onion, chopped
¼ cup vegetable oil
¼ cup tomato paste
¼ cup cider vinegar
½ teaspoon salt
1 tablespoon sugar
½ teaspoon black pepper

1. Cut cleaned squid into 1-inch pieces.

2. Sauté celery and onion in oil until tender. Add squid, cover and simmer for 5 minutes.

3. Add the tomato paste, vinegar, sugar, salt and pepper. Recover and simmer gently for 10 minutes until squid is tender. Serve with garlic bread.

To determine the cooking time for any cut of fish, lay the fish on a flat surface and measure at the thickest point from bottom to top. Allow 8 to 10 minutes cooking time per inch, doubling the time if the fish is frozen.

Broiled Swordfish with Mustard Butter   Serves 4

Any fresh garden herb such as thyme, tarragon, parsley or dill may be used.

4 8-ounce swordfish steaks, 1-inch thick
¼ cup dry white wine
2 tablespoons scallions, minced
⅔ cup heavy cream
¾ cup butter, chilled
2 tablespoons Dijon mustard
¼ cup lemon juice, freshly squeezed
salt and white pepper
2 tablespoons olive oil
2 tablespoons fresh basil, minced
basil sprigs for garnish

1. In a small saucepan, bring wine and scallions to a boil. Cook until liquid is reduced to 3 tablespoons. Add the cream and reduce mixture by half (about 3 to 4 minutes). Remove from heat.

2. Whisk in 2 tablespoons butter until blended. Return to low heat and whisk in remaining butter, 1 tablespoon at a time being sure each addition has blended smoothly. Move the pan on and off the heat if sauce begins to look oily on top. If sauce breaks, remove from heat and add 2 more tablespoons butter.

3. Add the lemon juice, mustard and salt and pepper to taste and whisk until smooth. Remove sauce from the heat and keep warm over hot water or in a double boiler.

4. Brush the swordfish steaks with the olive oil and sprinkle with basil. Let stand for 5 minutes. Broil fish for 3 to 5 minutes per side until firm to the touch. Divide sauce over 4 warm dinner plates, top with fish and garnish with basil sprigs.

Swordfish Block Island Fisherman Style

The fish remains plump, doesn't dry out, and is just delicious . . . .

8 ounces swordfish, freshly cut, ¾-inch
    thick, per person
2 strips bacon per person
1 small onion per person
big handful of parsley, chopped

1. In a large heavy skillet (cast iron if you have one) fry the bacon over medium heat until crisp. Remove from the pan and drain on paper towels.

2. Sauté the sliced onions in the bacon dripping until golden brown. Set aside.

3. Place the swordfish steaks in the remaining pan drippings, smother with onions and cook gently under a fitted lid, about 20 minutes.

4. Before serving swordfish, garnish with parsley and crumble the bacon on top.

Swordfish with Green Peppercorns   Serves 4

4 8-ounce swordfish steaks
2 tablespoons vegetable oil
2 tablespoons shallots, chopped
2 tablespoons green peppercorns, rinsed
6 tablespoons butter
¾ cup dry white wine
1 cup heavy cream
salt
parsley, chopped
cherry tomatoes

1. Choose a large frying pan and add the oil. Over medium heat cook the swordfish for 5 to 7 minutes on each side until golden brown. Remove fish and keep warm in a low oven.

2. Drain off most of the oil in the pan, leaving a scant teaspoon. Add the shallots and sauté for 1 minute. Add the wine and peppercorns and reduce by half over high heat.

3. Pour in the cream, increase heat and cook until sauce has thickened. Remove pan from the heat and whisk in the butter. Place swordfish on a hot platter and pour peppercorn sauce over. Garnish with warmed cherry tomatoes and chopped parsley.

Swordfish Steaks in Lime Marinade   Serves 8

**For an appetizer cut swordfish into bite-size pieces,
skewer and broil for 3 to 4 minutes.**

8 8-ounce swordfish steaks
¼ cup lime juice, freshly squeezed
2 teaspoons grated lime peel
3 garlic cloves, minced
⅓ cup soy sauce
1 tablespoon Dijon mustard
¼ cup oil
3 scallions, finely chopped
½ teaspoon black pepper, freshly ground
lime slices
scallion curls

1. Combine lime juice, lime peel, garlic, soy sauce, mustard, oil, scallions and pepper in a small bowl, mixing well.

2. Arrange the swordfish in a glass or stainless steel flat pan with sides. Pour the marinade over the swordfish, turning each piece to coat well. Cover and refrigerate for several hours.

3. Place the fish on a large broiling pan and cook under a preheated broiler, for 4 to 5 minutes on each side until fish flakes with a fork.

4. Transfer the swordfish to a serving platter and pour the pan juices and any remaining marinade over top. Garnish with lime slices and scallion curls.

Oriental Tuna Casserole   Serves 8 to 10

At last . . . an innovative twist to the basic recipe.

3 6½-ounce cans tuna, drained
1 cup celery, sliced
¼ cup onion, chopped
2 8-ounce cans water chestnuts, sliced
1 8-ounce can mushroom pieces, drained
2 teaspoons soy sauce
1 can cream of mushroom soup
1 cup cream of chicken soup
1 8-ounce can evaporated milk
1 5-ounce can Chinese noodles
6 ounces almonds, sliced
½ cup bread crumbs, buttered

1. In a large bowl, flake the tuna with a fork. Toss with celery, onion, water chestnuts mushrooms and soy sauce.

2. Stir in the mushroom soup, chicken soup and evaporated milk. Gently fold in the Chinese noodles and pour into a 6-quart buttered casserole. Sprinkle the top with bread crumbs and almonds and bake in a 350° oven for 45 minutes.

Semper Fidelis

Serves 4

1 pound cod, flounder, salmon or bluefish
4 tablespoons butter
2 cups onions, chopped
⅓ cup lemon juice, freshly squeezed
1 tablespoon dill
1 teaspoon "Krazy Mixed-Up Salt"
1 cup tomatoes, chopped or
    stewed tomatoes, drained
1 cup mushrooms, sliced
½ cup white wine

1. Melt the butter in a large skillet and sauté the onions until tender.
2. Place the fish fillets over the onions and sprinkle with lemon juice, dill and salt. Cover with tomatoes and mushrooms.
3. Pour the wine around the edges of the pan and cover tightly with a lid or aluminum foil. Simmer gently for 10 minutes.

Any leftover sauce can be strained and used as a base for soup or other dishes.

Kedaree

Serves 4

A very old Hindu recipe from India, via England.

1 cup rice
4 tablespoons butter
1 garlic clove, minced
1 cup cooked fish, flaked. Any fresh or
    leftover catch is fine . . . tuna is also
    delicious
1 cup cooked carrots, diced
salt and pepper
Cayenne pepper
4 eggs, hard-boiled and quartered
3 large tomatoes, sliced

1. Cook rice in 2 cups boiling salted water in a covered saucepan for 20 minutes. Cover and keep warm.
2. Melt butter in a large skillet and sauté garlic for 2 minutes. Add flaked fish, cooked carrots and heat for 3 to 4 minutes. Season with salt, pepper and Cayenne. Top with eggs.
3. Move mixture to one side of pan and put tomato slices on one side to warm. (You may omit this step and serve tomato slices as a cold ganish.)
4. On a round platter, make a ring of the hot rice. Mound the fish mixture in the center and surround with tomato slices.

This may be made ahead and assembled in a microwaveproof casserole. Cover and heat on high for 6 minutes, turning halfway through.

Fish in a Purse

This is an easy and quick way to cook fish; and can be varied with imagination, seasonings and types of fish. The key is to keep it simple, be flexible and experiment with different spice combinations.

Per person:

⅓ to ½ pound fish fillets, cod, bluefish or
   catch of the day
1 teaspoon butter
1 teaspoon lemon juice, freshly squeezed
⅛ teaspoon tarragon or dill
⅛ teaspoon salt
black pepper
pinch garlic powder or a little
   fresh garlic, minced
white wine

1. Place each serving of fish on a piece of heavy duty aluminum foil, large enough so the ends may be gathered and crimped together to form a purse.

2. Season with butter, lemon juice, tarragon or dill, salt, pepper and garlic. Gather up the ends of the foil, pour a splash of white wine on top of fish and close up foil completely, forming a purse. Be careful not to puncture foil while you are sealing.

3. Place a wire rack or inverted aluminum pie pan in a covered pot or large saucepan. Add ½-inch of boiling water to the pan and place the packages of fish on the rack. Cover the pan and bring water to a boil. Cook for 10 minutes. Turn heat off and let sit for 3 minutes before serving.

Fish in Champagne Cream

Serves 4

1 2-pound piece of a white fish such as
   haddock or cod
1 cup champagne
2 tablespoons butter
1 bay leaf
2 tablespoons onion, grated
½ cup mushrooms, chopped
2 tablespoons parsley, finely chopped
2 tablespoons heavy cream
2 tablespoons Parmesan cheese,
   freshly grated
salt and pepper

1. Place champagne, butter, onion, bay leaf, mushrooms and parsley in a small saucepan. Over medium heat, reduce mixture by half. Remove bay leaf.

2. In a small bowl, combine cream, Parmesan cheese and a pinch of salt and pepper. Stir in the reduced champagne mixture.

3. Dip fish in a little salted water and pat dry. Salt and pepper it lightly. Place in a large well-buttered baking dish and cover with the champagne sauce. Bake at 375° for 25 to 30 minutes until top is lightly browned.

Swedish Fish Pudding with Shrimp Sauce   Serves 4

Pudding:
1 pound haddock or cod, cut into strips
2 eggs
2 cups milk
½ teaspoon dill
1 tablespoon parsley, freshly chopped
salt and white pepper

Shrimp Sauce:
¼ pound tiny shrimp, cooked
2 tablespoons butter
2 tablespoons flour
1 cup milk
1 tablespoon sherry
½ teaspoon paprika
salt and Cayenne pepper

Pudding preparation:
1. Put the fish pieces in the bowl of a food processor fitted with the steel blade. Coarsely chop, about 30 seconds, pulsing on and off. Add the eggs, milk, dill, parsley and a pinch of salt and pepper. Process for 30 more seconds until fluffy.

2. Pour the mixture into a buttered glass ovenproof casserole that will fit into another baking dish, allowing 1 inch of water in the bottom baking dish. Place casserole with the fish on a metal trivet or rack in the bottom baking dish. Pour boiling water in to create a double boiler effect. Bake pudding at 350° for 1 hour.

Shrimp Sauce preparation:
1. Melt butter in a saucepan. Add the flour and mix well. Stir in the milk very slowly and add the sherry.

2. Cook for 2 to 3 minutes over low heat, stirring constantly, until thickened. Add the paprika, salt and Cayenne to taste. Stir in the shrimp and keep sauce warm.

To Serve:
Either unmold the fish pudding onto a hot platter or serve directly from the casserole, spooning the Shrimp Sauce over the top.

Can be served chilled the next day as a luncheon entrée. Omit the Shrimp Sauce and instead serve an herb mayonnaise with flecks of red pepper mixed in.

New Year's Eve Seafood Casserole   Serves 12

Always enjoyed the most when served BEFORE midnight . . .

4 tablespoons butter
1 pound fresh mushrooms
5 tablespoons flour
2 cups light cream
¼ cup sherry
2 cups mayonnaise
½ cup parsley, minced
½ cup scallions, chopped
2½ cups fresh bread crumbs
1 pound crabmeat, cartilage removed*
1 pound lobstermeat,* cut into chunks
2 14-ounce cans artichoke hearts, quartered
½ cup Parmesan cheese, freshly grated

***Cooked shrimp or scallops may be substituted
for either of these.**

1. In a large saucepan, melt the butter. add the mushrooms and sauté for 5 minutes. Stir in the flour and combine well.

2. Add the cream a little at a time, stirring constantly until sauce thickens. Add the sherry, cook for 2 minutes, remove from heat and cool.

3. Stir in the mayonnaise, parsley, scallions and bread crumbs. Lightly fold in the crabmeat and lobster.

4. Butter a 9x13-inch casserole dish. Layer the chopped artichokes in the dish and spread the crab and lobster mixture on top. Sprinkle the top with Parmesan cheese and bake at 350° for 30 to 40 minutes.

Seafood Casserole for a Crowd   Serves 24

**An excellent buffet entrée for the holidays or special occasions.
Serve it with a spinach soufflé, braised cherry tomatoes sprinkled
with dill and a green salad.**

4 pounds king crabmeat, remove shell
  pieces carefully
4 pounds large shrimp, cooked and cleaned
2 cups scallions, chopped
1 cup fresh parsley, chopped
8 cups white rice, cooked
4 cups mayonnaise
8 8-ounce cans sliced water chestnuts,
  drained
2 cups dry white wine
4 tablespoons sugar
salt and pepper to taste, freshly ground

Must be made ahead.

1. In a large bowl, lightly toss all above ingredients and divide into greased casseroles if you do not have one large enough to handle the whole batch.

2. Refrigerate overnight to blend flavors. Bake, 1 hour, covered in a 350° oven.

Crow's Nest Seafood Salad

Serves 10

The sophisticated side of a sandwich.

1 loaf Italian bread, crusts removed and cut into ½-inch cubes
4 hard-boiled eggs, chopped
½ cup Bermuda onion, chopped
½ cup scallions, chopped
2 4½-ounce cans small shrimp, rinsed and drained
1 7½-ounce can crabmeat, drained and flaked
1 cup celery, chopped
2 cups mayonnaise or salad dressing blend, (the light variety is very good if counting calories)
lettuce leaves

Must be made ahead.

1. Combine the bread cubes, chopped eggs, onions and scallions in a medium bowl. Toss lightly and cover. Place in the refrigerator overnight.

2. Several hours before serving, add the shrimp, crab, celery and mayonnaise or salad dressing. Gently mix with two forks until everything is well coated. Chill for 2 to 3 hours.

3. When ready to serve either line a large serving dish with lettuce leaves and mound salad on top or serve individually on lettuce cups.

Baked Seafood Newburg

Serves 8

4 tablespoons butter
½ pound mushrooms, sliced
1 cup scallions, chopped
⅓ cup flour
1 cup dry white wine
1 cup half-and-half cream
½ teaspoon curry powder
⅓ cup Parmesan cheese, freshly grated
1 pound medium shrimp, peeled and deveined
1 pound flounder, cut into finger-sized strips
½ pound scallops
salt and pepper to taste
½ cup corn flake crumbs
2 tablespoons butter, melted

1. Melt butter in a medium saucepan and sauté mushrooms and scallions until soft. Stir in the flour.

2. Gradually add the wine and half-and-half, stirring constantly. Add the curry powder and cheese, reduce heat and cook until sauce bubbles and thickens.

3. Gently fold in the shrimp, fish and scallops (all uncooked) until well coated with the sauce. Season with salt and pepper and pour into a buttered 3-quart casserole. Sprinkle crumbs on top. Drizzle with butter and bake at 350° for 40 to 60 minutes.

Bayou Seafood Gumbo II

Serves 6

A big plate of steamed greens and corn bread sticks with this are a family favorite.

4 slices bacon
2 onions, finely chopped
1 green pepper, chopped
2 garlic cloves, minced
1 pound okra, cut into ½-inch pieces
salt and Cayenne pepper
2 16-ounce cans whole tomatoes
1 bay leaf
1 cup water
1 pound medium shrimp, peeled and deveined
½ pound fish fillets, something firm and non-oily such as catfish, halibut or bass
parsley, freshly chopped

1. In a large pot, cook the bacon until crisp. Remove bacon, drain on paper towels and crumble.

2. Add the onions, pepper, garlic and okra. Sauté in bacon fat for 5 minutes until tender. Stir in the tomatoes and cook for 20 minutes until sauce is slightly thick.

3. Season mixture with salt and Cayenne pepper and add the water and bay leaf. Stir in the shrimp, crabmeat and fish fillets and simmer over medium-low heat for 30 minutes. Ladle over hot rice and sprinkle with parsley and crumbled bacon.

Paëlla Galley Style

Serves 6

1 pound fish fillets, cut into 2-inch pieces
1 pound large shrimp, peeled and deveined
6 pieces chicken, legs or breasts, cut in half
12 cherrystone clams, well rinsed
2 tablespoons olive oil
1 large white onion, chopped
1 garlic clove, minced
1 large green pepper, chopped
2 cups white rice
1 teaspoon oregano
½ teaspoon saffron
3 cups chicken broth
1 pound tomatoes, peeled and chopped
½ teaspoon salt
black pepper

1. In a large pot, brown the chicken pieces on both sides in the olive oil and set aside.

2. Add the onion, garlic, green pepper and oregano to the pan. Sauté for 3 minutes until tender and place the chicken on top.

3. Dissolve the saffron in the chicken broth and add along with the rice, tomatoes, salt and pepper. Cover and simmer for 30 minutes.

4. Layer the fish, shrimp and clams over the rice, nestling everything into the broth. Recover and cook for 10 minutes until shrimp are pink and clams have opened.

Seafood Fondue with Three Sauces   Serves 8

**That pot you received years ago as a wedding gift is not obsolete after all.
This dish is great fun for a crowd and can be prepared ahead.**

1 pound sea scallops
1½ pounds medium shrimp,
 peeled and deveined
2 pounds firm white fish such as cod,
 halibut or swordfish, cut into
 2-inch pieces
salt and pepper
1 lemon, freshly squeezed
½ cup dry white wine
3 tablespoons olive oil
3 pints mussels
2 cups mayonnaise
3 tablespoons ketchup
3 garlic cloves, minced
3 tablespoons mixed herbs: dill, parsley,
 chives, mint; chopped
2 pounds fish trimmings, bones, etc.
1 bay leaf
1 small onion stuck with 2 cloves
1 carrot, thinly sliced
1 lemon, quartered
1 bottle dry white wine

1. Place the scallops, shrimp and fish in a shallow dish and season with salt and pepper. Add the lemon juice, olive oil and ½ cup white wine and toss lightly and allow to marinate.

2. Rinse the mussels and remove the beards. Place in a large pot with ½ inch of water and steam, covered, for 6 to 8 minutes until shells have opened. Drain and remove mussel meats from their shells. Strain the cooking juices and return to the pot.

3. Add the fish trimmings, bay leaf, onion, carrot, lemon and wine. Simmer gently for 30 minutes, strain the stock and place in a fondue pot.

4. Meanwhile thread the marinated fish, shrimp, scallops and mussels on small wooden skewers.

5. Divide the mayonnaise between 3 bowls. Add the ketchup to one, the garlic to one, and the chopped herbs to one. Combine each sauce well.

6. When you are ready to serve, bring the stock to a boil and have each guest plunge a skewer into the hot stock for 4 to 5 minutes and season with the sauce of his choice. Be prepared with plenty of crusty bread for dipping.

ON BOARD

Edelweiss Baked Bluefish*

Serves 4

1 fillet of bluefish, skinned
1 tablespoon butter or oil
onions, scallions or shallots — anything
    "oniony" available on board
rosemary or oregano

Sauce:

2 tablespoons prepared mustard
5 tablespoons ketchup
1 tablespoon steak sauce
2 tablespoons dry sherry
2 tablespoons wine vinegar
liquid smoke to taste

*For boats with grills.

1. Tear off a large piece of heavy duty aluminum foil. Spread butter or oil on the foil where you will place the fish. Scatter onion and herbs on top and lay the fish to rest.

2. Mix all other ingredients for the sauce and spread over fish. Seal and crimp the foil around the fish and grill for 20 to 25 minutes depending on thickness of fillet.

Crab Melt on English*

Serves 8 as a luncheon

For a quick meal, mix the crab topping at home.

1 3-ounce package cream cheese
1 tablespoon onion, minced
2 tablespoons mayonnaise
2 tablespoons ketchup
1½ teaspoons Worcestershire sauce
dash salt
1 pound lump crab, cartilage removed
4 English muffins
2 tablespoons butter
8 thick slices of tomato
8 slices sharp cheese

*For boats with ovens.

1. Soften cream cheese with a fork until creamy. Add onion, mayonnaise, ketchup, Worcestershire, salt and crab. Stir until combined.

2. Split and butter English muffins. Place tomato slice on each half and spread with crab mixture. Put a slice of cheese on each. Bake at 350° for 20 to 30 minutes.

Off Soundings Clam Casserole*   Serves 6 to 8

May also be put in clam shells and served as a hearty appetizer.

¼ pound salt pork
6 medium onions, finely diced
3 pints hard-shell clams, shucked and
   ground or finely chopped
18 milk crackers
2 tablespoons butter, melted
⅛ teaspoon black pepper

*For boats with ovens.

1. Dice salt pork and sauté in a medium saucepan until golden. Add the onions and clams, crush the crackers and combine well.
2. Pour in the melted butter and pepper and moisten with any reserved clam juice.
3. Place in a sturdy casserole (9x14-inches is fine) and bake at 350° for 30 to 45 minutes. If your oven is small rotate pan once to avoid scorching.

Take-Along Linguine with Clam Sauce   Serves 4

1 pound linguine
3 6½-ounce cans minced clams
10 ounces bottled clam juice
⅓ cup olive oil
2 garlic cloves
1 small onion, minced
4 tablespoons dried parsley
1 teaspoon oregano
¼ teaspoon salt
¼ teaspoon crushed red pepper flakes
⅛ teaspoon black pepper

1. Cook linguine to taste in boiling water, drain and set aside.
2. Heat olive oil in saucepan, add onion and garlic. Sauté until golden.
3. Add the clams, clam juice and seasonings.
4. Cook until clams are heated through and toss with pasta.

Because the ingredients need no refrigeration, this recipe can be made on a boat with only a two burner stove. The dry ingredients can be pre-measured at home and brought aboard in a sandwich bag.

Hot Tomato Clam Broth   Serves 8

A mid-morning pick-me-up for a chilly day.

1 18-ounce cans tomato juice
2 8-ounce bottles clam broth
2 6½-ounce cans minced clams
1 tablespoon lemon juice, freshly squeezed
sour cream

1. Mix tomato juice and clam broth in a saucepan and bring to a slow boil.
2. Add the clams with their juice, stir for a minute and remove from heat. Add the lemon.
3. Pour into mugs and top with a spoonful of sour cream.

Fanciful Flounder*

Serves 6 to 8

For that night when rafted alongside with friends.

2 pounds flounder fillets
1 pound medium shrimp, peeled, deveined
  and cut into bite-size pieces
½ cup scallions, chopped
3 slices day old white bread, crumbled
1 teaspoon dill
1 teaspoon parsley
⅓ cup white wine
6 large slices Swiss cheese
paprika
butter

*For boats with ovens.

1. In a 9x12-inch baking dish, layer half of the flounder. Top with the shrimp and evenly sprinkle scallions and bread crumbs on top. Season with dill and parsley. Drizzle with melted butter.

2. Top with remaining flounder fillets. Pour wine over fish and cover with aluminum foil. If your boat has a snug galley, prepare this at home to this point the night before and refrigerate.

3. Bake at 350° for 20 minutes. Uncover, top with cheese and sprinkle with paprika. Cook for 5 minutes more until cheese has melted. Let casserole rest, replacing foil for 10 minutes before serving.

Five Minute Flounder

One minute to prepare, four minutes from the pan to the table.

2 good size flounder fillets per person
prepared mustard, any kind works, from
  brown to yellow to Dijon
butter, margarine or non-stick cooking spray,
  depending on availability or cholesterol
  count of diners
lemon, freshly squeezed

1. Spread mustard and dots of butter or margarine on white sides of fish fillets.

2. Heat large frying pan until drops of water dance on the surface. Place the fish, buttered side down and cook for 2 minutes. Turn and cook on other side for 2 more minutes. Give the fish a good squeeze of lemon and serve hot.

Salmon Slaw Rolls

Serves 6

This mixture can be put together and refrigerated after the breakfast dishes are done.

1 7½-ounce can salmon, drained, skin and bones removed
1 cup coleslaw
¼ cup mayonnaise
¼ teaspoon dill
6 onion rolls, split
2 medium tomatoes, sliced
1 cup bean or watercress sprouts

1. Combine salmon with coleslaw, mayonnaise and dill, tossing with a fork.
2. Divide mixture between six roll bottoms. Add tomato slices and sprouts. Top off with other half of roll.

Barefoot Smoked Salmon and Eggs Serves 4

With a very temperamental alcohol stove on board, one burner meals are a joy. Treat the crew to this for a late breakfast, or increase amount of eggs and serve for an easy supper with a fresh fruit salad.

4 slices rye or pumpernickel bread, lightly buttered
8 slices smoked salmon
¼ cup onion, finely chopped
2 tablespoons butter
6 to 8 eggs
2 tablespoons milk
2 teaspoons chives, chopped
salt and pepper
sour cream
chopped chives for garnish

1. Arrange 2 slices of smoked salmon on each piece of buttered bread.
2. Melt butter in a large frying pan and sauté onion until soft but not brown.
3. In a medium bowl, scramble eggs with milk, chives and salt and pepper to taste. Increase heat in frying pan with onions and cook eggs 2 to 3 minutes until nicely soft.
4. Divide scrambled eggs over each piece of bread and garnish with a spoonful of sour cream and chives on top.

Many of the more exotic fish such as salmon, mahi-mahi, orange roughy and giant whale halibut exhibit unusual flavors and very often do not need taste enhancement.

Salmon Kedgeree

Serves 4

This basic recipe has numerous twists, add other vegetables or cheese and spoon into scooped-out tomato halves to serve 8.

1½ cups cooked salmon (fresh or canned), flaked
3 tablespoons butter
1 medium onion, finely chopped
1½ cups cooked white rice
2 hard-boiled eggs, chopped
½ teaspoon dill
salt and pepper
2 tablespoons parsley, chopped

1. Lightly sauté the onion in the butter until translucent. Gently toss with the cooked rice, eggs, dill and seasonings.
2. Fold in the cooked salmon and heat for several minutes until ready to serve.

One-Burner Scallops with Mozzarella

Serves 4

A tasty addition to your boating repertoire.

1½ pounds scallops
1 tablespoon olive oil
1 carrot, chopped
1 large stalk celery, chopped
1 garlic clove, minced or ½ teaspoon garlic powder
1 15-ounce can stewed tomatoes
¼ cup Mozzarella cheese, shredded

1. In a medium saucepan, heat olive oil. Add the carrot, celery and garlic. Sauté for 3 minutes until just soft.
2. Add the scallops and sauté for 3 minutes. Pour the tomatoes over the scallops and heat thoroughly.
3. Lower the heat and sprinkle scallop-vegetable mixture with shredded cheese. Cover until cheese melts.
4. Serve over noodles or white rice.

Last Minute Scallop Sauté

Serves 2

So simple yet so delicious.

1 pound scallops
¼ cup butter
2 tablespoons scallions (or chives), chopped
½ cup onions, diced
1 tablespoon parsley, chopped
¼ cup sauterne or white wine
salt and pepper

1. Rinse scallops with cold water and pat dry.
2. Sauté the scallions and minced onion in butter for 2 minutes until translucent. Add the scallops, parsley, wine, salt and pepper.
3. Simmer for 4 to 5 minutes until scallops are done, but still soft. Serve with hot rice pilaf to absorb the divine pan juices.

Scallop Cheese Pudding*

Serves 4

Try this with shrimp or crab.

8 slices bread, buttered
1 pound scallops
½ cup celery, chopped
1 cup cheddar cheese, grated
3 eggs, slightly beaten
1 cup milk
½ teaspoon prepared mustard
½ teaspoon paprika
salt

*For boats with ovens.

1. Fit 4 slices bread, buttered side down in an 8x10-inch casserole dish.
2. Cover with scallops, celery and cheddar cheese. Place other 4 bread slices, buttered side up, on top of scallops.
3. Combine eggs, milk, mustard, paprika and a pinch of salt. Pour over casserole. Let rest 10 minutes and bake at 350° for 30 minutes until puffed and brown.

Scallop Surprise*

Serves 4

A surprise because of its richness and simplicity.

1½ pounds scallops
6 slices bread
1 pint light cream
24 saltine crackers, crushed
4 tablespoons butter

*For boats with ovens.

1. Break bread into small pieces and place in a bowl.
2. In a buttered 2-quart casserole dish, alternately layer the scallops and bread crumbs. Pour cream over the top.
3. Melt the butter in a frying pan and sauté crushed crackers for 2 minutes. Top the casserole with the buttered crumbs and bake at 375° for 30 minutes.

Bombay Scallops

Serves 4

A touch of India.

3 tablespoons vegetable oil
1 garlic clove, crushed
1 small onion, chopped
1 pound scallops
flour
½ teaspoon salt
2 teaspoons curry powder
3 tablespoons dry white wine
parsley

1. Heat oil in a heavy skillet. Add garlic and onion. Sauté for 3 minutes.
2. Roll scallops in flour and add to the pan. Brown quickly on all sides. Add salt, curry and wine, blend well. Stir until thickened over medium heat being careful not to overcook the scallops.
3. Serve over cooked rice and sprinkle with parsley.

Scrod Parmesan*

Serves 6

Your crew will suspect lasagna baking — voila, fish!

2 pounds scrod
1 26-ounce jar marinara sauce
2 4-ounce cans mushrooms
½ cup grated Parmesan cheese
6 ounces grated Mozzarella cheese
1 pound linguine
2 tablespoons olive oil
parsley, chopped

*For boats with ovens.

1. Cut the scrod into serving-size pieces and place in a baking pan. Pour the sauce evenly over the fish and top with the mushrooms.

2. Sprinkle grated cheeses over the fish and bake in a 350° oven for 30 minutes until cheese is nicely browned. In the meantime, cook the linguine according to package directions, drain and stir in the olive oil. Cover and keep warm.

3. When fish is ready, place a portion of hot linguine on each plate. Sprinkle the fish with parsley and serve, pouring the juices overall. Always remember to use good PAPER plates with any dish with tomato sauce on the boat as the sauce clings to everything in the sink.

Scrod Dijon*

Serves 4

Nothing nicer than the simplicity of this zesty fish topping.

1½ pounds scrod or haddock fillets
3 tablespoons butter, softened
3 tablespoons lemon juice
3 tablespoons Dijon mustard

*For boats with ovens.

1. Combine butter, lemon juice and Dijon mustard and blend well.

2. Place fish in a shallow pan and spread the mustard mixture evenly over the top. Let stand for 15 minutes.

3. This can be baked for 15 minutes at 350° or grilled over charcoal if you are lucky enough to still have the skin on the fish.

If you have been cutting or filleting fish on a wooden board or counter, rub the board or counter with half a fresh lemon to remove the odor.

Offshore Baked Shark*

Serves 6

Whoever caught the fish has to clean it and pass it down below to the cook.

1 2-pound shark
2 large celery stalks, chopped
1 small onion, minced
1 10-ounce can cream of mushroom soup
5 ounces milk
½ cup Mozzarella cheese, grated
salt and pepper

*For boats with ovens.

1. Cut fish into 1-inch strips and arrange in a buttered 8x12-inch baking dish. Cover with celery and onion.
2. Combine soup and milk until creamy. Stir in the Mozzarella, salt and pepper. Pour sauce over fish and cover with foil. Bake at 325° for 30 minutes and call the crew.

Vona's Super Easy Shrimp Curry

Serves 4 to 6

2 10-ounce cans, cream of mushroom soup, undiluted
2 tablespoons curry powder, add more to taste
1 pound medium shrimp, cooked and cleaned

4 tablespoons curry is medium hot and 6 tablespoons is very spicy.

Condiments:

crisp bacon, crumbled
bananas, sliced
coconut, shredded
peanuts, coarsely chopped
chutney
green pepper, finely diced
scallions, sliced
apple, finely diced

1. Stir curry powder into soup in a saucepan and warm. Add the shrimp and heat for 5 minutes.
2. Serve over hot, cooked rice and pass condiments, as many or as few as you have on board.

Use any leftover bacon, onions or pepper in your morning eggs and toss the leftover fruit in your cereal.

121

Emergency Shrimp and Rice   Serves 4

We have shared this with boating friends who have loved it. Keep ingredients on shelf at all times and this can save the day or night when you can't get ashore.

2 4-ounce cans medium shrimp, drained and rinsed
1 10-ounce can tomato soup
2 teaspoons parsley flakes
½ teaspoon instant minced onion
⅛ teaspoon Cayenne pepper
¼ teaspoon garlic salt
1 4-ounce can mushrooms
1 tablespoon butter
1½ cups Minute rice

1. In a 3-quart saucepan combine soup and 1 can of water. Heat until blended.
2. Add shrimp, seasonings, mushrooms and butter. Bring to a boil. Add the rice, remove from heat, cover and let stand for 10 minutes.

Floating Shrimp Marinara   Serves 8

2 10½-ounce cans whole baby clams
2 cups rice
1 tablespoon olive oil
½ teaspoon oregano
dash of salt, pepper and Cayenne
½ cup roasted red peppers, diced
1½ pounds medium shrimp, cooked, peeled and deveined
2 13-ounce cans vichyssoise
1 8-ounce can water chestnuts, drained and sliced
1 lemon, freshly squeezed

1. Drain clams, reserving liquid. In saucepan add enouth water to the clam liquid to make 1 quart.
2. Bring to a boil, add rice, olive oil, oregano and a few pinches of salt. Stir well, reduce heat, cover and cook until rice is tender, 18 to 20 minutes.
3. In a large pot, combine rice, clams, red peppers, shrimps, vichyssoise, water chestnuts and lemon.
4. Sprinkle a bit of Cayenne to taste and keep warm until the captain rounds up the crew. Give it a grind or two of black pepper at the table.

Artichoke Shrimp and Rice Salad   Serves 6

Keeps the cook cool on a hot summer night.

1½ pounds cooked large shrimp or
  4 4½-ounce cans shrimps,
  drained and rinsed
1 14-ounce can artichoke hearts, drained
  and quartered
3 cups cooked rice
½ cup scallions, chopped
¼ cup olives (green or black), chopped
¼ teaspoon dill
1 cup French dressing
olives
pickles

1. Cook rice while you are doing the breakfast dishes and place in ice chest along with cans of shrimp, artichoke hearts and olives.

2. When ready to serve toss rice with shrimp. Add artichoke hearts, scallions, olives and dill.

3. Moisten with French dressing and mix well, using more or less dressing if you prefer. Spoon onto lettuce leaves and garnish with additional whole olives and pickles.

Hot or Cold Shrimp and Crab Toss   Serves 4

If you don't want to light the stove, omit the crumb topping and serve as a salad on lettuce leaves.

2 4½-ounce cans medium shrimp, drained
  and rinsed
1 6-ounce can crabmeat, drained and rinsed
  with cartilage removed
1 green pepper, finely chopped
1 cup celery, finely chopped
½ small onion, minced
1 cup mayonnaise
1 teaspoon Worcestershire sauce
1 teaspoon parsley, chopped
salt and pepper
buttered crumbs

1. Place shrimp and crabmeat in bowl and combine with green pepper, onion and celery. Toss with the mayonnaise, Worcestershire sauce, parsley, salt and pepper, combining well.

2. Spoon mixture into individual shells or a 2-quart casserole. Sprinkle with buttered crumbs and bake at 350° for 30 minutes until browned.

If you are not on the boat and are serving this as a luncheon for 4, you can decrease the amount of shrimp by one can and still have a comfortable serving.

Garlic Shrimp and Linguine

Serves 4

Stop on the way to the boatyard and pick up a crusty loaf of bread and a salad at the deli. Better yet, just make this ahead and leave the mess at home.

1 pound medium shrimp, peeled and deveined
3 garlic cloves, chopped
1 tablespoon parsley, chopped
⅛ teaspoon black pepper, freshly ground
½ cup olive oil
1 pound linguine
4 tablespoons butter
white wine, if you have an open bottle aboard

Requires some advance preparation.

1. Place shrimp, garlic, parsley and black pepper in a plastic "take-along" container. Pour the olive oil over the shrimp to cover, adding a little more if needed. Marinate for serveral hours. Cover tightly and take to the boat.

2. On one burner, boil a pot of salted water and add the linguine.

3. On the other burner, melt butter in a skillet and add the shrimp and olive oil mixture. Cook for 2 to 3 minutes until the shrimp turns pink. Add a splash or two of white wine if you feel so inclined.

4. By now the linguine should be perfectly cooked. Drain it and pour the shrimp mixture overall. Serve immediately.

Sweet and Sour Tuna

Serves 6

A simple adaptation using ingredients from the pantry shelf.

2 7-ounce cans tuna, drained
3 tablespoons butter
¼ cup scallions, chopped
1 medium green pepper, cut into thin strips
4 tablespoons flour
1½ cups milk
1 15-ounce can pineapple chunks, drained with juice reserved
1 10-ounce can whole kernel corn, drained
¼ cup vinegar
salt and pepper
½ cup toasted almonds

1. Melt the butter in a medium saucepan. Add the scallions and green pepper. Sauté for 2 minutes.

2. Stir in the flour and mix well. Add the milk and reserved juice from the pineapple and cook, stirring constantly until sauce has thickened.

3. Add the vinegar and gently fold in the pineapple, corn and flaked tuna. Season with salt and pepper and simmer over low heat for a few minutes. Serve over white rice and sprinkle with almonds.

Tuna Aurora

Serves 4

8 ounces pasta (shells, ziti or your favorite)
2 7-ounce cans tuna, drained
2 tablespoons butter
1 medium onion, chopped
2 tablespoons flour
1 cup milk
2 teaspoons tomato paste
½ cup sharp cheddar cheese, grated
paprika

1. Cook the pasta in boiling salted water. Drain and set aside.

2. Melt the butter in a medium saucepan. Add the onion, chopped and sauté for 3 minutes until soft. Stir in the flour and remove from the heat.

3. Slowly add the milk, stirring constantly. Return to the heat and cook sauce for 3 more minutes until thickened.

4. Add the tomato paste, cheese and tuna to the sauce. Fold in the drained pasta and keep warm until ready to serve.

Serve with a salad of marinated cucumbers and tomatoes.

Italian Tuna and Bean Salad

Serves 4

The longer this sits, the better it tastes.

1 16-ounce can white or shell beans, drained
1 7-ounce can tuna, imported Italian if you can find it
1 tomato, diced
¼ cup red onion, chopped
2 celery stalks, chopped
½ green or red pepper, cut into strips
1 small cucumber, sliced
¼ teaspoon oregano
4 tablespoons olive oil
black pepper, freshly ground

1. Toss the beans with the tuna in a medium bowl. Add the chopped vegetables and oregano.

2. Drizzle olive oil overall and lightly mix — you may adjust the amount of oil, more or less to your liking. Give it some hearty grinds of pepper and serve on a lettuce leaf.

Cook's Day Off...
Scalloped Tuna and Potato Casserole*

Serves 4 to 6

For the night after a big dinner ashore.

4 cups potatoes, peeled and sliced
2 6½-ounce cans tuna, drained
4 tablespoons butter or margarine
4 tablespoons flour
2 cups milk
2 tablespoons prepared mustard
1 medium onion, diced
⅛ teaspoon black pepper
1 teaspoon parsley flakes
Parmesan cheese

*For boats with ovens.

**More milk may be added if casserole seems a bit dry after cooking — different kinds of potatoes seem to absorb more of the sauce.

1. Cook potatoes in salted water for 10 minutes. Drain.

2. In a medium saucepan, melt butter over low heat. Whisk in flour until combined.

3. Add the milk,** salt, mustard, onion, pepper and parsley. Cook for 2 to 3 minutes until sauce has thickened, stirring constantly.

4. Arrange some of the sliced potatoes in a 2-quart casserole to make a layer. Cover with a layer of tuna, then a layer of sauce.

5. Repeat until all ingredients are used, ending with a layer of sauce.

6. Bake at 350° for 45 minutes until bubbly. Sprinkle with Parmesan cheese before serving.

Tuna Bodenwein

Serves 6

Take along a piece of fresh ginger when cruising.
It's great for perking up chicken or vegetables.

2 7-ounce cans tuna (reserve oil). If using water packed tuna, substitute 1 tablespoon oil, 1 tablespoon butter
½ cup onion, chopped
1 8-ounce can water chestnuts, sliced
2 teaspoons ginger, freshly chopped or 1 tablespoon dry ginger
2 cups sour cream
salt and pepper

1. Drain tuna over a skillet if using oil packed tuna. If not, drain off water and add oil and butter to the pan.

2. Sauté the onion in the oil for 3 minutes until tender. Flake the tuna into the pan and add the water chestnuts and ginger. Sauté for a few minutes until heated throughout.

3. Add the sour cream, salt and pepper. Cook until steaming but do not boil. Serve over rice.

Fish at Sea*

This is a real "off shore" meal and improvisation is crucial!
The amount of fish will depend on two factors
— the success of the fisherman and how fast your boat is.

firm fleshed, freshly caught fish (such as
   tuna, bonito, dorade or mackerel) cleaned
   in salt water, but otherwise just as it
   comes from the hook.
parsley
rosemary
black pepper
lemon or lime, freshly sqeezed
scallions or red onions, diced
garlic, chopped
¼ pound butter or 2 tablespoons olive oil
   for drizzling

Variations:

• sliced tomatoes and basil, (omit the
   rosemary) and use a hint of oregano and
   thyme, garnish with black olives

• sprinkle liberally with crumbs and grated
   cheese (omit the rosemary)

• If you have let the fish marinate for a bit,
   chop up some celery and green peppers
   and spread on top. If you have some
   open white wine on board, pour a little
   overall. A can of chopped mushrooms
   may be added.

*For boats with ovens.

1. If the catch is tuna or dorade, cut it
   crosswise into steaks. Smaller fish should
   be filleted.

2. In a large, deep, well-buttered casserole
   (or plastic container if not to be cooked
   immediately), place the fish in one layer.
   Sprinkle liberally with herbs and spices.
   Layer another round of fish and repeat
   with herbs and spices. Top with ¼ pound
   of butter cut in chunks or drizzle olive
   oil over the fish.

3. Bake, uncovered, at 375° for 30 to 45
   minutes. The timing depends a lot on
   your method of cooking, that is, the type
   of fuel used. Some types of marine
   propane stoves cook much faster than
   the alcohol variety.

4. Serve with buttered noodles, corn
   bread or biscuits, accompanied by a
   green salad.

Fish Angelique*   Serves 4

A recipe from the Camden based ketch of the same name.

1½ pounds white fish (grouper, pollack,
   cod or haddock)
½ cup sour cream or plain yogurt
½ cup mayonnaise
2 tablespoons parsley
2 teaspoons dill
2 tablespoons milk
dash of pepper

1. Mix all ingredients, except fish, in a bowl.

2. Put fish in a well-buttered dish and spoon
   mixture over the top. Bake in 350° oven
   for 45 minutes until fish is done and
   sauce is slightly firm.

*For boats with ovens.   127

Whitehead Fisherman's Salad   Serves 6 to 8

This recipe was passed to a Seaport staff member by a fisherman from his native Northern Ireland. It has been used by generations of cooks at sea.

1 good-size fish. (What you catch is what
   you get!) Bass, blackfish or bluefish
   is best
vinegar
salt water
peppercorns, a handful
sliced tomatoes
lettuce leaves
mayonnaise

Requires some advance preparation.

1. The fish should be cleaned, but leave the skin and bones intact. Place in a pot with equal amounts of vinegar and salt water to cover. Add the peppercorns.
2. Put the lid on the pot and bring to a boil. Simmer for 10 minutes. Turn off the heat and let sit for 24 hours. Refrigerate as soon as it is well cooled off.
3. The next day skin and bone the fish. It will flake nicely and you will not believe how none of the "freshly caught" flavor is lost in cooking.
4. Serve the fish on a bed of lettuce, garnish with sliced tomatoes and serve with a side dish of mayonnaise if you wish.

Golden Fish Bake in Cream*   Serves 6

A hands down favorite with the cruising crowd.

2 pounds haddock or cod
4 tablespoons flour
½ teaspoon salt
¼ teaspoon black pepper
½ teaspoon paprika
1 cup milk
2 cups coarse bread crumbs
4 tablespoons butter
1 tablespoon parsley, chopped
1 cup sour cream

*For boats with ovens.

1. Cut fish into serving-size pieces, coat with mixture of flour, salt, pepper and paprika.
2. Arrange in a single layer in a 9x13x2-inch baking dish. Pour milk over the fish. Bake, uncovered in a 350° oven for ½ hour.
3. Toast bread crumbs lightly in butter in a medium-size frying pan. Stir parsley (and a pinch of any other seasonings you might have on board) into sour cream.
4. Remove fish from oven, spoon cream mixture over and top with butter and crumb mixture. Bake 10 minutes longer until sour cream is set and crumbs browned.

Summer Seafood Open-Face

A quick put-together lunch to enjoy at anchor after a long morning sail.

6 large slices French bread, toasted and
  buttered
lettuce leaves
2 large tomatoes, thickly sliced
1½ cups seafood salad, (your choice
  — tuna, shrimp or crab) made as you like
  with celery, mayonnaise, etc.
3 hard-boiled eggs, peeled and halved
French or Thousand Island dressing
½ cup pimento stuffed olives, sliced

1. On each plate place a piece of French
   bread and top with a lettuce leaf and
   some sliced tomato. Spoon some salad
   on each sandwich.
2. Make an indentation in the center of each
   serving and place ½ hard-boiled egg in
   the middle. Top with your choice of
   dressing and sprinkle with chopped olives.

Smothered Fish*

Serves 4

Makes a buttery baked onion sauce.

2 pounds fish fillets, a large slab of scrod
  or haddock is best
3 medium onions, thinly sliced
3 tablespoons flour
1 teaspoon Worcestershire sauce
4 tablespoons butter
salt, pepper, paprika
1 cup milk

*For boats with ovens.

1. Butter a 10x12-inch baking dish. Arrange
   the sliced onions over the bottom and
   top with the fish.
2. Sprinkle the flour over the fish, add the
   Worcestershire sauce, salt, pepper and a
   generous amount of paprika. Dot with
   little chips of butter.
3. Pour the milk over and around the fish.
   Cover with aluminum foil and bake at
   350° for 30 minutes.

Delmonico Haddock*

Serves 6

Simple boiled new potatoes are great with this sauce.

2 pounds haddock fillets, or any other firm
  white fish
1 large onion, minced
2 tablespoons butter
2 tablespoons flour
1 teaspoon dry mustard
1 cup milk
¾ cup sharp cheddar cheese, grated
salt and pepper
paprika

*For boats with ovens.

1. In a medium saucepan, sauté onion in
   butter until golden.
2. Quickly stir in the flour, mustard and
   milk. Cook over medium heat, stirring
   constantly until thickened. Stir in the
   cheese and combine until melted.
3. Place the haddock in a buttered 9x12-inch
   baking dish. Pour the sauce over fish.
   Sprinkle generously with paprika and
   bake at 350° for 30 minutes.

One Pot Jambalaya

Serves 4

You can adjust the amounts of most of these ingredients up or down to change the number of servings.

1 pound large shrimp, cooked
1 pound mussels, cleaned and debearded
½ pound sausage or ham, sliced
2 tablespoons oil
1 cup onion, chopped
½ cup green pepper, cubed
2 garlic cloves, minced
1 16-ounce can plum tomatoes
1 8-ounce can tomato sauce
1 cup water
⅔ cup rice
1 bay leaf
few dashes Tabasco sauce
parsley, chopped

1. In the bottom of a large pot, brown the sausage or ham. Add the oil and sauté the onion, pepper and garlic for a few minutes.
2. Stir in the tomatoes, tomato sauce, water, rice and seasonings. Bring to a boil, cover and cook over low heat for 10 minutes. Uncover and add the mussels, stirring lightly. Cover and cook for 5 more minutes.
3. Stir in the shrimp and cook for 5 minutes until mussels have opened and shrimp are hot. Ladle onto large plates. Add a green salad and serve with pita pockets cut into squares and buttered.

Scudding Along the Shore

Quantities are per person

Heralded as a four generation standby.

2 small onions per person
2 potatoes per person
1 1-inch cube salt fat back pork per person
1 to 2 tablespoons shortening
fish
pepper

Requires some advance preparation.

1. Peel and slice onions into thin rings.
2. Peel and slice potatoes into chips.
3. Slice salt pork into thin strips and fry in skillet for 5 minutes.
4. Add potatoes, onions, and a spoon or two of shortening if needed. Stir well and cook over low heat for an hour or so.
5. At this point, shove off in your boat, scud along the shore until you catch a nice fish. Return to the stove, cook fish as desired and serve with the potatoes and onions. If for some reason you did not catch a fish, the skillet meal will satisfy you.
6. Add pepper and serve.

Six Can Seafood Gumbo

Serves 6

Canned okra on the shelf is a cook's blessing. You can stretch any vegetable dish or salad with its addition.

1 medium onion, chopped
1 medium green pepper, chopped
2 garlic cloves, minced
4 tablespoons olive oil
1 16-ounce can whole tomatoes
1 12-ounce can cut okra
1 12-ounce can vegetable juice
1 teaspoon salt
1 teaspoon sugar
¼ teaspoon bottled hot pepper sauce
½ teaspoon oregano
1 tablespoon cornstarch
½ cup cold water
2 5-ounce cans whole shrimp
1 7-ounce can chopped clams
hot buttered rice

1. In a large saucepot sauté the onion, pepper and garlic in olive oil until soft. Add the tomatoes, okra, vegetable juice and seasonings. Cover and simmer for 10 minutes.

2. Blend the cornstarch with the water until smooth. Stir into the soup mixture and cook until thickened. Add the shrimp and clams and cook just to heat.

3. Spoon hot rice into bowls and ladle creole on top. Any combination of fresh seafood is an obvious plus to this recipe — chicken is another alternative.

Stovetop Portuguese Style Fish

Serves 4

Add some fresh clams or mussels if you have some.

1½ pounds cod, haddock or other thick flaky fish
2 14-ounce cans stewed tomatoes
1 green pepper, chopped
1 onion, chopped
1 garlic clove, minced
1 cup water
1 cup rice
2 tablespoons butter
salt and pepper
parsley, chopped

1. Cut fish into large chunks. Heat the stewed tomatoes in a saucepot and add green pepper, onion, garlic and water. Bring to a boil.

2. Add the fish, cover and simmer for 10 minutes. Add the rice, recover and simmer for 10 more minutes until rice is cooked. Swirl in the butter and season with salt and pepper. Spoon into soup bowls and sprinkle with parsley.

Seafood Delight
or What To Do With These Leftovers*

Serves 4

Make another good meal, what else?

1 pound fish fillets, cooked and flaked
2 cups cooked rice
1 cup last night's vegetables — green
    beans, zucchini, carrots, whatever
½ medium onion, chopped
1 garlic clove, minced
¼ teaspoon black pepper
⅓ cup Italian salad dressing
½ cup cheddar cheese, grated
1 cup croutons
¼ teaspoon paprika

*For boats with ovens.

1. Place the flaked fish (a non-oily type preferably), rice and vegetables in a buttered 2-quart casserole. Add the onion, garlic, black pepper and Italian dressing. Toss to combine well.

2. Spread the grated cheese and croutons on top. Sprinkle with paprika and bake for 45 minutes in a 350° oven until cheese bubbles and croutons are crisp.

Gulf Stream Slop

Serves 4 to 6

The redhead's specialty.

2 6½-ounce cans water packed tuna,
    drained
¾ pound crabmeat or 2 4-ounce cans crab,
    cartilage removed
1 tablespoon butter or olive oil
1 small onion, chopped
1 green or red pepper, chopped
1 10-ounce can Newburg or cheese sauce
1 8-ounce can sliced mushrooms, drained
1 8-ounce can petite peas, drained
dash each; garlic powder, dill,
    salt and pepper

1. In a medium saucepan, sauté the onion and pepper in the butter or oil until tender. Stir in the sauce mix and heat until melted and smooth.

2. Fold in the flaked tuna, crabmeat, mushrooms and peas. Add the seasonings and simmer gently for 5 minutes. Serve over your favorite rice mix.

**Leftovers can be reheated
and used as a hot dip with crackers.**

LUXURiOUS LOBSTER

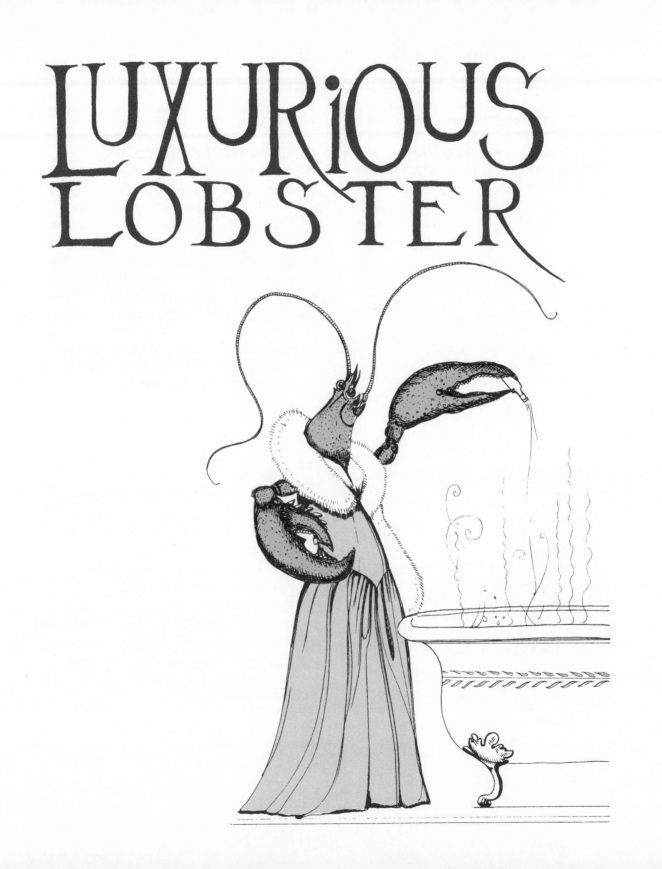

Tomatoes with Lobster and Chèvre

Best when the summer tomatoes are at their peak.

Serves 8 as a luncheon
or 16 as a first course

1½ pounds lobster meat, cooked and cut
  into ½-inch pieces
8 ripe Italian plum tomatoes
½ pound chèvre or other goat cheese
¼ cup olive oil
½ cup cloves, snipped
lettuce leaves

1. Cut tomatoes in half lengthwise and scoop out seeds with a spoon leaving just a shell. Drain upside down on paper towels.

2. In the bowl of a food processor soften the cheese slowly adding the oil and chives. This can also be done in a bowl with a fork.

3. Spoon some of the cheese mixture into each tomato half. Smooth with a knife.

4. Top each tomato with a mound of lobster chunks, pressing lightly into the cheese. Place each tomato on a lettuce leaf and sprinkle with additional chives. On each plate, serve a piece of thin French bread which has been brushed with olive oil and lightly toasted.

Lobster Parfait Royal

Serves 4

1 pound lobster meat, cooked and cut into
  ½-inch pieces
½ cup mayonnaise
1 tablespoon lemon juice, freshly squeezed
3 tablespoons chili sauce
1 tablespoon chives, chopped
½ cup celery, finely minced
1 small head bibb lettuce, 4 outside leaves
  reserved, centers shredded

Requires some advance preparation.

1. Combine mayonnaise, lemon juice, chili sauce, chives and celery in a medium bowl and mix thoroughly.

2. Add the lobster meat, cover and refrigerate until ready to serve.

3. Line 4 parfait or wine glasses with reserved lettuce leaves. Add the shredded lettuce in the bottom of each glass.

4. Divide the lobster mixture evenly between the 4 glasses and serve with crisp buttered toast fingers.

Paradise Island Lobster Salad

Serves 4 for dinner,
8 as a luncheon

4 1½-pound lobsters
1½ cups mayonnaise
3 tablespoons ketchup
¼ cup lime juice, freshly squeezed
2 teaspoons dry sherry
1 teaspoon sugar
½ teaspoon curry powder
½ teaspoon salt
1 cup celery, diced
dash Tabasco sauce
toasted coconut
1 orange, sliced
1 lime, sliced

Requires some advance preparation.

1. Steam the lobsters and cool. Remove meat and cut into small pieces. Reserve the lobster shells and chill the meat.
2. In a bowl, whisk the mayonnaise, ketchup, lime juice and sherry until creamy. Add the sugar, curry, salt and Tabasco. Refrigerate, covered, for at least 1 hour.
3. When ready to serve toss the lobster meat with the celery and add enough dressing to coat well. Spoon the salad into the reserved shells. Arrange on a platter with a bed of garden lettuce, sprinkle with coconut and garnish with orange and lime slices.

Lobster and Melon Salad

Serves 4

1 pound lobster meat, cooked and cut into ½-inch pieces
2 tablespoons dry sherry
¾ cup ripe melon, cubed
½ cup seedless grapes, cut in half
½ cup celery, finely chopped
¾ cup mayonnaise
¼ cup sour cream
fresh mint sprigs

Requires some advance preparation.

1. At least 6 hours before planning to serve the salad, combine the melon (cantaloupe or honeydew is best) with the grapes and toss with the sherry. Refrigerate.
2. In a mixing bowl combine the marinated fruit with the lobster meat and celery. Add the mayonnaise and sour cream, adjusting the combination to your taste.
3. Serve on chilled plates, mounded into a cup of garden lettuce. Garnish with fresh mint leaves.

If you ever spot a lobster on land, you will find it as clumsy as a newborn infant. It needs to support its weight in water in order to become agile.

Fresh Florida Lobster Salad

Serves 4 to 6

2 cups of fresh lobster meat, cooked
1 cup celery, finely chopped
2 tablespoons French dressing
1 tablespoon lemon juice, freshly squeezed
¾ cup mayonnaise
salt and pepper to taste
deviled eggs
stuffed olives
lemon wedges
garden lettuce

1. Combine lobster meat, French dressing, lemon juice, salt and pepper to taste. Toss and let stand for 5 minutes.

2. Drain off any liquid, add the mayonnaise and toss lightly.

3. Arrange a nice combination of lettuce, stuffed eggs and olives on a chilled plate. Spoon lobster salad in the center and garnish with lemon wedges.

Sherried Lobster Sauce

Sauce for 8

Serve this with your favorite fish mousse or poached flounder fillets.

1 pound fresh lobster meat, cooked and cut into ½-inch pieces
2 tablespoons butter
2 large shallots, minced
3 tablespoons flour
1 small tomato, peeled, seeded and finely chopped
¼ cup milk
¾ cup tomato juice
3 tablespoons dry sherry
½ cup heavy cream

1. Melt butter in a saucepan and sauté shallots for 2 to 3 minutes until tender. Do not brown.

2. Stir in the flour and cook for a minute or two over medium-low heat. In the meantime, heat the milk, chopped tomato and tomato juice in a separate pan, until steaming.

3. Slowly whisk the hot tomato-milk mixture into the flour mixture. Stir until smooth. Remove from the heat and add the lobster meat and sherry. May be made ahead to this point.

4. Before serving return sauce to heat and stir in the heavy cream until well blended and creamy pink.

Lobster Avgolemono

Serves 8

A light Greek lemon soup.

3 cups chicken broth, use canned or freshly
  made
½ cup rice
2 whole eggs
2 egg yolks
2 lemons, freshly squeezed
½ pound lobster meat, diced
parsley sprigs

1. Bring the chicken broth to a boil and add the rice. Cook for 10 minutes until tender.
2. In a small bowl, beat the eggs and egg yolks until light and foamy. Add the lemon juice slowly, beating with a fork. Add a little bit of the hot broth to the egg mixture, stirring quickly.
3. Slowly add the egg to the hot broth, blending it in well. Heat until soup has thickened and stir in the lobster meat. Warm for 2 minutes and spoon into china cups. Garnish with parsley.

Easy Lovely Lobster Bisque

Serves 4

When you want to serve a taste of lobster to your guests.

½ pound lobster meat, cooked
½ cup dry sherry
¼ cup butter
4 tablespoons flour
3 cups half-and-half,
  you may substitute milk
2 teaspoon white wine
2 teaspoons Worcestershire sauce
dash of salt and white pepper

Requires some advance preparation.

1. Soak lobster meat in sherry for ½ hour.
2. Melt butter in saucepan. Add flour and cook, stirring constantly for 1 minute, making a roux.
3. Whisk in the half-and-half and continue cooking. until thickened. Season with salt, pepper and Worcestershire sauce.
4. Add lobster meat and sherry. Cover and simmer over low heat for 10 minutes. Do not let boil. To serve, ladle into warmed soup bowls.

Lobster Stew for Two

Serves 2

Light the fire, light the candles.

¾ pound fresh lobster meat, cooked and cut
   into ½-inch pieces
2 tablespoons butter
1 cup clam juice
1 cup heavy cream
Dash of each:
   dry sherry
   Worcestershire sauce
   salt
   paprika
   parsley, chopped

1. In a small saucepan warm the clam juice and cream.
2. Sauté the lobster meat in the butter until the butter turns pink, about 1 minute. Do not overcook the meat.
3. Add the warm cream and clam juice and seasonings to taste. Simmer for several minutes.
4. Ladle into hot bowls and sprinkle with chopped parsley. Serve with hot buttered toast points.

Jane's Company Lobster

Serves 6

2 cups "pretty" macaroni shells, twists
   or bows
3 cups lobster meat, freshly cooked or
   canned and well rinsed
2 tablespoons butter
½ small onion, minced
2 tablespoons flour
⅛ teaspoon pepper
¼ teaspoon dry mustard
½ teaspoon salt
1½ cups milk
2 cups sharp cheddar cheese, grated;
   reserve ½ cup for topping casserole
¼ cup sherry
½ teaspoon mace
2 tablespoons lemon juice, freshly squeezed
½ cup crushed cracker crumbs

1. Cook macaroni as package directs, drain and set aside.
2. In a double boiler, combine butter, onion, flour, mustard, milk, salt and pepper until smooth. Add 1½ cups cheese and stir until blended. Add the sherry.
3. Place cooked macaroni in a buttered 8x12x2-inch baking dish or 2-quart shallow casserole. Arrange lobster meat on top and sprinkle with lemon juice and mace.
4. Pour sauce overall and sprinkle cracker crumbs around edge of casserole. Top with remaining ½ cup cheese. Bake casserole at 400° until hot and crumbs are browned.

Lobster and Linguine in Mustard Sauce   Serves 2

A celebration dinner for two.

¾ pound lobster meat, cooked
6 tablespoons butter
4 tablespoons olive oil
3 medium garlic cloves, minced
1 tablespoon capers, rinsed
2 to 3 tablespoons sweet prepared mustard
dash of cognac
fresh parsley and/or basil, chopped
6 tablespoons toasted pignoli nuts
½ pound linguine

1. Sauté lobster meat in 3 tablespoons of butter until warm. Cover and set aside in a warm oven. Meanwhile, put pot of salted water on to boil for the pasta.

2. Add remaining 3 tablespoons butter to a saucepan and sauté garlic until translucent. Add capers and mustard.

3. Whisk olive oil into butter mixture. Drain any liquid from lobster meat, adding to the pan and return lobster to oven to keep warm.

4. Drop pasta in boiling water and return to the sauce, continuing to blend until smooth. Add additional oil to thin, or mustard to thicken. Sauce should be thin enough to coat pasta.

5. Add cognac to simmering butter mixture and cook for 2 minutes to evaporate alcohol.

6. Drain pasta. Toss with ⅔ butter mixture. Put lobster on top and pour remaining butter over. Garnish with herbs and pignoli nuts.

One of the reasons a lobster molts, or looses its shell, in the summer is because it is related to the insect family and carries its skeleton on the outside.

Joan's Lobster Mold

Makes one 4-cup mold

1 envelope unflavored gelatin
¼ cup water
1 can cream of tomato soup, heated
  — do not dilute
2 tablespoons onion, chopped
4 tablespoons celery, chopped
1 8-ounce package cream cheese
1 cup mayonnaise
1 pound lobster meat, cooked and cut into
  small pieces
½ teaspoon vegetable oil

Requires some advance preparation.

1. Dissolve gelatin in water. Combine with heated tomato soup. Fold in onion, celery, cream cheese, mayonnaise and lobster meat.

2. Pour into a lightly oiled decorative mold; a lobster or fish shape is wonderful if you have one. Refrigerate overnight.

3. To unmold: place the bottom of the mold in a sink of warm water until you can shake it slightly free from the sides. Place your serving platter on top and flip — voila! Serve with crisp wafers.

Lobster and Asparagus on Toast with Pecan Butter Serves 4

1 pound asparagus, ends trimmed
½ cup butter
1 tablespoon lemon juice, freshly squeezed
3 tablespoons pecans, chopped
¾ pound fresh lobster meat
4 slices toast, crusts trimmed
  and cut in half
watercress sprigs
lemon wedges

1. Bring a medium pan of salted water to a boil. Drop in the asparagus spears and simmer for 4 minutes until still firm and crisp. Drain and refresh with cold water, set aside.

2. Melt the butter with the lemon juice and add the pecans. Sauté for 1 minute until pecans start to brown.

3. Put the lobster meat and asparagus spears side by side in a large non-stick pan. Warm with a drizzle of butter for 1 minute.

4. Arrange toast on individual plates, divide asparagus spears, and top each with lobster meat.

5. Pour pecan butter on top and garnish with watercress sprigs and lemon wedges.

Grilled Lobster Sandwich

Serves 2

A special occasion alternative to a hot lobster roll; the cheese holds the sandwich together nicely.

6 to 8 ounces lobster meat, cooked and cut into ½-inch pieces (one 1½- to 1¾-pound lobster or 2 small "culls," one claw apiece is plenty)
4 slices white bread, buttered
4 slices American cheese
1 tablespoon butter
1 tablespoon dry sherry
parsley sprigs

1. Place 2 slices of bread, buttered side down in a small frying pan. Top with cheese and other 2 bread slices, as with grilled cheese.

2. In another small pan, melt the butter with the sherry and cook for 1 minute. Add the lobster meat and keep warm.

3. Grill sandwiches on one side until nicely browned and turn. Gently open sandwhich and divide sherried lobster meat evenly. Recover and cook until bottom is browned. Remove to warm plates, cut in half and garnish with parsley.

Lobster and Gruyère Fondue

Makes 4 cups of fondue to serve 8

A late-evening supper party hit.

1½ cups lobster meat, cooked and cut into ½-inch pieces
1 cup dry white wine
1 pound Gruyère cheese, cubed
2 teaspoons prepared mustard
½ teaspoon anchovy paste
¼ cup cream
2 egg yolks
pinch Cayenne pepper

1. Pour wine into a chafing dish or fondue pot. Add the cheese and heat slowly, stirring with a fork, until cheese is melted.

2. Stir in the mustard and anchovy paste and cook until smooth.

3. Mix the egg yolks and cream together in a small bowl. Slowly whisk into sauce, being careful not to add too much at once.

4. Add the lobster meat and season fondue with Cayenne. Keep hot and serve with cubes of crusty French bread for dipping.

Lobster and Artichoke Surprise   Serves 4

A one plate meal for a picnic.

4 artichokes
12 ounces fresh lobster meat
½ cup celery, chopped
2 tablespoons green pepper, chopped
¼ teaspoon dill
¼ teaspoon paprika
8 tablespoons mayonnaise
1 teaspoon capers
garden or bibb lettuce

Requires some advance preparation.

Artichoke preparation:

1. Cut the stems of the artichokes at the base and cut ½-inch off the top. With scissors, trim the prickly tips off the leaves.

2. Place in a pot just large enough to hold them with ½ inch of salted water. Cover and steam for 35 to 40 minutes until the outer leaves pull off easily. Remove from pan to cool.

3. Pull out the center of small leaves. scrape out the furry choke with a spoon, being careful not to disturb the heart. Chill.

Dish preparation:

1. Mix the lobster meat with the celery, green pepper, dill, paprika and mayonnaise. Fill the center of each artichoke with the lobster salad and sprinkle with capers.

2. Arrange each artichoke on a bed of garden or bibb lettuce and pass a separate bowl of yogurt dill sauce or Maine Seafood Sauce (See index).

It takes almost 7 years for a lobster to reach a size of one pound.

Shore Road Steamed Lobster

A summertime Rhode Island lobster party.

1¼ to 1½ pound live lobster per person
plus extras
newspaper
very large pot
dish towels for each person
nutcrackers
small fish forks and picks
2 wastebaskets, lined with plastic bags
some seaweed
lemons
butter, melted

1. Cover table with thick layer of newspaper.
2. Boil 4 to 5 inches of water in large pot.
3. Dump in a handful of seaweed and cook for 2 minutes.
4. Put lobsters in pot.
5. Steam with lid on for 20 minutes or until lobsters are red and cooked.
6. Serve with lots of lemon and butter. Cook extra lobsters while you are enjoying the first cooked ones.

Lobster Stuffed Potatoes à la Southwest Harbor

Serves 4 for dinner or 8 for brunch

A Sunday night supper with no equal.

4 large Idaho potatoes
½ cup butter
½ cup sour cream or yogurt
2 tablespoons scallions, minced
¾ cup Jarlsberg cheese, shredded
½ pound lobster meat, cooked and cut into ½-inch pieces
salt and pepper
paprika

1. Bake potatoes in a 350° oven for 1 hour until soft when pricked with a fork. Let cool for 5 minutes.
2. Cut in half lengthwise, scoop out potato into a mixing bowl. Reserve potato skins. Add the butter, sour cream and scallions. Mash until well blended.
3. Stir in ½ cup of the cheese (reserve ¼ cup for topping) and the lobster meat. Season with salt and pepper.
4. Fill the potato skins with the mixture and sprinkle tops with reserved cheese. Dust with paprika and bake for 10 minutes at 450° or 20 minutes at 350°.

Over-Overstuffed Lobsters

Serves 8

For the devoted lobster lover.

8 1-pound lobsters
1 pound scallops, cut into small pieces
1 tablespoon vinegar
½ cup butter
1 garlic clove, minced
5 tablespoons flour
2 cups milk
2 tablespoons tomato paste
½ teaspoon salt
⅛ teaspoon Cayenne pepper
3 tablespoons parsley, chopped
1 bouillion cube, chicken
sliced lemons
stuffed olives

1. In a large steamer or pot, bring 2-inches of water to a boil. Add the vinegar. Place the lobsters in the pot with boiling water, cover and cook for 15 minutes.

2. Remove lobsters and let cool. With a good sturdy sharp knife slit each lobster in half down the center of underside. Remove the meat and cut into bite-size pieces. Reserve shells on a baking sheet.

3. Melt butter in a saucepan until bubbling; add the scallops and garlic and sauté for 3 minutes.

4. Blend in the flour and milk, stirring constantly and cook until mixture is thick and hot. Add remaining ingredients, except parsley and blend well. Stir in reserved lobster meat and heat mixture until bubbling.

5. Fill the 8 lobster shells and sprinkle with parsley. This may be done the day before, covered and refrigerated.

6. To serve, bake for 30 to 45 minutes at 425° until browned. Garnish with sliced lemon and stuffed olives.

Coral and Tomalley: the green material found in the body of most lobsters is the tomalley (or liver). The red material is coral (or roe) and is found in female lobsters only.

Slow Baked Stuffed Lobster

Serves 2 lobster lovers

2 1½-pound live lobster
2 small cull lobsters (lobsters that have
    lost a claw)
½ cup butter
2 tablespoons shallots, chopped
¼ cup sherry
1 to 2 garlic cloves, chopped
2 cups bread crumbs, fresh, toasted
salt and pepper

1. In a pot with ½ inch of water, steam the 2 cull lobsters for 5 minutes until pink. Cool and remove the meat, reserving the tomalley and roe (if you have a female lobster). Cut the meat into medium-size pieces.

2. Cook the 1½-pound lobsters as above. Split them down the underside of the body. Remove sac and again reserve tomalley and roe. Brush the shells and body meat with a little cooking oil and lay the four halves on a baking sheet.

3. Melt the butter in a large frying pan. Sauté the shallots and garlic for 5 minutes until tender. Add the tomalley and roe and sauté for 2 minutes more. Mix in the lobster meat from the culls, warm mixture for 3 minutes and remove from the heat. Stir in the sherry.

4. Toss the lobster mixture with the toasted bread crumbs and season with salt and pepper. Spoon the stuffing mixture into the cavity of each lobster.

5. Here is the trick — bake in a VERY slow oven, 200° for 6 hours. Cover with aluminum foil and dot with additional butter if dressing seems to be drying out. This cooking time may vary slightly between a gas and electric stove so monitor the lobsters after a few hours.

When splitting a live lobster to stuff, always remove and discard the stomach sac and intestinal vein. Save the coral, if there is any, and the tomalley.

Herbed Grilled Whole Lobsters   Serves 4

What a way to celebrate the 4th of July!

4 1¼- to 1½-pound live lobsters
½ cup vegetable oil
¼ cup red wine vinegar
½ teaspoon thyme
2 shallots, minced
1 tablespoon fresh parsley, minced
black pepper, freshly ground
butter, melted and clarified
lime or lemon wedges

1. Split and kill each lobster by placing it, shell side down, on cutting board, inserting a large knife into head and cutting along center through tail, leaving shell intact. Spread lobsters to expose meat.

2. Combine oil, vinegar, thyme, shallots and parsley; brush lobster meat generously with mixture. Season with black pepper to taste.

3. Place lobster, SHELL SIDE DOWN, on grill over white-hot coals and cook 7 to 8 minutes. Baste again with remaining oil mixture and turn meat side down; cook an additional 7 to 8 minutes, watching lobsters carefully to avoid burning.

4. When done, remove from grill and crack claws with flat side of heavy knife. Serve with drawn butter and lime or lemon wedges.

John's World's Best Bluefish

1 large bluefish fillet, from a 6 to 8
   pound fish
1 cup mayonnaise
2 lemons
lemon pepper seasoning
white wine

1. Place fish fillet skin side down on a large piece of heavy duty aluminum foil. Spread generously with mayonnaise.
2. Cut one lemon in half and squeeze juice over the fish. Sprinkle with lemon pepper seasoning and slice other lemon. Place lemon slices on top and pour enough wine (about ⅔ cup) over the fish so that it is quite moist.
3. Cover the fillet with a second piece of foil and fold up the sides so that you have an airtight rectangle of foil. It will become balloon-like when cooking.
4. Place fish package on a preheated hot grill and cook for 20 minutes. Do not turn over. You can now hold this for 5 to 10 minutes without opening while you finish other dinner preparations. Cut top of foil off and use a spatula to serve. Skin will stay on bottom piece of foil.

You will find that mayonnaise removes the strong flavor from a large bluefish or fillets that have been frozen for several months. Using this method really isn't necessary on anything under 5 pounds that is freshly caught. Without the mayonnaise use more lemon pepper seasoning and wine.

Dill Bluefish Grille

Serves 4

Nothing better when the fish is fresh off the hook.

1½ pounds fresh bluefish
⅓ cup olive oil
1 lemon, freshly squeezed
1 tablespoon dill

1. Mix olive oil, lemon juice and dill. Put fish into a shallow baking dish just large enough to hold it. Pour liquid over the fish and let stand for 30 minutes.
2. Grill over a hot fire for 15 minutes, turn once and baste as needed. Let the edges get crispy and a little burned for a wonderful flavor.

Spiced Cod Steaks

Serves 4

A taste of the Caribbean

4 8- to 10-ounce cod steaks. Bass or halibut may also be used
2 cloves
10 peppercorns
½ teaspoon cumin
½ teaspoon fennel
1 tablespoon curry powder
1 lemon, freshly squeezed
¼ cup oil
¼ cup white wine
2 garlic cloves, finely chopped
1 small onion, finely chopped

Requires some advance preparation.

1. In a kitchen mortar or wooden bowl, crush the cloves and peppercorns. Place in a mixing bowl and add remaining ingredients.
2. Place the fish steaks in dish large enough to hold them in one layer, pour marinade over fish and refrigerate for 4 to 6 hours, turning fish several times.
3. Grill fish steaks over hot coals for 5 minutes on each side. Don't play with the fish, just let it get crispy on each side before turning. Warm any remaining marinade and pour over fish before serving.

Honey Curried Cod

Serves 4

1½ pounds cod, skin on. Halibut
  or haddock are equally nice
¼ cup honey
¼ cup Dijon mustard
2 tablespoons lemon juice
2 teaspoons curry powder
½ teaspoon salt

1. Blend honey, mustard, lemon juice, curry powder and salt.

2. Brush both sides of fish with mixture and place in a shallow pan.

3. Spread remaining mixture over the fish. It should sit for 30 minutes before grilling.

4. Grill for 10 to 15 minutes until flaky.

This can also be done in an under-the-oven broiler during the cooler months to keep the cook warmer.

Foil Barbequed Cod

Serves 2

Any other thick flaky fish is successful with this recipe.

2 8-ounce pieces cod fillet
1 medium onion, thinly sliced
1 green pepper, finely chopped
1 tomato sliced
1 garlic clove, chopped
salt and pepper
½ cup bread crumbs
¼ teaspoon paprika
¼ teaspoon oregano
¼ cup lemon juice
¼ cup white wine
parsley

1. Place sliced onions on a large piece of heavy duty aluminum foil. Place cod fillets on top of onions. Top with green pepper, tomato slices, garlic and season with salt and pepper.

2. Cover with second fish fillet. Sprinkle with bread crumbs, paprika and oregano.

3. Pour lemon juice around edges and pour wine over top of fish and crumbs. Seal aluminum foil tightly and cook on a hot grill for 10 to 15 minutes depending on thickness of fish. Open foil and serve fish with crusty bread for dipping in the juices.

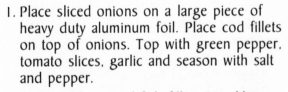

Mahi-Mahi Palm Beach Style

Serves 4

One of those easy, elegant party dishes.

4 fillets of mahi-mahi, 8-ounces each, cut
    ½-inch thick. Swordfish with the skin
    trimmed off may be substituted
½ cup olive oil
½ cup white wine
2 tablespoons sherry
1 tablespoon balsamic vinegar
½ cup chopped fresh mint leaves
1 teaspoon hot red pepper flakes

Requires some advance preparation.

1. Place the fish fillets in a pan large
   enough to hold them in one layer.
2. Combine the oil, wine, sherry, vinegar,
   mint leaves and red pepper in a mixing
   bowl. Pour the marinade over the fish
   and marinate, refrigerated, for 4 hours,
   turning several times.
3. Grill the mahi-mahi over a hot fire for
   6 to 8 minutes per side basting with the
   marinade several times. Serve on a colorful
   platter, surrounded by slices of fresh
   pineapple, avocado and papaya. For a
   hot summer night all that is needed to
   accompany this is a buttery rice pilaf.

Tabor Boy Mussels

Serves a crowd

Reminiscent of a schooner cruise along the Maine coast.

1 large pot of mussels, about 10-quarts
½ bottle white zinfandel or whatever
    white wine is on board
8 tomatoes, halved
10 garlic cloves, sliced
2 onions, sliced
2 tablespoons basil
1 teaspoon (approx.) each:
    thyme, marjoram, dry mustard, and
    rosemary
lots of black pepper, freshly ground

1. Pick over the mussels, removing the
   beards and any stones attached. Rinse
   them with lots of salt water and put in
   the pot.
2. Throw in the tomatoes, garlic (don't
   bother to peel) and onions. Sprinkle
   all the seasonings on top, being very
   generous with each addition. Pour the
   wine over the mussels and add enough
   water to give you lots of soupy broth
   when finished. Toss the mussels a bit
   so as to get some of the vegetables
   to the bottom.
3. Cover and place on a grate over a hot
   wood fire. Bring to a boil and steam for
   10 minutes until all mussels are opened.
   Gather 'round, roll up your sleeves and
   eat the mussels right out of the pot
   with lots of bread to dip in the juice.

Chinese Barbequed Salmon

Serves 4

2 pounds salmon steaks or fillets,
 ¾-inch thick
¼ cup soy sauce
¼ cup teriyaki sauce
¼ cup white wine
1 tablespoon sugar
2 garlic cloves, minced
1 teaspoon ginger, freshly grated
⅛ teaspoon Chinese chili paste
½ teaspoon onion powder
½ teaspoon white pepper
3 tablespoons peanut oil

1. Combine all of the marinade ingredients in a mixing bowl, whisking in the peanut oil last.
2. Place salmon in a shallow dish and pour mixture overall. Marinate for at least 30 minutes, basting occasionally.
3. If grilling steaks, brush hot grill with additional peanut oil to prevent from sticking. Grill 4 to 6 minutes on each side, basting often.

or

If broiling, place salmon on a rack and cook for 5 minutes. Baste, turn and broil 4 to 6 minutes more.

Sesame Salmon

Serves 4

4 8-ounce salmon steaks
2 garlic cloves, crushed
2 tablespoons olive oil
2 tablespoons lemon juice, freshly squeezed
1 teaspoon dill
½ teaspoon salt
⅛ teaspoon pepper
2 tablespoons sesame seeds

1. Rub fish steaks on both side with crushed garlic. Brush with oil and sprinkle with dill, salt, pepper and sesame seeds.
2. Place salmon in an oiled, hinged wire grilling rack. Cook over glowing coals for 4 to 5 minutes until browned. Turn and cook on other side until fish flakes with a fork.

Try some spicy Chinese noodles for a side dish.

Grilled Herb Marinated Salmon   Serves 4

4 8-ounce salmon steaks
½ cup dry vermouth
½ cup salad oil
2 tablespoons lemon juice, freshly squeezed
¾ teaspoon salt
⅛ teaspoon black pepper, freshly ground
½ teaspoon thyme
½ teaspoon marjoram
¼ teaspoon sage
1 tablespoon fresh parsley, minced

Requires some advance preparation.

1. Combine vermouth, oil, lemon juice, salt, pepper, thyme, marjoram, sage and parsley. Place salmon in a shallow pan and pour sauce over. Marinate salmon steaks for 2 to 3 hours in the mixture.

2. Place steaks on a greased, hot charcoal grill and cook, basting frequently with the marinade, for 7 to 8 minutes on each side or until salmon flakes easily with a fork.

Delicious with fresh green peas, parsley buttered potatoes and an avocado salad.

Teriyaki Salmon Steaks   Serves 4

4 8-ounce salmon steaks
¾ cup soy sauce
¼ cup brown sugar
½ cup rice wine (sake)
1 lemon, freshly squeezed
¼ cup vegetable oil

Requires some advance preparation.

1. Mix soy sauce, brown sugar, rice wine, lemon juice and oil until well blended.

2. Place salmon steaks in a shallow dish and pour soy sauce mixture on top. Marinate steaks for at least 1 hour.

3. Grill or broil for 5 minutes until nicely browned. Carefully turn steaks and cook on other side for 5 more minutes, basting several times. Remove to a platter.

4. Heat leftover soy sauce mixture and drizzle over salmon before serving. Steamed Chinese vegetables and pea pods on each end of the platter make an attractive accompaniment.

Rosey Salmon

Serves 6

The rosé keeps the salmon pink.

6 8-ounce salmon steaks,
   1- to 1½-inches thick
1 cup rosé wine
1 tablespoon olive oil
½ teaspoon thyme
1 small red onion, finely minced
⅛ teaspoon black pepper
sea salt

Requires some advance preparation.

1. Combine the wine, olive oil, thyme, onion and black pepper. Pour marinade over the uncooked salmon in a shallow glass or enamel pan.
2. Refrigerate for several hours, turning steaks occasionally.
3. Drain salmon and grill over a hot charcoal fire. Allow 5 minutes per side for a 1-inch steak and increase to 7 minutes per side for a 1½-inch steak. Sprinkle with a little sea salt as steaks cook and baste occasionally with the wine sauce.

Sunset Scallop Kebobs

Serves 4

1½ pounds sea scallops
⅓ cup vegetable oil
⅓ cup white wine or vermouth
2 tablespoons lemon juice
1 teaspoon basil
1 garlic clove, minced
4 slices uncooked bacon, cut into
   2-inch pieces
1 large green pepper, cut in 1½-inch squares
12 cherry tomatoes
12 whole mushrooms

Requires some advance preparation.

1. Combine oil, wine lemon juice, basil and garlic in a medium bowl. Add scallops and cover. Refrigerate for 24 hours.
2. Skewer scallops with alternating bacon, peppers, onions and mushrooms, dividing among 4 large skewers or 8 small ones. If you use bamboo skewers, rather than metal, soak for 15 minutes in warm water to prevent from burning.
3. Place on a hot grill and cook for 10 minutes, turning once and basting often.

Shark Steak with Rice Pilaf

Serves 2

This can be broiled indoors and stays equally as moist as cooking on the grill.

2 ¾- to 1-pound shark steaks, boned and skin removed
2 tablespoons peanut oil
1 tablespoon lemon juice, freshly squeezed
1 tablespoon lime juice, freshly squeezed
½ teaspoon dill
1 cup white rice, cooked
1 small onion, chopped
½ cup mushrooms, sliced
2 tablespoons butter
½ cup peas, freshly cooked or frozen and defrosted

1. With a sharp knife, make small incisions in both sides of each steak.
2. Combine the peanut oil with lemon juice, lime juice and dill. Rub generously over steaks, allowing slits to absorb the mixture.
3. Grill over a hot fire for 7 to 10 minutes per side, depending on the thickness of the fish.
4. Meanwhile, make the quick rice pilaf. Sauté the onions and mushrooms in the butter until soft and golden brown. Stir in the cooked rice and peas and toss. Cover and keep hot until fish is cooked.

Shrimp Pierre

Serves 4

A great picnic finger food.

2 pounds large shrimp, peeled and deveined, leave the tails on
3 garlic cloves, finely chopped
1 medium onion, finely chopped
¼ cup parsley, chopped
1 teaspoon basil
1 teaspoon dry mustard
1 teaspoon salt
½ cup olive oil
1 lemon, freshly squeezed

Requires some advance preparation.

1. Prepare the marinade combining garlic, onion, parsley, basil, mustard, salt, oil and lemon juice.
2. Place shrimp in marinade and toss lightly. Cover bowl tightly and refrigerate for 24 hours.
3. Cook shrimp on a hot grill for 3 to 4 minutes on each side, basting often. You may cook them individually or place them on skewers. You will find that turning them with tongs is the most successful method to use.

Hawaiian Shrimp and Bacon Skewers   Serves 8

Prepare in the morning for grilling that evening.

3 pounds shrimp, shelled
½ pound sliced bacon
1 cup soy sauce
¼ cup dry sherry
¼ cup lemon juice, freshly squeezed
1 8-ounce can water chestnuts
1 cup fresh or canned pineapple chunks

1. Combine soy sauce, sherry and lemon juice in a large bowl.
2. Add the shrimp and let marinate at room temperature for 30 minutes.
3. Cut bacon slices in thirds and wrap a strip around each shrimp. Thread shrimp on skewers, alternating with pineapple and water chestnuts.
4. Grill for 5 minutes on each side, basting occasionally. Bacon should be crisp and shrimps pink.

Susie's Barbequed Shrimp   Serves 4

1 pound large shrimp, deveined
2 lemons, freshly squeezed
1 garlic clove, crushed
¼ teaspoon pepper
½ teaspoon salt
1 teaspoon Accent
1 teaspoon oregano
3 tablespoons soy sauce
1 cup vegetable oil

Requires some advance preparation.

1. Whisk all of the ingredients except shrimp together in a medium bowl. Add the shrimp and marinate for several hours or overnight in the refrigerator.
2. Divide the shrimp on 4 skewers and cook over a medium hot grill. Brush with the marinade and cook 6 to 8 minutes, turning once. They are done when the shrimp turn pink.

If you marinate extra thick fish steaks in lemon juice before broiling, it partially cooks the flesh and cuts down on broiling time without drying it out.

Swordfish Chinoise

Serves 4

4 8-ounce slices swordfish
¼ cup soy sauce
2 tablespoons sesame oil
2 tablespoons sesame seeds
2 tablespoons sherry
1 teaspoon garlic, minced
1 teaspoon fresh ginger, minced
8 scallions, cut into 2-inch julienne strips
1 8-ounce can water chestnuts, sliced

1. In a small bowl make sauce combining soy sauce, sesame oil, sesame seeds, sherry, ginger and garlic.
2. Make 4 12-inch squares of heavy duty aluminum foil. Place a piece of swordfish on the right hand section of each piece.
3. Divide scallions and water chestnuts over the top of the fish. Pour sauce over fish, working one piece at a time. Fold foil from left to right and crimp edges to form a package.
4. Place packages on a hot grill and cook for 10 minutes. Shake each package to be sure the fish is not sticking and cook 5 more minutes. Cut open and serve.

Serve with hot white rice to spoon right in the sauce.

Lemon Sword and Cukes

Serves 6

2 pounds swordfish cut into 1-inch cubes
¾ cup oil
½ cup lemon juice, freshly squeezed
1 bay leaf, crumbled
½ teaspoon oregano
hot red pepper flakes
2 cucumbers cut into 1-inch thick slices
½ cup pimento stuffed olives

1. Combine oil, lemon juice, bay leaf, oregano and a few shakes of hot pepper flakes to taste.
2. Add the swordfish and cucumber pieces to the marinade and coat thoroughly.
3. Thread on skewers, alternating fish with cucumbers and olives. Broil for 10 minutes, turning frequently and basting with marinade.

Complete this dinner with wild rice and a tossed green salad.

Swordfish Kebobs with Citrus Marinade   Serves 6

A real splash of summer.

2½ pounds swordfish
12 pearl onions
2 medium green peppers, cut in
   ¾-inch strips
2 medium red peppers, cut in
   ¾-inch strips
12 mushrooms
6 cherry tomatoes

Citrus Marinade:

6 tablespoons rice vinegar
3 tablespoons water
8 tablespoons orange juice, freshly squeezed
8 tablespoons lemon juice, freshly squeezed
6 tablespoons lime juice, freshly squeezed
1 tablespoon Dijon mustard
2 tablespoons honey
6 tablespoons vegetable oil
2 tablespoons fresh chive or dill, snipped

Requires some advance preparation.

1. Whisk together, in order, the marinade ingredients. This may be done well ahead and kept refrigerated for up to 2 weeks.

2. Peel pearl onions and blanch in boiling water for 10 minutes.

3. Cut swordfish into 1-inch cubes and place in a glass or plastic bowl. Pour marinade over fish, cover and refrigerate for 4 hours. Add vegetables to bowl, lightly toss and marinate for 1 hour.

4. Arrange swordfish, peppers, onions and mushrooms on skewers. Grill for 7 minutes over a hot fire, add a cherry tomato to each skewer and turn.

5. Baste kebobs well and grill for 5 minutes until nicely browned.

6. Serve on hot buttered white rice and sprinkle with additional chopped chive or dill.

Mediterranean Grilled Tuna

Serves 4

4 8-ounce fresh tuna fillets
2 tablespoons olive oil
1 small onion, finely chopped
1 green pepper, finely chopped
2 garlic cloves, minced
1 bay leaf
½ teaspoon rosemary, crushed
¼ cup parsley, freshly chopped
⅛ teaspoon black pepper
1 28-ounce can crushed tomatoes
⅓ cup pitted black olives, sliced

1. Heat the olive oil in a medium saucepan and add onion, green pepper and garlic. Sauté for 2 to 3 minutes until transparent.

2. Add the bay leaf, rosemary, parsley, black pepper and tomatoes. Simmer the sauce over medium heat for 20 minutes and stir in the black olives.

3. Meanwhile, brush the tuna fillets with a little olive oil and grill over a hot fire for 6 to 8 minutes per side depending on the thickness of the fish. This fish will be nice and flaky when ready.

4. To serve, spoon some of the hot tomato sauce onto a plate and top it off with a fish fillet. This sauce can also be poured over any other thick white fish such as bass or scrod, and baked in the oven if you prefer.

Fish on the Rocks

Ingredients are per person

Have all the ingredients on hand and let your guests make their own package. Just don't mix them up on the coals!

1 small fish or 8-ounce fillet of bass, halibut or bluefish
½ small onion, thinly sliced
2 tomato, sliced
few strips of pepper (mix of red, green or yellow)
1 pat of butter
1 tablespoon fresh herbs; thyme, tarragon and parsley
salt and pepper

1. Pass out large squares of heavy duty aluminum foil to your guests. Invite everyone to build their own dinner, starting with fish and vegetable, finishing off with the butter, salt and pepper. Top with minced herbs and carefully wrap each fish in the foil. Seal well at edges.

2. Place on hot coals or charcoal grill. Cook for 10 to 15 minutes depending on thickness of fish.

If you have a nice big fire, accompany the fish with roast corn on the cob.

159

Flaming Grilled Fish with Herbs Serves 4

If no one caught a fish for you, have the fish dealer prepare it for you.

1 whole fish, 5 to 6 pounds, salmon or
   striped bass, cleaned
½ cup butter
¼ cup olive oil
1 tablespoon lemon juice, freshly squeezed
handfuls of herbs: parsley, thyme,
   dill, fennel
a little cognac

1. Split the fish open for broiling. In a small saucepan, melt the butter, add the olive oil and lemon juice.
2. Brush the fish on both sides with butter mixture and grill for 10 minutes on each side, basting occasionally. Length of grilling time will depend on thickness of the fish. Test for doneness with a fork, fish should flake easily.
3. Put a good layer of fresh herbs on a serving platter — be sure it is flameproof. Place the broiled fish on top.
4. In a small saucepan warm the cognac slightly. Turn down the lights and pour over the fish. Ignite and bring the flaming platter to the table.

Lois's Blackened Fish Serves 4

This may also be done stovetop but be ready to evacuate!

4 fresh fillets, a firm fish such as sword,
   tuna or mahi-mahi
½ teaspoon each; crushed red pepper, garlic
   salt, onion powder and dried basil
¼ teaspoon each; ground white pepper,
   dried crushed thyme, black pepper,
   and sage
¼ cup butter, melted

1. Combine all of the seasonings in a bowl. Brush both sides of fish fillets with melted butter and coat each side generously with seasoning mixture.
2. Remove rack from charcoal grill. Place a 12-inch IRON skillet directly on hot coals. Heat pan until smoking.
3. Add the fish fillets to the pan. Drizzle 2 tablespoons of melted butter over fish. Grill 2½ to 3 minutes until blackened, turning once.

PASTA

Linguine with White Clam Sauce I

1 dozen cherrystone clams per person.
These will keep well for about 4 days
stored in a plastic bag on ice. Leave the
bag opened so the clams can breathe.

5 large garlic cloves per 3 servings

3 tablespoons olive oil

1 handful linguine per person, uncooked,
although the correct amount per serving
bedevils any cook

crushed Italian dried hot red pepper

sprigs of Italian parsley

1. Put clams in a metal basket or steamer
   and place in a large pot. Add water to
   underside of basket, not deeper than
   ¼-inch. The trick is not to dilute clam
   broth that is produced during steaming.
   Cover pot and steam until clams just
   begin to open.

2. Open clams over the pot, allowing all of
   the broth to mix in with the juices in the
   pan. Place the clam meat on a flat
   surface and mince with a sharp knife
   and fork.

3. Heat the olive oil in a frying pan and
   sauté the garlic until soft, being careful
   to stir well so it does not brown.

4. Strain the clam broth through cheesecloth to remove any shell or grit and add
   to the pan with the garlic and olive oil.
   Simmer for 1 minute and add the minced
   clams. Do not let this get too hot or the
   clams will toughen.

5. Place cooked pasta on individual plates
   and spoon the clams and broth on top.
   Garnish with parsley and hot red pepper
   to taste.

**One generous cup of cooked crabmeat equals 6 ounces. One pound
of crabmeat yields approximately 3 cups, flaked.**

Linguine with White Clam Sauce II   Serves 2

Keep a few cans of chopped clams on the shelf, and dinner can be ready in 10 minutes, from start to finish.

2 6½-ounce cans chopped clams
½ cup olive oil
4 garlic cloves, minced
1 shallot, minced
½ teaspoon dried oregano
¼ teaspoon dried basil
¼ cup fresh parsley, chopped
½ teaspoon salt
⅛ teaspoon pepper
½ lemon, freshly squeezed
1 tablespoon butter
8 ounces linguine, cooked and drained

1. Drain the clams into a small bowl and reserve the juice.

2. Sauté the garlic and shallots in the olive oil for 3 minutes until soft. Add the clam juice, oregano, basil, parsley, salt and pepper. Cook until the mixture has reduced and thickened.

3. Add the clams and stir until the clams are just heated through. Stir in the lemon juice and butter and combine well. Serve over hot cooked linguine.

Gangway Linguine with Crab   Serves 4

This recipe has sailed up and down the New England coast with great success.

1 pound linguine
¾ pound crabmeat
4 ounces butter
1 cup green pepper, chopped
1 cup Spanish onion, chopped
½ cup mushrooms, sliced
2 garlic cloves, minced
½ teaspoon oregano
½ teaspoon salt
⅛ teaspoon black pepper, freshly ground
1 16-ounce can stewed tomatoes
½ cup water
Parmesan cheese, grated

1. Bring a large pot of water to a boil. Cook linguine according to package directions.

2. At the same time melt the butter in a skillet and sauté peppers, onions and mushrooms for 3 minutes until tender.

3. Add the crabmeat, salt, garlic, oregano and pepper and simmer for 5 minutes. Stir in the stewed tomatoes and water. Cover and simmer until pasta is done.

4. Drain the pasta and toss with the sauce in a large bowl. Serve with lots of grated Parmesan cheese.

Mussels Marinara with Pasta   Serves 6

**An easy dinner to prepare when you have had
a successful day of musseling on the shore.**

4 pounds mussels, always best when used
  the same day as picked
1 large onion, chopped
1 large garlic clove, chopped
1 tablespoon olive oil
½ teaspoon dried basil
1 8-ounce can tomato sauce
1 pound of your favorite pasta, cooked
  and drained
salt and pepper to taste

1. Scrub and debeard the mussels and
   steam in a large pot with ½ inch of water
   for 8 to 10 minutes. Shake the pot half
   way through cooking.
2. Remove mussels from their shells and
   place in a bowl with one cup of their
   strained broth.
3. In a large skillet sauté the onion in the
   olive oil until tender. Add the minced
   garlic and cook for 2 more minutes.
   Add the basil, tomato sauce and ¼ cup
   reserved mussel broth. Simmer for
   30 minutes.
4. Add the cooked pasta to the sauce and
   gently toss with the mussels and remaining
   broth. Season to taste and serve
   immediately.

Salmon and Pasta in Asiago Cream   Serves 4 to 6

**If you are preparing a whole salmon for guests,
plan on enough left over to serve this the next day.**

1 pound spinach fusilli or other small pasta
2 to 3 cups cooked salmon, flaked
2 cups cream
2 tablespoons butter
4 tablespoons Asiago cheese, grated
2 tablespoons capers, drained
8 ounces frozen petite peas, unthawed
1 handful fresh dill, chopped
½ handful fresh parsley, chopped

1. In a pot of boiling water, cook fusilli for
   6 to 8 minutes, being careful not to
   overcook. Drain and butter.
2. in a medium saucepan, reduce cream and
   butter by one-third. Stir in Asiago cheese,
   capers, peas, dill and parsley. Simmer
   until cheese melts and gently add
   flaked salmon.
3. To serve, pour hot sauce over salmon
   and buttered fusilli.

Fettucine Alfredo with Smoked Salmon and Capers

Serves 4 as dinner, 8 as first course

A blackboard specialty at one of our favorite local restaurants.

¾ pound fettucine or egg noodles
½ cup butter
1½ cups Parmesan cheese, grated
black pepper, freshly ground
1½ cups heavy cream
½ cup smoked salmon (about 8 slices), chopped
2 tablespoons capers, rinsed
parsley, chopped
Parmesan cheese, for serving

1. Cook the fettucine in a pot of boiling salted water for 8 to 10 minutes. If using fresh pasta, adjust cooking time to 3 to 4 minutes once water has returned to a boil. Drain and set aside.

2. Meanwhile, melt butter in a large saucepan. Add Parmesan cheese, pepper and cream. Cook over low heat, stirring constantly until slightly thickened.

3. Gently stir in the smoked salmon and capers. Toss with the drained pasta until well coated. Place in a hot serving dish, sprinkle with parsley and Parmesan cheese, serve immediately.

Seashells

Serves 4

. . . by the seashore.

1 pound scallops
¼ cup olive oil
2 garlic cloves, finely chopped
1 small onion, finely chopped
¼ cup dry white wine
1 teaspoon Old Bay Seasoning
2 tablespoons parsley, chopped
8 ounces pasta shells, cooked, drained and drizzled with olive oil
Parmesan cheese, grated

1. In a medium frying pan heat olive oil. Add the garlic and onion and sauté for 2 minutes until soft.

2. Add the scallops and cook over medium heat for 4 to 5 minutes until mixture is golden. Pour in the wine and add the Old Bay Seasoning and parsley.

3. Stir the cooked shells into the scallop mixture and heat until nicely blended. Spoon onto hot plates and pass the Parmesan.

Scallops and Avocado Provençal with Linguine   Serves 4

Invite some guests who might enjoy sharing in dinner preparations. You will have a great time chopping, mincing, tasting and conversing.

3 tablespoons olive oil
3 tablespoons butter
1 pound sea scallops, quartered
8 shallots, minced
8 scallions, minced
2 large garlic cloves, minced
2 tablespoons fresh basil, minced,
   or 2 teaspoons dried basil
2 tablespoons fresh tarragon, minced,
   or 2 teaspoons dried tarragon
¾ teaspoon fresh thyme, minced,
   or ¼ teaspoon dried thyme
½ cup dry white wine
4 cups crushed tomatoes, well-drained or
   10 large tomatoes, peeled, seeded
   and chopped
½ cup whipping cream
2 teaspoons sugar or to taste
salt and black pepper, freshly ground
1 pound linguine, cooked and drained
1 large avocado, peeled and chopped

1. Heat olive oil and butter in a large non-aluminum frying pan. Add the scallops and sauté over medium heat for 2 minutes until just firm. Transfer scallops to a bowl and set aside.

2. To the remaining olive oil-butter mixture add shallots and scallions. Cook until soft. Stir in the garlic and herbs. Cook 1 minute.

3. Add the wine and tomatoes. Increase heat to high and boil briefly until thickened. Stir in cream and sugar, let simmer for 20 seconds.

4. Combine the hot sauce with the scallops and season with salt and pepper to taste. Gently toss with hot pasta until coated and finally, add the chopped avocado and mix.

Pasta and Scallop Chowder   Serves 4

Start with the basic chowder preparation and add any other seafood you care to at the end.

2 cups water
1 12-ounce can V-8 juice
½ cup medium shell macaroni
2 tablespoons Parmesan cheese, grated
1 tablespoon onion, minced
1 tablespoon instant chicken bouillon
½ teaspoon oregano
½ teaspoon basil
1 garlic clove, minced
1 cup frozen mixed vegetables
12 ounces bay scallops

1. In a large saucepan mix the first 9 ingredients and bring to a boil. Reduce heat, cover and simmer for 10 minutes.

2. Add vegetables and return to a boil. Reduce heat, cover and simmer for 15 minutes until pasta and vegetables are tender.

3. Add scallops, return to a slow simmer. Reduce heat, cover and simmer gently for 5 minutes.

4. To serve, ladle into big bowls and pass additional Parmesan and garlic bread.

Fettucine with Scallop and Mushroom Cream   Serves 6 to 8

1 pound fettucine
1 pound scallops
½ pound mushrooms, sliced
6 tablespoons olive oil
¼ cup dry sherry or white wine
8 tablespoons water
1 16-ounce can evaporated milk
8 garlic cloves, minced
½ teaspoon white pepper
6 tablespoons Parmesan or Romano cheese, freshly grated
2 tablespoons cornstarch

Variation:

An attractive variation to this dish — use half spinach fettucine and half regular fettucine, adding one package of drained frozen chopped spinach to the sauce.

1. In a skillet, sauté the mushrooms in 2 tablespoons olive oil for a few minutes until they begin to become tender. Remove mushrooms with a slotted spoon and reserve.

2. Add the scallops and sherry or white wine to the pan and cook until done, about 5 minutes. Return the mushrooms to the pan, remove from heat and cover to keep warm.

3. In a saucepan, heat remaining 4 tablespoons olive oil and the 6 tablespoons of water. Add the garlic and white pepper.

4. Slowly pour in the evaporated milk and increase heat to bring mixture almost to a boil. Drain and remove the mushrooms and scallops from the skillet and add this liquid to the hot sauce. Stir in the cheese and heat until melted.

5. Mix the cornstarch with 2 tablespoons cold water. Add the mixture to the sauce and stir constantly until sauce thickens.

6. Cook pasta per package instructions and drain. Arrange in a large serving bowl and top with scallops and mushrooms. Pour the hot sauce overall and serve immediately.

To get the most flavor from dried herbs, crush them with a mortar and let them steep in a tablespoon of dry white wine for 10 minutes.

Capellini with Scallops and Lemon Mustard Serves 2

Serve with a nice pepper and tomato salad.

1 cup dry white wine
½ teaspoon lemon peel, grated
½ pound bay scallops
2 teaspoons Dijon mustard
¼ cup chilled butter
5 ounces capellini
1 tablespoon butter
1 tablespoon chives, snipped

1. Bring wine and lemon peel to a slow simmer in a medium saucepan.

2. Add the scallops and cook for 1 minute until opaque. Remove with a slotted spoon.

3. Increase heat and reduce wine mixture to ¼ cup.

4. Reduce heat to low and whisk in the mustard and butter a little at a time. Add the scallops and heat thoroughly.

5. While you are preparing the sauce, cook pasta in boiling water until al dente, about 5 minutes. Drain and toss with 1 tablespoon butter. Spoon scallops and sauce over hot pasta and sprinkle with chives.

Marseillaise Shrimp and Scallop Pasta Serves 4

For a variation try adding mushrooms or zucchini.

1 pound medium shrimp, peeled and deveined
1 pound scallops
3 tablespoons olive oil
3 medium onions, sliced
3 garlic cloves, crushed
1 28-ounce can crushed tomatoes
1 teaspoon oregano
1 teaspoon basil
4 tablespoons parsley, chopped
⅛ teaspoon pepper
½ cup dry red or white wine
1 pound pasta (twists look very nice with this dish)

1. In a Dutch oven, heat olive oil and add onions and garlic. Sauté until soft.

2. Add crushed tomatoes, oregano, basil, parsley, pepper and wine. Simmer for 15 minutes to thicken.

3. Add the shrimp and scallops, stir in well. Cook over medium heat for 8 minutes until firm.

4. Pour sauce over cooked hot pasta and pass with grated Parmesan cheese and garlic bread.

Smoked Scallops and Capellini   Serves 4 to 6

Hard to believe, a no-guilt, low fat pasta dish.

1 pound scallops
1 tablespoon liquid smoke
1 cup white wine
½ teaspoon thyme
1 teaspoon garlic, crushed
1 cup clam juice
1 tablespoon butter
1½ tablespoons cornstarch
2 cups low fat (2%) milk
pepper
¾ pound capellini

1. Cook capellini according to directions. Drain and keep warm.

2. In a heavy medium-size saucepan combine wine, thyme, garlic and clam juice. Cook over medium-high heat for 10 minutes until reduced by half. Stir in the butter.

3. Rinse scallops in cold water and drain well. Add liquid smoke to a dry skillet. Toss with scallops and cook over medium heat, pouring off the juice. The scallops will start to dry, tighten and turn a light honey color. Gauge about 10 to 15 minutes depending on whether you use small bay scallops or the larger sea scallops.

4. Stir cornstarch into the milk and add to the reduced wine-clam mixture. Cook over low heat, stirring occasionally until mixture thickens. Add scallops to the saucepan and heat for 5 minutes until bubbly. Season to taste with black pepper. Spoon creamy scallop sauce over hot capellini and serve.

BUTTERED SHRIMPS AND SAUCE

"Stew a quart of shrimp in half a pint of white-wine, a nutmeg grated, and a good piece of butter; when the butter is melted, and they are not through, beat the yolks of four eggs with a little white-wine, and pour it in, and shake it well, till it is of the thickness you like; then dish it on sippets, and garnish with sliced lemon."

MRS. E. SMITH'S COMPLEAT HOUSEWIFE, 1739

Lover's Linguine with Galliano   Serves 2

**A sweet and spicy special occasion dinner for two
that won't keep you in the kitchen all day.**

½ pound linguine
¾ pound large shrimp, peeled and deveined
2 garlic cloves, minced
2 scallions, chopped
3 tablespoons parsley, freshly chopped
2 tablespoons pimento, chopped
4 tablespoons olive oil
2 tablespoons butter
¼ cup Galliano liqueur

1. Cook the linguine in boiling salted water for 7 minutes until firm. Drain and cover to keep warm.

2. In a large skillet, sauté the shrimp and garlic in olive oil for 3 minutes. Add the scallions and parsley and cook for another minute until shrimp are pink.

3. Stir in pimento, butter and Galliano. Add the hot pasta and toss until well coated.

Gatehouse Company Fettucine with Shrimp   Serves 8

**Equally delicious served hot or cold, a great dish to do ahead
for entertaining on a hot summer night.**

1½ pounds large shrimp, cooked and peeled
1 pound fettucine
4 teaspoons sesame oil
1 cup chicken broth
1 cup sundried tomatoes, cut into strips. Use the ones packed in olive oil so you can use the oil to moisten the salad. If not available, soak dried tomatoes in oil overnight to soften
3 garlic cloves, finely minced
8 ounces mushrooms, sliced
1 cup parsley, chopped
salt and black pepper, freshly ground

1. Cook the fettucine according to package directions, being careful not to overcook as you want it to be al dente. Drain and place in a large bowl.

2. Pour the sesame oil and chicken broth overall and toss well to coat fettucine.

3. Add the shrimp, sun dried tomatoes, garlic, mushrooms and parsley. Season with salt and lots of black pepper to taste and moisten with olive oil drained from the tomatoes or add more, if desired.

Father Don's "Fetuchina"

Serves 12 or more

From a Louisiana priest.

3 onions, chopped
3 celery stalks, chopped
3 medium green peppers, chopped
3 8-ounce sticks butter
¼ cup flour
3 tablespoons parsley, chopped
3 garlic cloves, minced
¾ pint half-and-half cream
3 pounds large shrimp or crayfish, cleaned and tails removed
1 pound Velveeta processed cheese, cubed. If you substitute any other harder cheese such as cheddar, you will need to add more half-and-half
2 tablespoons jalapeño relish
1 16-ounce box flat noodles — "fetuchina"
salt and pepper to taste

1. In a large saucepan, sauté the onions, celery and peppers in butter until soft.
2. Stir in the flour and cook over low heat for 10 minutes, making a roux. Be careful to stir mixture around in pan so as not to scorch. Add the parsley.
3. Add the half-and-half, cheese, garlic, relish, salt and pepper to taste and combine thoroughly. If you are using crayfish, add at this point and cook gently until sauce is smooth and crayfish pink. If you are using shrimp, cook sauce alone for 15 minutes add shrimp and cook for 5 more minutes.
4. Cook the noodles in a pot of boiling salted water and drain thoroughly Combine the shrimp/crayfish sauce with noodles and pour into a large buttered casserole. Bake at 350° for 15 minutes until bubbling. This makes a big recipe and will fill several smaller casseroles if needed. Divine!

If you're wondering why the garlic is not included in the sautéeing of the onions, celery, and pepper; it is because in creole and cajun cooking the sautéeing of those three things are referred to as "The Holy Trilogy," so the garlic is always added later.

Baked Shrimp and Green Noodles   Serves 8

This delicious casserole can be prepared ahead of time and reheated.

1   8-ounce package spinach noodles or
fettucine
2   pounds large shrimp, peeled and deveined
4   tablespoons butter
1   cup sour cream
1   cup mayonnaise
1   10-ounce can cream of mushroom soup
4   tablespoons dry sherry
1   tablespoon chives, chopped
1   teaspoon Dijon mustard
1   cup sharp cheddar cheese, grated

1. Cook the noodles in boiling water according to package directions, but cut the cooking time in half as they will cook more later. Drain well and place in a large buttered casserole dish.

2. Melt the butter in a skillet and sauté the shrimp for about 5 minutes until pink and just tender. Pour the shrimp and cooking butter over the noodles.

3. In a medium bowl combine the sour cream, mayonnaise, mushroom soup, sherry, chives and mustard until well blended. Pour sauce over shrimp.

4. Sprinkle cheddar cheese overall (a strong colored cheese makes a nice contrast). Bake at 350° for 30 minutes until cheese is melted and bubbly.

Savannah Shrimp Pilaf

Serves 4

A favorite low country Georgia recipe. Use cast nets and go "shrimping"!

1   pound medium shrimp, peeled,
or a combination of half shrimp
and half oysters
4   slices bacon, chopped
½ cup celery, chopped
1   medium onion, diced
1½ cups water
1   cup rice
1½ cups tomatoes, chopped
⅓ cup green pepper, chopped

1. In a medium-heavy saucepan, sauté bacon, onion and celery for 3 minutes until lightly browned.

2. Add the raw shrimp and cook, uncovered for 5 more minutes.

3. Add the water and rice. Cover and cook for 10 minutes. Top with the tomatoes and peppers, recover, stir and finish cooking for 5 minutes. Let rest for 10 minutes before serving.

Shrimp and Shells in Chili Sauce   Serves 4

A surprise Mexican pasta dish that your friends will love.

½ cup olive oil
2 medium onions, chopped
1 garlic clove, minced
2 green peppers, cut into julienne strips
3 8-ounce cans tomato sauce
1 4-ounce can jalapeño peppers, drained
1 teaspoon chili powder
1 teaspoon sugar
1 pound cooked large shrimp, shelled
  and cleaned
½ pound shells, cooked and drained
¼ cup sour cream
avocado or black olives, chopped to garnish

1. Heat the olive oil in a saucepan and add the onions, garlic and green peppers. Sauté for 5 minutes until limp but still crisp.

2. Add the tomato sauce, jalapeño, chili powder and sugar. Simmer over low heat for 15 minutes.*

3. Stir in the shrimp and shells. Mix lightly and heat thoroughly over medium heat.

4. To serve, spoon onto individual plates, top with sour cream and pass the avocado and olives.

*This can be made ahead to this point and reheated.

Savory Scampi Primavera   Serves 8

This need not always be served hot, try it chilled as a picnic entrée.

1 1-pound package linguine
¾ cup olive oil
3 large garlic cloves, minced
  (2 tablespoons)
½ teaspoon lemon peel, finely chopped
2 carrots, cut in 2-inch strips
1 medium zucchini, cut in 2-inch strips
1 medium red pepper, cut in 2-inch strips
1½ pounds medium shrimp,
  cleaned and peeled
2 tablespoons lemon juice
¾ teaspoon salt
⅛ teaspoon black pepper, freshly ground
2 tablespoons fresh basil, torn or substitute
  2 teaspoons dried basil
2 tablespoons parsley, torn

1. Cook pasta as directed on package, drain.

2. Meanwhile, heat oil in a large skillet, add garlic and lemon peel, stirring for 30 seconds.

3. Add vegetables and shrimp, cook and stir over medium heat until shrimp turns pink, about 3 or 4 minutes.

4. Sprinkle with lemon juice, salt and pepper. Stir in basil and parsley. Spoon sauce over pasta and toss well.

Shrimp and Pasta in a Pot   Serves 4

**If fresh pasta is available, try something different
— perhaps the tomato, garlic or spinach variety.**

1 pound medium shrimp, uncooked
  and cleaned
1 8-ounce box of petite peas
1 pound of your favorite pasta
½ cup butter
1 cup heavy cream
½ cup imported Swiss cheese, shredded
½ cup Romano cheese, grated
½ cup Parmesan cheese, grated
salt and pepper to taste

1. Bring a large pot of water to a full boil.
   Add the pasta and peas. Stir to make
   sure it does not stick.
2. Bring to a second boil, add shrimp and
   cook until pasta is al dente (about
   5 minutes).
3. Melt butter over medium heat, add the
   cream and stir. Before the mixture
   reaches a boil add all of the cheeses
   and stir.
4. Drain the shrimp, pasta and peas. Mix
   with the cheese sauce, season with salt
   and pepper, and serve immediately.

Spaghetti with Mussels, Scallops and Shrimp   Serves 4 to 6

1 pound spaghetti, cooked and drained
3 tablespoons olive oil
1 large onion, chopped
1 medium green pepper, chopped
4 garlic cloves, minced
¼ cup white wine
½ teaspoon basil
1 teaspoon marjoram
1 teaspoon oregano
1½ cups canned tomatoes, well drained
1½ pounds mussels, well scrubbed
  and debearded
1 pound large shrimp, peeled
  and deveined
1 pound scallops, cut in half, if large
salt and black pepper, freshly ground
Parmesan cheese, grated

1. Heat oil in a large saucepan over medium
   heat. Add onion and green pepper and
   sauté until golden. Add the garlic and
   cook for another minute.
2. Stir in the wine, basil, marjoram, oregano
   and tomatoes. Cook over high heat for
   5 minutes and then add the mussels.
   Cover and reduce heat. Cook for 3 to 4
   minutes until shells just begin to open.
3. Add the shrimp and scallops to the pan
   and recover. Cook for an additional 3 to
   4 minutes until shrimp and scallops are
   just firm.
4. Gently toss with cooked spaghetti and
   season with salt and pepper. Serve in
   large bowls with grated cheese.

**For company, prepare the sauce ahead, drizzle a
little olive oil over the spaghetti and toss at the
last minute.**

174

Seafood and Cheese Medley

Serves 10 to 12

A perfect Sunday brunch for a bunch.

1 12-ounce box flat noodles or shells, cooked and drained
4 ounces pimentos, chopped
8 ounces mushrooms, sliced
1 8-ounce can lobster meat, rinsed and cut into ½-inch pieces
½ pound medium shrimp, peeled and cooked
1 8-ounce can crabmeat
½ cup butter
½ cup flour
1 teaspoon salt
4 cups milk
½ pound sharp cheddar cheese, grated

1. In a saucepan melt butter and stir in flour. Add salt and slowly whisk in the milk, stirring constantly to make a light cream sauce.

2. Fold in the grated cheese and cook until melted.

3. In a large mixing bowl, combine noodles, pimentos, mushrooms, lobster, shrimp and crab. Pour cheese sauce overall and mix well.

4. Divide mixture into two 3-quart buttered casseroles and bake at 350° for 45 minutes.

Special Occasion Seafood Salad

Serves 6 to 8

Bring this along on the boat for a simple cruising weekend meal.

1 pound medium pasta shells
2 cups crabmeat
1 6-ounce can shrimp, drained
2 eggs, hard-boiled and diced
½ cup green pepper, chopped
¾ cup celery, diced
1 to 1½ cups mayonnaise
½ teaspoon dry mustard
¼ teaspoon black pepper
paprika
additional hard-boiled eggs
   and sliced tomatoes for garnish

1. Cook, drain and cool pasta shells.

2. In a large bowl, combine crabmeat, shrimp, eggs, green pepper and celery. Fold in mayonnaise and seasonings.

3. Line a large bowl with lettuce leaves and fill with salad. Dust with paprika and garnish outside edges with egg and sliced tomatoes.

Because fish is so perishable it should ideally be frozen the same day as it is caught. If it sits in the refrigerator for more than 2 days, feed it to the neighbors cat.

Dué Pasta Pesto

Serves 6 to 8

Be prepared with plenty of crusty Italian bread and chilled soave.

Pesto:

2 cups fresh basil leaves
½ cup parsley
½ teaspoon salt
3 ounces pine nuts
3 medium garlic cloves
1 tablespoon Romano cheese
1 tablespoon Parmesan cheese
¾ to 1 cup olive oil

Pasta:

1 10-ounce package two-color
   (spinach and egg) fettucine
6 tablespoons olive oil
6 garlic cloves, chopped
1 medium onion, diced
1 small zucchini, cubed
1 small yellow squash, cubed
8 ounces mushrooms, sliced
1 pound swordfish, cut into 1-inch pieces
1 pound scallops
6 tablespoons Pesto (see above)
Parmesan and Romano cheese,
   freshly grated
black pepper

Pesto preparation:

1. In the bowl of a food processor fitted with a steel blade, combine basil, parsley, salt, pine nuts, garlic and cheeses. Chop for 10 sceonds and slowly add enough olive oil until you have a thick paste. Depending on how moist the basil leaves and cheeses are, you may need a little more or less olive oil to reach the right consistency.

Pasta preparation:

1. Cook fettucine in boiling water according to package instructions for al dente. Drain.

2. Add 3 tablespoons olive oil to a medium saucepan and sauté garlic, onion, zucchini, yellow squash and mushrooms until soft. Remove from pan.

3. Add remaining 3 tablespoons olive oil to pan and sauté swordfish cubes and scallops (or any other combination of seafood) for 3 minutes until firm.

4. Place drained fettucine in a large pot and combine with cooked vegetables and seafood. Gently toss with pesto and heat over medium heat for 3 to 4 minutes until steaming. Serve on heated plates and sprinkle with freshly grated cheese and pepper.

Paprika and Cayenne pepper, because of their color, are affected by light, and therefore have a short shelf life. Buy them in small quantities and store them in the refrigerator for maximum flavor.

Jamestown Fish and Pasta Combo   Serves 6

Almost a working man's Bouillabaisse, depending on what you choose to add . . . easy, hearty and low cholesterol.

1 pound fish fillets, cod, haddock or sole, cut into 2-inch pieces
1 10-ounce can baby clams
1 tablespoon olive oil
1 cup onion, chopped
1 garlic clove, minced
1 16-ounce can Italian plum tomatoes
2 cups clam-tomato juice cocktail
1 cup parsley, chopped
1 teaspoon lemon peel, shredded
1 teaspoon dried basil
1 teaspoon Cayenne pepper
1 cup pasta, small-size, such as bows, shells or capellini
½ cup white wine

1. In a 3-quart saucepan sauté onions and garlic in oil until soft.
2. Add undrained tomatoes with juice, breaking up with a spoon. Stir in the clam-tomato juice, parsley, lemon peel, basil and Cayenne. Cover and simmer for 25 minutes.
3. Add the seafood and pasta. Cook for 8 to 10 minutes until fish flakes and pasta is cooked. Pour in the white wine and simmer for a few minutes to blend flavors. Serve in deep soup plates.

Seagoing Linguine Capriccio II   Serves 4

A taste of the Mediterranean.

1 pound fresh skinless fish, preferably monkfish
1 pint bay scallops
1 large leek, washed
3 tablespoons olive oil
1 tablespoon fresh garlic, minced
1 teaspoon dried hot red pepper flakes
1 cup onion, finely chopped
½ cup celery, finely chopped
1 teaspoon saffron threads (optional)
2 cups canned crushed tomatoes
½ cup dry white wine
1 bay leaf
2 tablespoons parsley
¼ teaspoon fennel seed
1 10-ounce package linguine, cooked and drained

1. Cut fish into 1-inch chunks.
2. Finely dice white part of leek.
3. In a large pot, heat oil. Add garlic, hot pepper, leeks, onions and celery.
4. Stir in the saffron and cook over medium heat for 2 minutes.
5. Add the tomatoes, wine, bay leaf, parsley and fennel; cover and bring to a boil.
6. Simmer for 15 minutes, stirring often.
7. Add the fish, cook for 4 minutes, then add the scallops and continue cooking for 2 minutes. Serve over hot linguine.

Sauce improves if made ahead and gently warmed before serving.

Seafood Pasta Primavera

Serves 4

A great way to get a lot of mileage out of a small amount of shellfish.

1 tablespoon butter
4 ounces medium shrimp, shelled
   and deveined
4 ounces scallops
1 cup broccoli, broken into pieces
½ cup mushrooms, sliced
½ cup onion, chopped
¼ cup green pepper, chopped
2 tablespoons butter
2 tablespoons flour
¼ teaspoon ground pepper
2 cups milk
2 ounces Swiss cheese, shredded
½ cup Parmesan cheese, grated
2 cups cooked spaghetti

1. In skillet, heat 1 tablespoon butter until hot; add shrimp and scallops, sauté until shrimp are pink. With slotted spoon, remove from skillet.

2. In same skillet, add broccoli, mushrooms, peppers and onions, sauté until tender. With slotted spoon remove vegetables from pan.

3. In same pan add 2 tablespoons butter, heat until hot. Sprinkle butter with flour and pepper, stir quickly to combine. Cook for 1 minute, stirring constantly. Gradually stir in milk; cook over medium heat, stirring constantly, until smooth and thick.

4. Add cheese and cook, stirring frequently, until melted. Return sautéed vegetables and seafood to pan, add pasta and toss to combine. Reduce heat to low and cook until thoroughly heated.

TRADITIONAL FLAVOR ADAPTATION

Savory Stuffing

Serves 8

This is a basic stuffing for any type of seafood from lobster to squid.

2 cups cracker crumbs
2 tablespoons Parmesan cheese, grated
1 dash ground pepper
1 tablespoon parsley, chopped
2 tablespoons olive oil
2 tablespoons water

1. Mix all the ingredients together in a large bowl taking care to moisten the cracker crumbs just enough so they hold together but are not wet.
2. That's all there is to it.

Mother Higgins' Secret

Serves 4 as an entrée, 8 as an appetizer

For people who don't like fish.

2½ to 3 pounds fresh blackfish or bluefish, cut into bite-size cubes
6 strips bacon, chopped
½ medium onion, chopped
1 green pepper, finely diced
2 cups fresh bread crumbs or cracker crumbs
2 tablespoons olive oil
lemon-pepper seasoning

1. In a large frying pan, cook the bacon until crisp. Remove and drain on paper towels.
2. To the remaining fat in the pan, add the onion and green pepper. Sauté until tender and remove from the pan.
3. Roll or shake the fish cubes in the crumbs. Add a little olive oil to the pan and fry the fish cubes over medium heat until browned on both sides. Season to taste with lemon-pepper and add the cooked bacon, onions, and peppers to the pan.
4. Continue cooking for a few minutes, lightly tossing vegetables with the fish. Serve hot with forks (as an entrée) or toothpicks (as an appetizer).

Microwave Baked Bluefish

Serves 4

The chef's idea to use milk with bluefish came from her brother-in-law, a commercial fisherman out of Point Judith, Rhode Island. The milk seems to mellow the strong bluefish flavor to which some people object.

1½ pounds bluefish fillets
½ cup milk to marinate
2 cups herb seasoned stuffing mix
2 large celery stalks, finely diced
1 medium onion, finely chopped or
　1 tablespoon instant minced onion
4 sprigs parsley, snipped or 1 tablespoon
　parsley flakes
2 tablespoons butter, melted

1. Place fillets fleshy side up in a greased microwave-safe baking dish. Pour milk over fish to marinate while preparing dressing.

2. Combine stuffing mix with celery, onion, parsley and butter. Moisten with milk used to marinate fish (add more if necessary).

3. Spread fish evenly with dressing. Cover casserole and microwave on high for 8 to 10 minutes, rotating dish halfway through cooking time. Fish is done when it flakes with a fork.

4. Allow to stand 2 to 3 minutes before serving. Cooking time may vary slightly depending on power of microwave.

Baked Bluefish with Garlic Potatoes   Serves 4 to 6

**You can bake almost any variety of fish this way,
adding butter, lemon, dill or sour cream if you choose to.**

2 bluefish fillets, fresh from the ocean or
    better still, Long Island Sound
1½ pounds potatoes, thinly sliced
    (about 5 large Idaho potatoes)
⅔ cup olive oil
2 tablespoons garlic, chopped
⅓ cup parsley, chopped

1. If you are preparing this ahead, slice potatoes and put in cold water until ready to prepare fish. Drain and pat dry before using.
2. Layer potato slices in a shallow baking dish. Pour ⅓ cup olive oil over potatoes and spread half of garlic and parsley on top. Sprinkle with salt and pepper and bake at 400° to 425° for 15 minutes.
3. Put bluefish fillets, skin side down, over potatoes and pour over remaining ⅓ cup olive oil. Spread the rest of the garlic and parsley over the fish. Bake 10 to 15 minutes longer until fish flakes easily with a fork.

**Rule of thumb for any other fish with this recipe
— 400° for 10 minutes per inch of thickness.**

U.S.S. George Washington Carver Bluefish   Serves 4 To 6

**Offered by a friend whose husband was stationed
at the sub base in Groton, Connecticut.**

1 2-pound slab of bluefish (filleted)
1 small onion, finely chopped
¼ pound mushrooms, sliced
4 tablespoons butter
2 tablespoons fresh parsley, chopped
2 to 3 cups herb stuffing mix
½ cup white wine
3 lemons

1. Place the bluefish, skin side down, on a baking sheet that is covered with a heavy large-size brown bag from the market.
2. Sauté the onions and mushrooms in the butter for 2 to 3 minutes until tender-crisp. Add the parsley, herb crumbs and moisten with white wine.
3. Spread the stuffing evenly over the blue-fish and drown the stuffing with the juice of the three lemons. Bake for 25 minutes at 350° until fish flakes. You will be surprised how light the fish comes out as the brown bag absorbs most of the oiliness.

Captain's Clam Pie

Serves 6 to 8

If you want a more filling pie, fold some diced cooked potatoes into the sauce before baking.

2 cups minced clams, drained
    (juice reserved)
¼ cup butter
¼ cup flour
I cup milk
½ cup clam liquid
¼ cup heavy cream
2 tablespoons scallions, chopped
½ cup celery, minced
I tablespoon parsley, chopped
pinch of salt and pepper
pastry for a 9-inch 2 crust pie

1. Melt butter in a medium saucepan, whisk in the flour and cook for I minute.
2. Remove pan from heat, add milk and clam juice, stirring quickly to avoid any lumps.
3. Return to heat, add the cream and stir over medium heat until thickened.
4. Add scallions, celery, pepper, parsley, clams, salt and pepper. Pour filling into bottom crust in pie pan, cover with top crust and crimp the edges.
5. Bake pie for 40 minutes in a 400° oven. Let stand 10 minutes before cutting.

Clamburger Special

Serves 6

A light summer supper to serve after a day at the beach.

I pint clams, finely chopped
I cup cracker crumbs
I egg, well beaten
½ teaspoon salt
½ teaspoon parsley
¼ teaspoon black pepper
¼ cup vegetable oil

1. Mix clams, crumbs, egg, salt, parsley and pepper. Refrigerate for 30 minutes.
2. Form into 3-inch round cakes and fry in hot oil for 2 minutes on each side until crisp. Drain on paper towels.
3. Serve on toasted rolls with sliced tomato, lettuce and tartar sauce.

If you are digging your own clams, wash them well with sea water and place them in a pail. Cover with fresh sea water and let stand for 10 to 15 minutes to allow the clams to cleanse themselves of sand. The sand will settle to the bottom, then you can carefully remove the clams without disturbing the sand.

At Home Clambake

Here are the steps to follow for an at home celebration which is ideal for either the backyard charcoal grill or the kitchen range.

beer
lobsters, 1 per person, plus a few extras
steamer clams, 1-dozen per person
corn on the cob

1. Pour beer, about 1 inch deep, into a large pot and heat until it steams.
2. Plunge live lobsters into the steaming beer.
3. Add rinsed steamer clams. The portions of clams may be placed in individual packages made out of aluminum foil or tied in a cheesecloth bag.
4. Husk the corn and add it to the pot, wiggling in down between the lobsters and clams. Cover the pot and steam for 20 minutes. Serve with Hot Deviled Butter.

Hot Deviled Butter:

1 cup butter
2 tablespoons Worcestershire sauce
2 teaspoons prepared mustard
2 tablespoons chili sauce
4 teaspoons lemon or lime juice, freshly squeezed
1 tablespoon parsley, chopped
dash Tabasco sauce

Hot Deviled Butter preparation:

Melt the butter and add remaining ingredients. Heat until bubbly hot. Makes 1½ cups.

Cape Cod Cod Steaks

Serves 6

Sweet and saucy, serve with white or wild rice.

6 8-ounce cod steaks or fillets
4 tablespoons butter
1 onion, finely chopped
2 garlic cloves, minced
2 tablespoons lemon juice
1 16-ounce can whole-berry cranberry sauce
salt and pepper
parsley sprigs

1. In a medium saucepan, melt the butter. Sauté the onion and garlic until translucent.
2. Stir in the lemon juice and cranberry sauce and heat until sauce has just melted.
3. Place cod steaks in a 10x14-inch baking dish. Sprinkle with salt and pepper and pour cranberry sauce overall. Bake at 350° for 30 minutes until bubbling. Garnish with lots of parsley.

Point Club Fish Cakes

Makes 3 dozen cakes

1 pound salt cod
8 medium potatoes, peeled and cubed
2 tablespoons butter
2 eggs, well beaten
black pepper, freshly ground
parsley, chopped
vegetable oil

1. Rinse the fish under cold water for 5 minutes. Place the potatoes in a large saucepot and top with the codfish. Add cold water to cover and bring to a boil. Reduce heat and cook for 35 to 40 minutes until potatoes are tender and fish flakes with a fork. Drain well and place in large bowl.

2. Add the butter to the fish mixture and mash with a fork. Stir in the eggs and continue to combine. Do not overmix, you want a coarse blend. Season with black pepper and a few pinches of parsley, refrigerate for several hours.

3. When ready to serve, form the mixture into 2-inch cakes. Fry in a thin layer of hot oil in a skillet, cooking 3 to 4 minutes on each side until crisp and golden. Drain and serve with cups of cocktail sauce, tartar sauce and lemon wedges.

Fish Cakes may be cooked well ahead of time, placed on a baking sheet and reheated in a 375° oven.

Starting back in 1940 a group of Stonington men got together after church and drove down to "the Point." They would squeeze into one car and spend an hour or so socializing before heading to the local fishermen's club. Since several of them were fine cooks, there was often a great rivalry over who could make the best fishcakes. This recipe emerged after several of the men put their heads together, made a batch and served it in the car.

Creamed Codfish

Serves 6

Remembered as a special occasion dinner at the grandparents — still a treat when mother comes to visit.

1 2-pound box salt codfish
2 tablespoons butter
4 tablespoons flour
1 egg, beaten
2 cups milk
dash of Worcestershire sauce
1 tablespoon parsley, chopped
salt and pepper to taste

1. Place codfish in cold water for several hours to freshen. Change water, as it will become too salty.

2. In a medium saucepan, place the fish in 2 cups of water and cook slowly over medium heat for 15 minutes. Drain.

3. Melt the butter in a medium saucepan and whisk in the flour. Cook for several minutes, stirring constantly. Remove from heat.

4. Combine the beaten egg and milk. Quickly combine with the butter-flour mixture in the pan and return to heat. Cook for 3 to 4 minutes until thickened.

5. Gently fold in the fish and season with Worcestershire, parsley, salt and pepper to taste. Spoon over hot mashed potatoes.

Other family favorites, stewed tomatoes and fresh green beans, make a colorful meal.

Fried Cod Cheeks

Serves 4

1 pound fresh cod cheeks
1 lemon
¾ cup flour
¼ cup cornmeal
½ teaspoon salt
black pepper, freshly ground
cooking oil

Traditionally accompanied by boiled potatoes, coleslaw and brown bread.

1. Rinse the cod cheeks under cold water and pat dry. Lay them out on a baking sheet and squeeze the lemon overall.

2. Combine the flour, cornmeal, salt and pepper in a paper or plastic bag. A few at a time, add the cheeks to the bag and shake until well coated.

3. In a large heavy skillet heat ¼-inch of oil over medium heat. Fry the cod cheeks for 7 to 8 minutes on each side until crusty. Drain on paper towels and serve immediately.

Chesebrough Cheese Fish

Serves 6

This recipe was handed down though the family of Edward Eugene Bradley, one of the three original founders of Mystic Seaport.

2½ pounds fish fillets, flounder is preferred
    but catch of the day is fine
½ cup flour
2 teaspoons dry mustard
4 tablespoons butter
1 cup milk
1 cup sharp cheddar cheese, diced
salt and pepper

1. Lightly butter a 3-quart casserole, line with the fish fillets, folded in half, end to end.

2. In a medium bowl, mix flour, mustard, butter, milk and cheese together with a fork. Season with salt and pepper. The mixture will be lumpy.

3. Pour mixture over fillets and bake in a 350° oven for 30 minutes.

Results—a creamy cheese-sauced fish with no work.

Roman's Market Crispy Fried Flounder   Serves 6

A 75 year-old family tradition. A platter of this in the center of the table, served with fresh vegetables, makes a delicious meal for a hungry family.

12 medium flounder fillets
4 eggs
3 cups fresh bread crumbs
vegetable oil

1. Pat fish fillets dry. Carve yourself a little counter space and begin.
2. Beat 2 eggs in a large soup bowl. Do this 2 at a time as you go along.
3. Dip the fish in the egg and then in the bread crumbs. Redip in beaten eggs and then again in the crumbs, being sure fish is nicely coated on both sides.
4. Heat ⅛-inch of oil in a large heavy skillet and add several fillets being sure not to crowd the pan. Cook gently for 4 to 5 minutes on each side until crisp and tender. Keep cooked fillets warm in the oven while you finish cooking the remaining fish. Place on a large platter and serve with lemon wedges.

One Dish Haddock Dinner   Serves 4

Let it cook while you relax.

2 ¾-pound haddock fillets
4 onions, thinly sliced
½ pound mushrooms, quartered
8 new potatoes, skin on, sliced
1 cup dry white wine
1 cup water
1 bay leaf
½ cup fresh bread crumbs
⅓ cup melted butter
salt and pepper
parsley, chopped

1. Butter an ovenproof casserole and cover the bottom with the sliced onions.
2. Place the fish fillets on top and surround with the mushrooms and potatoes. Pour the wine and water over the fish and add the bay leaf.
3. Sprinkle fish with bread crumbs, pour the melted butter overall and season with salt and pepper. Bake at 350° for 30 to 40 minutes stirring the vegetables around in the juices once or twice. Serve very hot, sprinkled with parsley.

Finnan Haddie, Dearborn Station Serves 4

The wonderful aroma of this is infectious.

1 pound finnan haddie (smoked haddock)
1½ cups milk
2 medium potatoes, cooked and cut into
  thick slices
¼ cup butter, melted
¼ teaspoon salt
black pepper
1 cup medium cream
paprika
2 hard-boiled eggs, diced
parsley sprigs

1. In a small saucepan, simmer the fish in the milk for 10 minutes. If you wish save the milk to use in a chowder.
2. Place fish in a shallow casserole and arrange potato slices in each end. Drizzle with butter and season with salt and pepper.
3. Pour cream over fish and potatoes and sprinkle generously with paprika. Bake at 350° for 10 minutes. Add eggs around edge of casserole and bake for 10 more minutes until hot and bubbly. Garnish with parsley sprigs.

Baked Finnan Haddie   Serves 4

**The character of the fish stands out here,
as it is not masked by a heavy cream sauce.**

1½ pounds finnan haddie (smoked haddock)
4 potatoes, peeled and cut into large cubes
4 carrots, cut into 2-inch pieces
2 medium onions, quartered
1 12-ounce can unsweetened condensed
  milk
pepper
parsley, chopped

1. Try to fit the fish in a pot that will not make in necessary to cut the fillets up too much; they will flake later in cooking. Cover with water and simmer for 10 minutes. Drain and save ½ cup of liquid.
2. Layer potatoes, carrots and onions in a medium pan, cover with water and cook for 20 minutes. Vegetables should be tender but not soft.
3. Arrange pieces of fish and drained vegetables in a large oven-to-table serving dish. You will not want to have to transfer this again before serving.
4. Pour condensed milk and ½ cup reserved cooking liquid over the dish. Season with a little pepper. Bake at 350° for 30 minutes, basting occasionally with the pan juices. Sprinkle with parsley and dot with butter, if you wish, before serving.

Herring and Potato Salad

Serves 6 to 8

An innovative take-along to a summer picnic.

1 12-ounce jar marinated herring and
  onions in wine sauce
6 cups potatoes, peeled and sliced
1 cup celery, chopped
1 medium red onion, thinly sliced
½ cup olive oil
½ cup white wine
2 tablespoons parsley, chopped
1 teaspoon dill
1 tablespoon capers, rinsed

Must be made ahead.

1. Drain the herring and cut into bite-size pieces. Set aside.

2. Cook potatoes in boiling salted water for 10 minutes until tender. Be careful not to overcook as you want them firm. Place in a large bowl.

3. While potatoes are still hot, add celery, onion, olive oil and white wine. Gently toss in dill and parsley.

4. Add the herring and mix well. Cover and refrigerate until ready to serve. Garnish with lettuce leaves and sprinkle with capers.

Crazy About Scalloped Oysters

Serves 4

From a Seaport member living in Tennessee who picked up this recipe from a neighbor while stationed at the submarine base in Groton years ago.

1 pint oysters
2 to 2½ cups cracker crumbs,
  coarsely crushed, or lightly seasoned
  bread crumbs
½ cup butter, melted
½ teaspoon salt
1½ teaspoons celery seed
¼ teaspoon black pepper
⅓ cup oyster liquor
¾ cup light cream
½ teaspoon Worcestershire sauce

1. Drain oysters, reserving ⅓ cup liquor in a small bowl.

2. Combine the cracker crumbs and the melted butter. Spread one-third of the crumbs in a well greased 8x2-inch high round baking dish.

3. Cover with half of the oysters. Sprinkle with a little salt pepper and celery seed. You will love what this little spice adds to the dish.

4. Using half of the remaining cracker crumbs, make another layer over the oysters. Finish with the remaining oysters and again season with salt, pepper and celery seed.

5. Combine the oyster liquor, cream and Worcestershire sauce. Pour evenly over the oysters. Top with the remaining crumbs and bake at 350° for 40 minutes.

Rhode Island Oyster Cakes

Makes 2 dozen cakes

2 pints oysters, fresh shucked
1 egg
2 tablespoons oyster broth
1 can cream of mushroom soup (undiluted)
1 tablespoon white onions or scallions,
  finely chopped
4 shakes of Worcestershire sauce
2 teaspoons lemon juice
¼ cup fried bread crumbs
2 cups of rolled cracker crumbs
  (Chicken in a Basket, if available)
½ cup butter

1. Simmer oysters and their liquor gently for
   2 minutes in a medium saucepan. Cool
   and pick over carefully for any
   shell fragments.

2. In a medium bowl, combine oysters with
   broth, soup, onion, seasonings and
   cracker crumbs. Refrigerate several hours.

3. To assemble, mold mixture into palm-size
   patties. Melt the butter and sauté cakes
   over low heat in a frying pan until hot
   and brown on both sides. Drain well and
   serve with melted butter or cocktail-
   horseradish sauce.

Buzzards Bay Scalloped Oysters Serves 4

**There is nothing as special with a Thanksgiving or Christmas turkey
as an oyster casserole.**

1 pint oysters and liquor
20 buttery crackers, crushed
½ cup stale bread crumbs
⅓ cup butter, melted
salt and pepper
2 tablespoons cream
2 tablespoons dry sherry

**4x the recipe nicely Serves 20 people.
6x the recipe for 30.**

1. Mix cracker crumbs with bread crumbs
   and the melted butter. Place one-third of
   the crumbs in the bottom of a buttered
   casserole.

2. Put half of the oysters and their liquor
   on top of the crumbs. Sprinkle with salt,
   pepper, 1 tablespoon of cream and add
   1 tablespoon of sherry.

3. Make another layer of crumbs and
   another layer of the remaining oysters,
   salt, pepper, cream and sherry.

4. Finally cover with crumbs and bake at
   425° for 30 minutes.

**Some holiday dishes can be made well ahead, but
this one should be assembled at the last minute
so it does not get soggy.**

Sherried Scalloped Oysters

Serves 12 to 16 people

**Don't always wait to have this for the holidays. Serve it
as a main dish for a buffet and your guests will rave!**

3 pints oysters (about 6 dozen medium
   size, if you are shucking)
4 cups coarse crumbs, use a mixture of
   toasted bread, saltines and herb seasoned
   stuffing mix
¾ cup butter, melted
1 cup oyster liquor
½ teaspoon salt
pinch of Cayenne pepper or
   few dashes Tabasco sauce
¾ cup light cream
1½ teaspoons Worcestershire sauce
3 tablespoons dry sherry

1. Drain oyster liquor, reserving 1 cup.
2. Combine crumbs and melted butter,
   mixing well. Layer crumbs and oysters in
   shallow baking dish, starting and ending
   with crumbs.
3. To the reserved oyster liquor, add the
   salt, Cayenne or Tabasco, cream,
   Worcestershire sauce and sherry. Pour
   this mixture evenly over the casserole. If
   it seems too dry, drizzle a little extra
   cream and sherry on top. Bake at 375°
   for 30 minutes. If you prepare this ahead,
   do not pour the seasoned cream on the
   casserole until you are ready to bake it.

Plymouth Oyster Pie

Serves 4

**A wonderful way to greet new neighbors.
Tie it up in a colorful dish towel for them to keep.**

4 tablespoons butter
8 tablespoons flour
3 cups warm milk
1 pint oysters, drained and
   liquor reserved
4 carrots, diced and cooked
2 potatoes, diced and cooked
1 medium onion, chopped
2 tablespoons green pepper, finely chopped
salt and pepper
⅛ teaspoon nutmeg
1 tablespoon parsley
1 9-inch pie crust

1. Melt butter in a saucepan. When
   bubbling, whisk in the flour. Remove
   from heat and add the oyster liquor and
   milk, stirring constantly. Cook over
   medium heat until sauce has thickened.
   Drop in the oysters and simmer for
   2 minutes until edges are curled.
2. Fold in the carrots, potatoes, onion and
   green pepper. Season to taste with salt
   and pepper. Add parsley and nutmeg.
3. Put the filling in a deep casserole and
   top with crust. Crimp the edges. Bake at
   375° for 25 minutes until crust is brown
   and filling is bubbling hot.

Grandpa K's Oyster Stuffing for Turkey

For a 12-pound turkey, double for 18- to 25-pound turkey

This recipe comes from years of following Grandpa around the kitchen at Thanksgiving and watching carefully to see everything that went into the mixing bowl.

½ pound pork sausage
3 strips bacon
turkey giblets (heart, liver, wing tips, neck)
½ teaspoon salt
½ teaspoon pepper
½ teaspoon poultry seasoning
¼ teaspoon thyme
2 to 3 celery stalks
1 medium onion
½ pint oysters, coarsely chopped
large loaf French bread
1 tablespoon butter, melted

1. Precook giblets in water for 45 minutes. This can be done a day ahead.

2. In a food grinder or processor, grind the giblets with the bacon until coarse.

3. Put sausage meat in a large pot and add ground giblets, bacon and seasonings. Sauté for 15 minutes.

4. Coarsely grind or process the celery and onion and add to the sausage-giblet mixture. Cook for 8 minutes until vegetables are tender. Add the oysters and sauté for 2 to 3 minutes.

5. Soak the French bread in water for 5 minutes. Remove and squeeze out the moisture. Break the bread up and combine well with other ingredients. Drizzle melted butter on top and toss.

6. Stuff the bird and enjoy the holiday.

Baked Oyster "Pie"

Serves 4

Mother always served this with a chilled tomato aspic.

½ cup dry bread crumbs
1 cup cracker crumbs, freshly ground
8 ounces butter, melted
1 pint oysters with liquid
6 tablespoons light cream

1. Mix bread crumbs and cracker crumbs in a small bowl. Pour melted butter over crumb mixture and toss with a fork until well combined.

2. Butter a 10-inch pie plate and spread half the crumbs evenly over the bottom.

3. Drain the oysters and reserve the liquid. Place oysters on top of the crumbs.

4. Mix the cream with reserved oyster liquor and pour half over the oysters. Place remaining crumbs on top and cover with remaining liquid. Bake in a 400° oven for 20 minutes.

Mimi's Oyster Pie

Serves 6 to 8

1 pie-crust dough for a one-crust pie
1 quart shucked oysters
8 tablespoons butter
2 tablespoons flour
1 cup milk
½ cup onion, finely chopped
1 large celery stalk with leaves, chopped
salt and pepper
2 cups saltine crackers, ground

1. Drain the oysters and reserve ½ cup liquor.

2. Melt 4 tablespoons butter in a saucepan and whisk in the flour. Cook for 3 to 4 minutes, stirring constantly.

3. Meanwhile, heat the milk and the reserved oyster liquor almost to a boil. Quickly stir into the flour-butter mixture. Cook until thickened and smooth. Season with salt and pepper.

4. In the remaining 4 tablespoons butter, sauté the onion and celery until tender. Combine with the cream sauce.

5. Press the cracker crumbs into a well buttered 9-inch pie plate or shallow casserole, being sure to build up the sides. Spread the oysters on top and cover with the cream sauce.

6. Roll out the pie crust to fit the pan and cover the dish. Crimp the edges and bake for 45 minutes until golden brown. This is not meant to be served as "a piece of pie" such as a fruit pie but spooned on the plate as with deep dish pie.

BAKED SHAD

"Keep on the head and fins. Make a forcemeat or stuffing of grated bread crumbs, cold boiled ham or bacon minced fine, sweet marjoram, pepper, salt, and a little powdered mace or cloves. Moisten it with beaten yolk of egg. Lay the fish in a deep pan, putting it's tail to it's mouth. Pour into the bottom of the pan a little water, and add a jill of port wine, and a piece of butter rolled in flour. Bake it well, and when it is done, send it to table with the gravy poured round it. Garnish with slices of lemon.

Any fish may be baked in the same manner. A large fish of ten or twelve pounds weight, will require about two hours baking."

MISS LESLIE'S DIRECTIONS OF COOKERY, 1839

Salmon à la King

Serves 4 to 6

May also be made with cooked pasta, and baked in a casserole with a topping of buttered crumbs.

2 cups canned or cooked salmon
4 tablespoons butter
½ cup celery, chopped
½ cup green pepper, chopped
1 cup mushrooms, sliced
¼ cup flour
½ teaspoon salt
1½ cups milk (if you are using canned salmon, measure the juice and add milk to make 1½ cups)
2 tablespoons pimento, chopped
2 tablespoons parsley, chopped
paprika

1. Break salmon into chunks being careful to remove any skin and bones.

2. Melt the butter in a saucepan and sauté celery, green peppers and mushrooms until tender-crisp.

3. Add the flour and salt and stir until combined. Slowly add the liquid and simmer, stirring until sauce is thick and creamy.

4. Fold in the salmon, pimento and parsley. Heat and serve in a patty shell, on buttered toast, or over white rice.

Roast Salmon with Lobster Sauce

Serves 4

A glorious way to serve a whole fish.

1 2-pound salmon
¼ pound salt pork
½ cup Madeira
½ cup beef stock
1 teaspoon salt
⅛ teaspoon pepper

Sauce:
1 tablespoon butter
2 tablespoons flour
½ cup milk
½ cup light cream
2 tablespoons dry sherry
1 1-pound lobster, boiled, meat removed (about ⅔ cup)
salt, pepper and paprika
watercress or parsley for garnish

1. Cut the salt pork into thin slivers. Make slits overall the fish and poke salt pork under the skin. Rub the fish and cavity with salt and pepper and place in a buttered roasting pan.

2. Pour the Madeira and stock into the pan. Cover the fish and bake for 30 minutes, basting often.

3. Meanwhile, melt the butter in a small saucepan. Stir in the flour and cook for one minute. Add the milk, cream and sherry, stirring constantly, and simmer until thickened. Season with salt, pepper and paprika. Add the lobster meat and keep warm.

4. When the fish is done, remove it to a heated platter and garnish with fresh greens. To serve, split the fish down the back and lay each fillet to the side. Remove the backbone and delicate stalkcage with a fork and slice the fish. Spoon the hot lobster sauce on each serving or pass it in a sauceboat.

Poached Salmon à la Dishwasher
(or How To Have Fun While Poaching)

Your guests love it, are impressed with the poached salmon, laugh at the recipe, want a copy, and can't wait to try it out.

salmon fillets, 6 to 8-ounces per person
disposable aluminum turkey roasting pan
aluminum foil
champagne or white wine
empty dishwasher
kale
parsley
red pepper strips
lemon
your favorite cucumber dill sauce or
   see suggestions in "Top It Off"
plastic wrap

1. Place fillets in bottom of aluminum pan, skin side down.

2. Pour in enough wine or champagne to cover fish — don't worry, I have never put in too much or too little and I've never measured — if you're uneasy about cooking like this, pour a glass of the wine or champagne and sip slowly.

3. Splurge on aluminum foil; seal top of roasting pan, then wrap over and under pan so that water CAN NOT enter roasting pan.

4. Place pan on top dishwasher rack. Be sure dishwasher is empty . . . DO NOT add soap.

5. Start dishwasher — I use wash cycle and cancel dry cycle; (if you can't cancel dry cycle, don't worry — this is a wonderful, flexible recipe). Allow dishwasher to cool down, then remove pan. Allow the pan to cool completely, and then place in refrigerator (after removing all extra aluminum foil).

6. Next day, wash kale and place on serving dish.

7. Place salmon skin side down. Decorate with parsley sprigs, lemon slices and red pepper strips. Cover with plastic wrap until ready to serve. Serve with dill sauce on the side.

Gullybridge Scallops

Serves 4

This recipe comes from the kitchens of several "native island women" from Nantucket ... simple, but rich (the scallops not the women).

1¼ to 1½ pounds scallops
6 tablespoons butter, melted
1¼ cups cracker crumbs, crushed
⅔ cup light cream

1. Melt butter in a saucepan and stir in cracker crumbs. Mix well.
2. In a 1-quart casserole, layer scallops and buttered crumbs, ending with a layer of crumbs.
3. Pour cream over the top and bake in a 400° oven for 30 minutes.

Scalloped Scallops

Serves 6 to 8

Have this ready to pop in the oven after an evening of carol singing.

2 pounds scallops
8 tablespoons butter
1½ cups fresh bread crumbs
1½ cups cracker crumbs, crumbled
⅔ cup medium cream
2 teaspoons prepared brown or Dijon mustard
parsley, chopped

1. Melt the butter in a medium saucepan and remove from heat. Stir in the bread crumbs and cracker crumbs, tossing lightly.
2. Spread a layer of the buttered crumbs in a large 2- to 3-quart casserole. Cover with the scallops and top with the remaining crumbs.
3. Mix the cream with the mustard and pour over the casserole. Bake at 350° for 30 minutes until crumbs are light brown and casserole is bubbling hot. Sprinkle with parsley and serve.

One pound of fresh scallops yields approximately 2 cups of cooked meat. One cup of fresh scallops weighs approximately 5 ounces.

Cuttyhunk Paprika Scallops   Serves 4

With summertime memories of sunsets across Vineyard Sound.

1¾ pounds scallops
¾ cup seasoned bread crumbs
1 tablespoon paprika
¼ cup flour
4 tablespoons butter
½ cup scallions, chopped
2 tablespoons parsley, chopped

1. Combine bread crumbs, paprika and flour in a mixing bowl. Add the scallops and toss thoroughly to coat.
2. Melt the butter over medium-high heat in a large frying pan. If you do not have a pan large enough to hold scallops in one layer, cook them in two batches.
3. Add the scallops and cook for 5 minutes, stirring gently. Let them brown nicely then add the scallions and parsley. Cook for 3 more minutes and serve on hot plates, garnished with lemon slices. The nutty flavor of short grain brown rice is perfect with this scallop dish.

New Haven Railroad Lemon Scrod   Serves 4

When rail dining car service was at its best . . . GBT favorite

4 8-ounce scrod fillets
8 tablespoons butter
2 tablespoons lemon juice, freshly squeezed
½ teaspoon salt
2 tablespoons parsley, minced
white pepper, freshly ground
6 tablespoons fine bread crumbs

1. Preheat the broiler for 10 minutes.
2. Melt butter in a heavy saucepan. Add lemon juice, salt, parsley and pepper to taste.
3. Arrange scrod fillets in one layer in a shallow baking dish or individual oval casseroles. Pour lemon butter overall, covering thoroughly. Broil fish for 5 minutes, basting with butter sauce several times.
4. Sprinkle bread crumbs over the fish and baste several times. Broil for 5 more minutes and spoon lemon butter over fish before serving.

Scrod is a young codfish. It is preferred over the cod because of its manageable shape and resemblance to sole.

Mustard Microwave Shrimp   Serves 2

A special favorite from a Kennett Square kitchen.

1 pound shrimp, peeled and deveined
1 lemon
½ cup butter
2 tablespoons Dijon mustard
2 garlic cloves, minced
1 tablespoon capers, rinsed
2 tablespoons parsley, freshly chopped

1. Place the shrimp in one layer in a 2-quart microwaveable casserole. Squeeze the lemon over the shrimp and let stand for 15 minutes.

2. In a small dish, melt the butter at medium heat and stir in the mustard, garlic, capers and parsley.

3. Pour butter sauce over the shrimp and loosely cover with plastic wrap. Cook for 1 to 1½ minutes on high heat, turn casserole and cook for another minute until shrimp are pink. Serve the shrimp and juice over hot rice.

Sole Rarebit   Serves 4

4 large sole fillets, about 5-ounces each
3 tablespoons butter
8 ounces sharp cheddar cheese, grated
½ cup beer or ale
1 egg
½ teaspoon paprika
¼ teaspoon dry mustard
1 teaspoon Worcestershire sauce
½ cup flour
salt and pepper
4 slices bread, toasted and buttered
8 slices tomato
8 slices bacon, cooked and crumbled
parsley, chopped

1. In a heavy medium saucepan, melt 1 tablespoon butter. Add the grated cheese and as the cheese starts to melt, gradually add the beer, stirring constantly.

2. Beat the egg in a small bowl with the paprika, mustard and Worcestershire sauce. Add a few spoonfuls of the cheese to the egg and then slowly stir the egg mixture into the cheese. Simmer over low heat, stirring constantly for a minute. Cover and keep warm.

3. Season the flour with salt and pepper and dredge each sole fillet on both sides. Melt the remaining 2 tablespoons butter in a large skillet and fry the fish for 2 minutes on each side until lightly browned.

4. Place a piece of toast on each dinner plate and top with a sole fillet. Put 2 slices of tomato on each piece of fish and spoon welsh rarebit overall. Sprinkle with bacon, chopped parsley and additional paprika and serve immediately.

Buttermilk Sole

Serves 2

Try cooking shucked oysters this way and serve them on buttered toast points with a horseradish sauce.

4 to 6 sole fillets, about ¾ pound
½ cup flour
salt, pepper and dill
½ cup buttermilk
3 tablespoons butter
paprika

1. Season the flour with salt, pepper and a few pinches of dill. Place on a plate.
2. Dredge the fish fillets on both sides in the flour. Melt the butter in a skillet over medium heat.
3. Quickly dip the fish into the buttermilk and place in the hot pan. Cook for 2 minutes on each side until crispy and browned. Sprinkle with paprika before serving.

Christmas Eve Special Squid

Serves 6

A true feast with some Roman influence in the seasoning.

2 pounds squid, dressed (head and tentacles separated, mantle removed and the pen discarded)
2 garlic cloves, minced
1 onion, finely chopped
3 tablespoons olive oil
2 cups canned peeled tomatoes
½ cup water
salt and pepper
12 Italian black olives, pitted and chopped
¼ cup raisins
2 tablespoons pine nuts

1. Cut the squid into small pieces and wash well.
2. In a medium saucepan, sauté the garlic and onion in the olive oil until golden brown.
3. Add the squid, tomatoes, water and season with salt and pepper. Cover the pan and simmer for 10 minutes.
4. Stir in the olives, raisins and pine nuts, adding extra of any if you wish. Cover again and simmer for 10 more minutes until squid is tender. Arrange slices of crusty Italian bread in serving bowls and spoon the squid and sauce over the bread.

Toaster Trout for Two

Serves 2

This recipe would be considered especially quick and easy — it's designed for a counter-top toaster-oven with a broiler.

2 whole trout, 9- to 10-inch size, dressed
2 tablespoons oil or butter, melted
4 ounces sliced mushrooms, fresh or canned
2 tablespoons Parmesan cheese,
  freshly grated
I small onion, thinly sliced and buttered
salt and pepper

1. Coat the trout inside and out with some of the oil or melted butter. Fill the cavities with mushrooms and sprinkle with Parmesan cheese.

2. Place trout on the broiler pan to fit into the toaster oven and set to broil. Cook until you see small spots of burnt skin.

3. Turn trout and place buttered onion slices, seasoned with salt and pepper on the body of the fish. Continue to broil until small spots of burn appear — then it's time to serve.

Contributor's Illustration

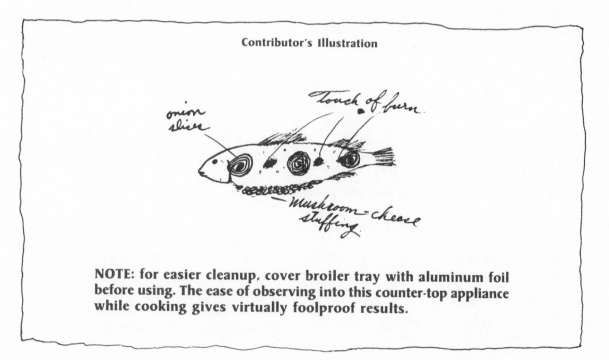

NOTE: for easier cleanup, cover broiler tray with aluminum foil before using. The ease of observing into this counter-top appliance while cooking gives virtually foolproof results.

Blue Ribbon New England Pie   Serves 6

A good Sunday night supper dish, it can be doubled or baked as individual pies.

2 cups quahogs, coarsely chopped, or
  cherrystones, cut in half
2 chicken breasts, skinned, boned, cooked
  and cubed
8 tablespoons butter
18 small white onions, peeled
½ cup celery, chopped
½ cup flour
1 teaspoon thyme
1½ cups chicken broth
1½ cups light cream
salt and pepper
1 8-ounce package corn kernels, defrosted
3 eggs, hard-boiled and quartered
pastry for 1 pie shell
1 egg yolk, beaten with 1 teaspoon of water

1. Melt 4 tablespoons of butter in a medium saucepan. Add the onions and celery, cover and cook gently for 10 minutes. Stir several times so as not to brown the vegetables.
2. Add the remaining 4 tablespoons of butter and stir in the flour and thyme. Whisk in the chicken broth and cream, cook until sauce has thickened and season with salt and pepper.
3. Add the clams, corn and chicken, mixing thoroughly. Gently fold in the eggs and pour into a buttered ovenproof casserole.
4. Roll the pie crust to fit the casserole, cover and seal the edges. Brush the top generously with the beaten egg and make several slits in the top. Bake in a 400° oven for 30 minutes until pastry is browned.

Stonington Baked Fish Fillets   Serves 6

We love this with fresh peas and red potatoes.

2 pounds fish fillets (a thick fish, haddock
  or cod is best)
¼ teaspoon paprika
3 tablespoons lemon juice

White Sauce for step 2:
2 tablespoons butter
3 tablespoons flour
1 tablespoon dry mustard
1¼ cups milk
salt and pepper
½ cup bread crumbs, buttered
1 tablespoon parsley, minced

1. Cut fish fillets into serving pieces. Place in a buttered shallow baking dish. Sprinkle with paprika and lemon juice.
2. In a small saucepan, melt butter over medium heat. Whisk in flour quickly and add dry mustard and milk. Cook, stirring constantly for 3 or 4 minutes until thickened.
3. Pour the sauce over the fish, sprinkle with crumbs and parsley. Bake at 350° for 35 minutes until browned.

New England Style Bouillabaisse   Serves 6

Anything goes here — use whatever combination of fish and shellfish is freshest.

1½ to 2 pounds firm fleshed fish fillets,
  skin on, cut into 3-inch pieces (sea trout,
  bass, cod, blackfish or halibut are good
  choices. Use at least 2 varieties. Add a
  few squid if you have them)
1 pound sea scallops
2 dozen cherrystone clams, rinsed
2 dozen mussels, rinsed and debearded
2 tablespoons olive oil
2 leeks, washed and chopped
4 garlic cloves, minced
1 28-ounce can whole tomatoes
2 8-ounce bottles clam juice
½ cup dry white wine
1 teaspoon fennel seed or 1 tablespoon
  Pernod or Anisette
1 teaspoon thyme
1 bay leaf
1 teaspoon orange peel, grated
pinch saffron
Cayenne pepper

1. In a large soup pot sauté the leeks and
   garlic in olive oil until soft. Add the
   tomatoes, clam juice, white wine and
   seasonings. Cover and simmer for 30
   minutes.

2. Add the cut up fish, cover and cook for
   10 minutes over medium-low heat. Stir in
   the scallops and top with cherrystones
   and mussels. Shake the pot. Cover and
   cook for 10 more minutes until clams
   and mussels are opened and fish flakes
   nicely. Divide seafood into 6 large
   shallow bowls and give everyone a bowl
   for shells. Pour sauce over top. Serve
   with garlic French bread.

Cranberry Stuffed Fish

What to do with that big bass or bluefish.

1 2½- to 3-pound fresh fish, cleaned
1 apple, unpeeled and chopped
½ cup onion, chopped
½ cup celery, chopped
1 lemon, freshly squeezed and
  rind grated
½ cup whole-berry cranberry sauce
2 tablespoons parsley, chopped
2 cups cooked rice, white or brown
1 egg, well beaten
¼ cup butter, melted

1. Mix all ingredients except fish in a large
   bowl and combine well. Whatever the
   catch of the day may be, sprinkle whole
   fish or fillets with salt and pepper. If you
   have a whole fish, stuff the fish and sew
   or skewer the opening. If not, layer fillets
   with stuffing in a buttered baking dish.

2. For a whole fish, cover and bake for
   40 minutes; for fillets adjust time to
   25 to 30 minutes. Carefully remove fish
   and garnish with lemon slices and parsley
   sprigs, drizzle with extra butter if you
   care to.

Leftover Fish Pie without Parsnips

Dough:

1⅔ cups flour, sifted all-purpose
pinch of salt
1 stick cold salted butter
1 tablespoon vegetable oil
1 egg yolk
¼ cup cold water

Dough preparation:

1. In a large mixing bowl put the sifted flour, salt and butter, chopping the butter up quickly into small bits as you put it in. Use a pastry blender to mix until the texture is like rolled oats.

2. Beat the oil, egg and water together and pour into a well made in the center of the flour mixture.

3. Mix with a fork and gather into a ball using your fingers only. (The heat of your hand will melt the butter.)

4. Wrap the dough in wax paper and refrigerate until firm, 20 minutes — longer in the summer.

5. Roll out ⅔ of the dough on floured waxed paper. If it gets sticky, put it in the freezer for a few minutes to re-harden. Using the paper to transfer the dough, turn the paper, dough side down, over a large deep casserole dish. Line the bottom and sides with the dough. Butter it lightly, top with foil and weigh it down with dried beans. Set aside.

6. Roll remaining ⅓ of the dough into a shape that will cover the dish. It will shrink so make it a little larger.

7. Bake crust lined casserole and pastry cover at 475° for 10 to 25 minutes depending on the kind of pan you use and dough thickness. It's done if it looks flaky, not soft. Remove from oven and fill.

"Leftover" filling:

1½ cups potatoes, diced
½ cup carrots, sliced
1 small can peas
2 small onions, chopped
3 tablespoons butter
3 tablespoons flour
2 cups milk
½ teaspoon salt
grind of black pepper
2 teaspoons dried parsley
dash of lemon juice
1 pound cooked fish, flaked (light flavored, such as salmon, cod or haddock)

Filling preparation:

1. Cook potatoes and carrots together in a small amount of boiling salted water, drain. Drain can of peas.

2. Cook onion in butter until tender. Remove from heat.

3. Beat flour into milk until smooth and add to onion and butter. Add salt, pepper and parsley. Cook until thickened, stirring constantly. Stir in lemon.

4. Layer vegetables and fish in precooked pastry shell in casserole. Cover with sauce.

5. Bake at 400° for about 45 minutes. Add the pastry cover and continue baking for 15 minutes more.

This pie makes impressive eating no matter what leftovers one tosses in, with one exception — parsnip. A parsnip was once added to this recipe when guests were to come for dinner, and it was totally inedible.

This French style pastry will keep frozen for weeks, or 3 or 4 days wrapped in waxed paper in the refrigerator. One could probably cook water in this crust and it would turn out flaky.

A DOWNEAST CLAMBAKE

With a tip of the hat to Bob Bryan and the late Marshall Dodge — "Bert and I"

"Sarah, remember that lady in Connecticut — the one we met when we went to the Seaport at Mystic — we had suppa at her restrant?"

"Yes, Charles."

"Waal, she's sold the restrant and's making a cookbook for the Seaport — she wants to put in a recipe for a real Maine clambake."

"Why don't ya tell her how I do it in our L.L. Bean cooker right heya in the kitchin."

"Noo — what I think she wants is how the summa people do it. Ya know, they get up real early — bout eight — course I've been out since four hawlin the darned pots. But, early for them I guess. First, they set about diggin a hole near the shore — bout four by four and two foot deep. Then they lug a bunch of big rocks from under the water and put em in the hole. On top of that they build the Biggest bonfire y'uv ever seen and keep it rorin most of the day.

"When they're fixin to eat, they shuck the corn, partly boil some potatas, and peel some nice big onions. By that time I've showed up with the lobstas and clams in the pickup.

"When the fire's pretty well burned down, they throw a couple of buckets of sea water on the rocks — boy don't it steam like the devil — then lay on a piece of chicken wire and put on the potatas, corn, onions and clams. Then another chicken wire and a bunch of seaweed if its handy and the lobstas on top of that. Finally, more seaweed or a clean sheet (won't be clean after that) and a nice heavy tarp, weighed down round the edges with stones.

"In just over half hour, they lift the tarp and the first chicken wire with the lobstas — right onto the back of my pickup — yup, I'm still there, sippin on a nice cold beer — there was plenty. Then the next layer of clams and vegetables. By then, ya can't hold em back and they swarm round that pickup like black flies in May.

"Sarah, those summa people go to a lotta trouble to croak down a lobsta, but gotta admit they taste pretty fancy — with melted butter and all the fixins — right down there on the shore with the sun settin behind the Camden Hills and the last ferry from Rockland roundin the Monument. — Course don't get me wrong, I like em right here at the kitchin table, too."

Good Hot-Hot Sauce

Makes 1 cup

Easy to remember — one of everything.

1 cup chili sauce
1 tablespoon horseradish
1 tablespoon Worcestershire sauce
1 tablespoon lemon juice, freshly squeezed
1 heavy dash Tabasco

Must be made ahead.

1. Combine all ingredients and chill.
2. Serve with your favorite bivalve — cherrystones, clams or mussels.

Brown Caper Butter Sauce

Makes ¾ cup

Serve this hot as a change with your bucket of steamed clams.
Make a double batch at home and take along to a beach picnic.

8 tablespoons butter
⅓ cup capers, drained
2 teaspoons lemon juice, freshly squeezed
2 teaspoon parsley, minced
1 teaspoon dry white wine

1. Melt the butter and cook over medium heat until brown.
2. Remove from heat and add capers, lemon juice, parsley and wine.

Caper Sauce Tartare

Makes 1½ cups

A hit with fish and chips.

1 cup mayonnaise
1 tablespoon lemon juice
2 teaspoons parsley, chopped
2 tablespoons gherkins, finely chopped
1 tablespoon onion, finely chopped
1 tablespoon capers, rinsed

Must be made ahead.

1. Add the lemon juice, parsley, gherkins, onion and capers to mayonnaise. Stir thoroughly and chill.

Rosey Red Onion and Basil Butter   Makes ¾ cup

**This adds a heavenly color to any grilled or poached fresh fish.
You may also toss with yellow squash or pasta.**

1 large red onion, finely chopped
2 tablespoons butter
2 tablespoons red wine
1 tablespoon fresh basil, chopped
½ cup butter

Must be made ahead.

1. In a small saucepan sauté red onion in 2 tablespoons butter until soft.
2. Add red wine and cook until liquid has evaporated. Cool.
3. In a blender or food processor, combine onion mixture, ½ cup butter and basil. Whirl until fluffy. Refrigerate.

Pomegranate Mint Sauce   Makes 3 cups

A lovely color and taste combination.

2 large handfuls of mint leaves
1 teaspoon sugar
1 cup fresh cream
1½ cups sour cream or yogurt
3 limes, freshly squeezed
1 small pomegranate

**Pomegranates stay refrigerated
in a sealed bag for a week.**

1. In the food processor, chop the mint, pulsing for just a few seconds.
2. Add the sugar, cream, sour cream and lime juice and quickly blend. Remove mixture to a small bowl.
3. CAREFULLY break pomegranate in half with a fork. (Remember that the juice stains terribly — the Indians used to use this for paint and dye.) With a small spoon, scrape the seeds away from the membrane. One fruit should yield about ¾ cup. If you like, save a few tablespoons to garnish a salad. Stir the pomagranate seeds into the mixture.

Maine Seafood Sauce

Makes 1½ cups

Pink and creamy.

½ cup mayonnaise
2 tablespoons sweet pickle relish
½ cup chili sauce
1 teaspoon prepared mustard
1 tablespoon chives, chopped
3 hard-boiled eggs, chopped
½ cup celery, chopped
1 tablespoon lemon juice, freshly squeezed

1. Combine all of the ingredients and blend well.
2. Serve with Maine shrimp or other chilled seafood on lettuce leaves or in a salad.

Summer Fish Salad Dressing

Makes 2½ cups

Also nice on cold vegetables.

½ cup scallions, chopped
1 cup mayonnaise
½ cup sour cream
1 garlic clove, minced
1 cup parsley, chopped
½ cup sour cream
1 teaspoon Worcestershire sauce
1 tablespoon fresh basil, chopped
½ teaspoon thyme
1 tablespoon lemon juice

Must be made ahead.

1. Combine mayonnaise with sour cream.
2. Add remaining ingredients and chill.

Roman Garlic Sauce

makes 1 cup

Toss with chilled seafood and pasta.

1 lemon, freshly squeezed
2 garlic cloves, chopped
2 tablespoons fresh parsley, chopped
2 tablespoons capers, chopped
6 tablespoons olive oil
⅛ teaspoon coarse black pepper
1 bay leaf

Must be made ahead.

1. Squeeze lemon into a small bowl. Add garlic, parsley and capers.
2. Slowly whisk in the olive oil, 1 tablespoon at a time.
3. Season with pepper, add the bay leaf and cover. Refrigerate overnight.

Honey Fruit Dressing

Makes 1 cup

**A lovely dressing to pour over a salad plate of chilled shrimp,
avocado and fresh fruit slices.**

1 pint mayonnaise
⅓ cup honey
2 tablespoons orange juice,
   freshly squeezed
1 tablespoon orange rind, grated

Must be made ahead.

1. Mix mayonnaise with other ingredients.
Chill well.

"Bleu" and Green Dressing

Makes 3½ cups

Spread this on a thick fish fillet before broiling.

½ pound bleu cheese
1 cup scallions, chopped
½ cup parsley, chopped
2 cups mayonnaise
1 cup sour cream
½ cup tarragon or herb vinegar

Must be made ahead.

1. Crumble the cheese, mix with the
scallions and parsley.
2. Stir in the mayonnaise, sour cream
and vinegar. Refrigerate overnight
before serving.

Bourbon Street Sauce Creole

Makes 1 quart

**At the end of the summer when you can't stand looking at the garden,
make a batch of this and freeze. On a cold snowy night poured
over baked fish or shrimp — it is heaven!**

3 tablespoons olive oil
1 medium onion, diced
1 green pepper, diced
2 celery stalks, diced
2 garlic cloves, finely chopped
1 cup chicken stock
2 cups chopped tomato
1 tablespoon vermouth
1 8-ounce can tomato sauce
1 bay leaf
¼ teaspoon Cayenne pepper

1. In a medium saucepan, heat olive oil.
Add onion, pepper, celery and garlic.
2. Sauté vegetables for 2 to 3 minutes until
translucent.
3. Add remaining ingredients, reduce heat
and simmer uncovered for 15 minutes.

Indonesian Sate Dipping Sauce   Makes 3 cups

A spicy dip for fish kebobs or fried shrimp.

1 4-ounce can mild whole green chilies,
   drained
6 garlic cloves
½ cup lime juice, freshly squeezed
6 scallions
1½ cups chicken stock
2 cups smooth peanut butter
1 tablespoon fresh ginger, chopped

Must be made ahead.

1. Rinse chilies, drain.
2. Coarsely chop garlic and scallions.
3. Add to the bowl of the food processor with lime juice and ginger. Pulse on and off for 30 seconds.
4. Slowly add chicken broth and peanut butter, mix well.
5. Transfer to bowl and refrigerate for several hours. If sauce separates, whisk until smooth before serving.

Rick's Cocktail Salsa   Makes 2 cups

This salsa is an alternative topping for clams, oysters on the half shell or shrimp cocktail.

1 red bell pepper
1 jalapeño pepper
2 large tomatoes, chopped
½ medium yellow onion, chopped
3 sprigs fresh coriander (cilantro)
½ lime, freshly squeezed
½ teaspoon salt
½ teaspoon cumin

Must be made ahead.

1. Place red bell pepper and jalapeño pepper directly on center rack of 400° oven for 10 to 15 minutes or until pepper skin is bubbling and brownish in color. Remove from oven, let cool, and cut in half. Remove seeds and stem from red pepper and place in food processor. Remove stem from jalapeño and add to the bowl.
2. Place remaining ingredients in processor and purée to a cocktail sauce consistency. Chill for 2 to 3 hours for maximum flavor. Add more salt if desired, before serving.

This salsa can also be served warm to top off grilled seafood.

Spiced Parsley Sauce

Makes 1½ cups

Looks great over grilled salmon.

½ cup olive oil
¼ cup lemon juice
½ cup onion, finely chopped
1 teaspoon garlic, minced
1 teaspoon oregano
¼ cup Italian flat leaf parsley, finely chopped
¼ teaspoon Cayenne pepper
¼ teaspoon salt
1 teaspoon black pepper, freshly ground
1 tablespoon pignoli nuts

Must be made ahead.

1. In a bowl combine the olive oil and lemon juice. Whisk until smooth.
2. Add remaining ingredients and let stand for several hours to mellow flavors.

West Indies Barbeque Sauce

Makes 1½ cups

Make a double batch and try it on chicken.

1 onion, finely chopped
1 celery stalk, finely chopped
1 apple, peeled and chopped
¼ cup vegetable oil
3 tablespoons curry powder
2 cups chicken stock
3 medium tomatoes, peeled and chopped
salt and pepper
toasted cashews or almonds

1. Sauté the onion, celery and apple in the oil until soft.
2. Add the curry powder, chicken stock and tomatoes. Simmer for 30 minutes over low heat and season with salt and pepper. Serve with grilled fish and garnish with toasted cashews or almonds.

Salsa Fresca

Makes 3 to 4 cups

This salsa makes an excellent light topping for grilled swordfish, tuna, mahi-mahi, or any other firm fish.

5 large ripe tomatoes, diced
1 medium yellow onion, diced
¼ cup fresh coriander (cilantro), chopped
½ tablespoon salt
1 lemon, freshly squeezed
1 teaspoon cumin
1 fresh jalapeño, chopped fine

Must be made ahead.

1. Mix together all ingredients, let stand in refrigerator one day before serving.

Anchovy Dill Sauce

Makes 2 cups

**Spread over a whole poached fish
and garnish with additional herbs.**

½ cup watercress leaves
½ cup parsley sprigs
¼ cup fresh dill, chopped
¼ cup scallions, sliced
2 garlic cloves, minced
2 tablespoons lemon juice, freshly squeezed
4 anchovy fillets, chopped
½ teaspoon salt
¼ teaspoon black pepper
1 cup mayonnaise
½ cup sour cream or yogurt

Must be made ahead.

1. In the bowl of a food processor or blender, chop the watercress, parsley, dill, scallions, garlic, anchovies and lemon juice. Remove to a bowl and add the salt, pepper, mayonnaise and sour cream. Mix well and chill overnight before serving.

Black Olive Baste and Marinade

Makes 1 cup

A zesty marinade for any "steaked fish," such as swordfish, salmon, tuna and even steak steak! This makes an excellent quick sauce for pasta and is good to bring on board a boat to improvise other dishes.

1 12-ounce can of black pitted olives, drained
2 tablespoons fresh basil
2 tablespoons garlic, minced
olive oil, enough for a thin paste
  — add more for pasta

Must be made ahead.

1. Place all of the ingredients in the bowl of a food processor and blend until smooth but still chunky.

2. Spread top and bottom of fish steaks with the paste and marinate for several hours.

3. Either grill over charcoal or place in a baking dish and bake at 400° for 20 minutes until fish is firm.

For pasta:

1. Cook pasta and drain, add black olive paste and cooked seafood, such as scallops or shrimp, and diced cooked vegetables — mushrooms, sweet red pepper and zucchini.

2. Serve with lots of fresh grated Romano or Parmesan cheese.

Fourth of July Red Pepper Sauce   Makes 3 cups

Serve with a big platter of chilled shrimp.

3 7-ounce jars roasted red peppers, drained
   and rinsed
½ cup fresh mint
½ cup flat leaf Italian parsley
6 tablespoons lime juice, freshly squeezed
4 large garlic cloves
6 tablespoons corn oil

Must be made ahead.

1. Combine peppers, mint and parsley with
   lime juice and garlic in the bowl of a
   food processor and spin for 30 seconds.
2. Slowly drizzle in oil through feed tube
   and process until smooth.
3. Transfer to a bowl and refrigerate until
   ready to use.

Parmesan Cheese Topping   Makes 1 cup

Turns a weeknight fish dinner into something special.

½ cup Parmesan cheese, freshly grated
¼ cup butter
3 tablespoons mayonnaise
3 scallions, chopped
¼ teaspoon salt
dash hot pepper sauce

1. Mix all ingredients into a thick paste.
2. Broil any type fish fillets until almost done.
3. Spread topping ¼-inch thick over fillets.
4. Continue broiling until topping turns a
   light golden brown.

Mussel Power   Makes 1½ cups

You might never serve butter again.

2 shallots, minced
2 sweet dill pickles, chopped
1 small bunch of mixed fresh herbs
   (tarragon, parsley, chives chervil)
1 tablespoon capers, drained
1 tablespoon lemon juice, freshly squeezed
1 cup mayonnaise

Must be made ahead.

1. Combine all of the ingredients in a
   medium bowl and refrigerate at least
   4 hours or overnight, if possible.
2. Serve with a big pot of steamed mussels
   in the shell, hot or cold.

Orange Dill Vinaigrette

Makes 1 cup

**A great dressing for a salad of romaine lettuce and shrimp
or cold fish garnished with walnuts, orange and red pepper.**

½ cup orange juice, freshly squeezed
1½ teaspoons fresh dill, chopped
1 medium egg yolk
1½ teaspoons red wine vinegar
½ teaspoon orange peel, grated
2 tablespoons vegetable oil
dash salt and white pepper

1. In a saucepan, reduce the orange juice by half over medium heat, about 3 minutes. Cool.
2. In a bowl whisk egg yolk until creamy and add the vinegar, orange peel and dill.
3. Whisk in the orange juice and slowly add the oil. Season to taste with salt and pepper.

Yogurt Dill Sauce

Makes 1½ cups

Experiment with other fresh herb combinations.

⅔ cup yogurt
⅔ cup mayonnaise
2 tablespoons scallion, finely chopped
2 tablespoons parsley, finely chopped
1 tablespoon fresh dill, chopped
   or 1 teaspoon dry dill weed
salt and pepper to taste

1. Blend all ingredients and serve at room temperature over hot poached salmon, or chilled with a salmon salad.

Swedish Mustard Sauce

Makes 1 cup

Brush over fish fillets while grilling.

2 tablespoons brown prepared mustard
1 teaspoon dry mustard
¼ cup sugar
¼ cup vinegar
¾ cup salad oil
½ teaspoon salt
white pepper

1. In a small bowl whisk mustards, sugar and vinegar.
2. Gradually add oil, whisking constantly until sauce is creamy smooth and thickened. Season with salt and pepper to taste.
3. Cover and chill. Before serving, stir again to combine well.

Chinese Sweet and Spicy Sauce   Makes 2 cups

This makes a spicy marinade or basting sauce for swordfish or shrimp.

4 tablespoons soy sauce
¾ cup ketchup
¾ cup water
2 tablespoons vinegar
½ cup brown sugar
I onion, finely diced
I garlic clove, minced
I teaspoon ginger, grated

Must be made ahead.

1. Combine all ingredients and refrigerate overnight.
2. Besides using on swordfish or shrimp, this can be poured over a thick piece of cod or haddock and baked for 30 minutes.

The pan juices over white rice are heavenly.

Oma's Cocktail Sauce   Makes 1½ cups

Add yogurt or mayonnaise to this for a creamy summer salad dressing.

½ cup ketchup
½ cup chili sauce
I teaspoon black pepper, freshly ground
I teaspoon tarragon vinegar
I shallot, minced
¼ cup cream
I teaspoon horseradish

1. In a medium saucepan combine ketchup, chili sauce, pepper, tarragon, vinegar and shallot. Simmer over medium heat until bubbling.
2. In a small pan heat the cream gently. Whisk the hot cream very slowly into the sauce. Cool. Stir in the horseradish and chill until ready to use on any shrimp, lobster or avocado salad.

Quick n' Easy Clam Sauce   Makes 4 servings

3 tablespoon butter
I tablespoon garlic, minced
½ small onion, finely chopped
4 6½-ounce cans minced clams, do not drain
I tablespoon fresh parsley, chopped

1. Melt butter in a saucepan. Add the onion and sauté until translucent.
2. Add the garlic, clams and liquid. Heat until bubbling. Stir in the parsley. Serve over spaghetti or linguine.

No-Guilt Fish Topping

Add any fresh herbs to this sauce.

1 cup lowfat plain yogurt
2 tablespoons reduced calorie mayonnaise
1 tablespoon Dijon mustard
1 tablespoon lemon or lime juice,
   freshly squeezed

1. Combine all ingredients and spread over flounder or cod fillets. Bake at 375° for 10 to 15 minutes until fish is flaky and sauce creamy.

You may also spoon this sauce over a cold flaked fish salad as a low fat alternative to mayonnaise.

GO WiTH

Curried Apple Scallop

Serve hot or cold as a side dish with grilled fish or shrimp.

8 apples, peeled and sliced
2 tablespoons butter
½ cup honey
⅓ cup lemon juice, freshly squeezed
½ teaspoon curry powder
¼ teaspoon dry mustard
½ teaspoon salt
½ cup almonds, slivered

1. Melt the butter in a small saucepan. Add the honey, lemon juice, curry powder, dry mustard and salt. Combine well.
2. Arrange the sliced apples in a 2-quart baking dish. Pour the sauce overall and toss lightly to coat the apples. Sprinkle with almonds and bake for 40 minutes at 375°, basting apples with the juices several times.

Sherried Mushrooms and Artichokes Serves 6 to 8

Can be reheated quickly in a microwave oven.

4 tablespoons butter
2 9-ounce packages frozen artichoke hearts, thawed
1 pound mushrooms, sliced
¼ teaspoon thyme
½ teaspoon salt
¼ teaspoon black pepper, freshly ground
½ cup dry sherry

1. Melt the butter in a medium frying pan. Add the artichoke hearts and sauté for 3 minutes.
2. Stir in the mushrooms and continue cooking for 2 minutes. Season with thyme, salt and pepper. Add the sherry, increase heat and cook for 3 minutes. Do not overcook, the vegetables should still be tender.

Oysters are graded and sold in the following sizes: Standards — 30 to 40 to a pint; Selects — 26 to 30 to a pint; and Extra Selects — 21 to 26 to a pint. Shelf life in the refrigerator is 2 to 3 weeks. Shelf life of shucked oysters is 1 week.

Artichoke and Parmesan Struedel   Serves 12

2 9-ounce packages frozen artichoke hearts
1½ cups Ricotta or cottage cheese
1½ cups Parmesan cheese, freshly grated
3 eggs, beaten
½ cup scallions, minced
½ cup fresh breadcrumbs
¾ teaspoon tarragon
black pepper, freshly ground
1 pound phyllo pastry sheets
1 cup butter, melted

1. Simmer artichokes in lightly salted water for 3 minutes. Drain, pat dry and cut into small ½-inch pieces. Cool for 10 minutes.

2. In a medium bowl place the artichoke hearts, cheeses, eggs, scallions, breadcrumbs, tarragon and pepper, mix well.

3. Open phyllo pastry out on a work surface. Cut entire stack into 12x16-inch rectangle, if necessary. Working quickly, brush one phyllo sheet with butter (keep remaining sheets covered with a damp towel). Top with another phyllo sheet and brush with butter. Continue with 6 more sheets, making a total of 8 in the layer.

4. Mound 2 cups filling crosswise 3-inches from the edge. Leave a 1-inch border at each end. Fold the 3-inch border over the filling, fold both ends in and roll jelly roll style. Brush with butter.

5. Repeat with remaining phyllo and filling, forming 2 more rolls. Struedel may be made ahead and refrigerated up to 24 hours.

6. Arrange rolls, seam side down, on baking sheets leaving 6-inches between them. Brush again with butter and bake at 400° for 25 to 30 minutes. Cool 5 minutes before slicing.

If you don't need all three struedel, wrap them tightly and freeze, defrost thoroughly before baking.

Asparagus Parmesan

Serves 4

A do-ahead asparagus dish for an evening with guests.

1 pound fresh asparagus
2 tablespoons butter
½ cup scallions, chopped
2 tablespoons lemon juice, freshly squeezed
⅛ teaspoon dry mustard
½ cup mayonnaise
¼ teaspoon salt
⅛ teaspoon black pepper
½ cup breadcrumbs, buttered
⅓ cup Parmesan cheese, grated

1. Trim the tough ends off the asparagus. Drop into a pan of boiling, salted water and cook 3 to 4 minutes until tender-crisp. Drain and immediately rinse with cold water to retain color. Re-drain and lay stalks out in a 2-quart baking dish.

2. Heat butter and sauté scallions for one minute. Remove pan from heat and add lemon juice, dry mustard, mayonnaise and salt and pepper.

3. Pour mixture over asparagus spears and sprinkle bread crumbs overall. Top with cheese and bake 10 to 15 minutes or until brown.

Lemon Green Bean Salad

Serves 6

Arrange on a pretty platter and garnish with twists of lemon peel.

1 pound green beans, ends snipped
  but left whole
¼ cup olive oil
2 garlic cloves, finely minced
¼ cup red onion, chopped
¼ teaspoon thyme
¼ teaspoon salt
1 lemon, freshly squeezed and rind grated
black pepper

1. Cook the beans in lightly salted water for 5 to 7 minutes until tender-crisp. Drain and refresh with cold water to keep the beans nice and green.

2. In a shallow container, mix the remaining ingredients. Add the beans and toss well to coat. Cover and refrigerate for 3 or more hours until ready to serve, mixing several times to marinate.

Cuban Lima Bean Salad

Serves 6

2 8-ounce packages lima beans
1 red onion, thinly sliced
2 garlic cloves, minced
1 cup scallions, chopped
1 tomato, cubed
¾ cup pimento stuffed olives
4 tablespoons olive oil
2 tablespoons wine vinegar
2 teaspoons lemon juice
½ teaspoon each: thyme and oregano
½ teaspoon salt
black pepper, freshly ground

1. Cook lima beans for 3 to 4 minutes according to package directions until still firm. Refresh with cold water and drain.

2. Combine lima beans with onions, garlic, tomato and pimentoes. Pour olive oil, vinegar and lemon juice overall. Sprinkle with seasonings and gently toss until vegetables are well coated.

This improves the longer it refrigerates, so chill it at least 24 hours.

Tipsy Carrots

Serves 4

Carrots always look as though they belong with fish.

1 pound carrots, peeled and cut diagonally into "coins"
2 tablespoons butter
2 tablespoons honey
½ cup amber rum
⅛ teaspoon nutmeg
⅛ teaspoon cinnamon
salt and pepper

1. Cook the carrots for 8 minutes and drain well.

2. Add remaining ingredients and toss to coat the carrots. Pour into a hot serving dish.

Chilled Carrots and Yogurt

Serves 6

This makes an interesting side dish for a seafood curry or grilled fish steaks.

6 large carrots
½ cup scallions, finely chopped
¼ cup parsley, finely chopped
1 cup yogurt
1 teaspoon cumin
1 teaspoon sugar
½ teaspoon hot red pepper flakes

Must be made ahead.

1. Cut the carrots into very thin 1½-inch matchsticks. This can be done with the slicing blade in the food processor if you prefer.
2. In a mixing bowl, combine the carrots with the remaining ingredients. Chill for at least 24 hours, stirring a few times to combine flavors.

Company Carrots

Serves 6

Looks elegant, but is quick, inexpensive and easy.

1½ pounds carrots, cut into thin strips
½ cup mayonnaise
1 tablespoon onion, minced
1 tablespoon prepared horseradish
½ teaspoon salt
⅛ teaspoon black pepper
⅓ cup cracker crumbs, finely crushed
3 tablespoons butter
paprika
parsley, chopped

1. Cook the carrots in salted water for 8 to 10 minutes until fork tender. Drain and reserve ¼ cup cooking liquid. Arrange carrots in a 9-inch casserole dish or pie plate.
2. Combine reserved cooking liquid with mayonnaise, onion, horseradish, salt and pepper. Pour sauce over carrots.
3. Sprinkle cracker crumbs on top and dot with butter. Generously dust with paprika and bake for 20 minutes in a 375° oven. Sprinkle with parsley before serving.

Barbados Celery Purée

Serves 4

A pretty and light dish to serve with some of the oilier fish such as bluefish or mackerel.

6 large celery stalks with leaves, chopped
2 baking potatoes, peeled and cubed
1 tablespoon butter
½ cup heavy cream
1 tablespoon light rum
¼ teaspoon nutmeg
salt and pepper, freshly ground
parsley, chopped

1. In a medium saucepan of boiling water, cook the celery and potatoes for 20 minutes until tender. Drain.

2. Place vegetables in bowl of food processor or blender and pureé until smooth.

3. Place the pureé in a saucepan and stir in butter, cream, rum and nutmeg. Cook over low heat for 5 minutes, stirring frequently. Season with salt and pepper and sprinkle with chopped parsley.

Celestial Celery Casserole

Serves 8

How often we overlook the possibilities of a humble bunch of celery . . . a divine accompaniment with seafood.

4 cups celery, cut in ½-inch pieces
1 medium onion, chopped
1 cup sour cream
1 can cream of celery soup
1 8-ounce can water chestnuts, sliced
½ cup slivered almonds
salt and pepper
¾ cup herb stuffing mix
¼ cup Parmesan cheese
2 tablespoons butter

1. Place celery and onion in a medium saucepan and cover with water. Cook for 5 minutes and drain.

2. In a mixing bowl, combine the celery and onions with sour cream, soup, water chestnuts and almonds. Season to taste with salt and pepper, combine well.

3. Pour the mixture into a 1½-quart baking dish and top with crumbs and cheese. Dot the top with butter and bake at 350° for 30 minutes until bubbly and brown.

Haddock, hake, pollack, cusk and Boston bluefish are related to the codfish. They exhibit a firmer texture, sometimes with a grayish flesh.

Indian Corncakes

Makes 18

Pick up a few extra ears of corn at the farm and make these the next day.

2 cups corn kernels, cooked
⅓ cup flour
3 eggs
salt and pepper
2 tablespoons vegetable oil

1. In a food processor fitted with the steel blade or in a blender, coarsely chop the corn, add the flour and eggs. If you do this in the blender, you will need to do it in two batches. The mixture should be lumpy. Season to taste with salt and pepper.

2. In a heavy skillet heat 1 tablespoon oil over medium heat, and drop mixture into pan in 2½-inch rounds. Cook for a minute or two until undersides are golden. Turn and cook on the other side. Transfer cakes to a warm platter and repeat process using other tablespoon of oil and the rest of the batter.

Sunset Skillet Corn Dowdy

Serves 6

This also can be served as a luncheon dish with a green salad.

1 tablespoon butter
½ cup onion, finely minced
2 eggs
2 cups fresh corn, grated (8 ears)
2 tablespoons parsley, chopped
¼ cup sour cream
¾ teaspoon salt
pinch Cayenne pepper or few drops
   of hot pepper sauce
½ cup fresh white bread crumbs

1. Melt the butter in a small frying pan and sauté the onion until soft.

2. Beat the eggs in a mixing bowl and add the corn, parsley, sour cream, salt and pepper. Add the sautéed onions and combine well.

3. Butter a heavy bottomed 10-inch skillet, preferably with a non-stick coating. Pour in the batter, sprinkle with crumbs and cover. Cook over medium-low heat for 15 to 20 minutes until bottom has browned nicely and custard top has set. Place pan, uncovered, under a preheated broiler and brown the top lightly. Slide the corn dowdy onto a hot platter or serve right from the skillet.

Note: may be kept warm for 20 to 30 minutes before serving, also may be served cold.

Cheesy Eggplant Slices   Serves 4

Kids devour this and then ask, "What is it?"

1 large eggplant
1 egg
2 tablespoons vegetable oil
2 tablespoons milk
⅔ cup fine dry breadcrumbs
½ cup cheddar cheese, grated
¼ cup Parmesan cheese, grated
½ teaspoon salt
¾ teaspoon oregano
dash Cayenne pepper
3 tablespoons butter, melted

1. Peel eggplant and cut into ¼-inch slices. In a small bowl, beat egg with oil and milk.

2. Mix bread crumbs, cheeses, salt, oregano and Cayenne together. Dip eggplant slices into egg mixture, letting excess drip off, then dip into the crumb mixture.

3. Arrange slices on a greased baking sheet and drizzle with butter. Bake on the top shelf in a 450° oven for 8 to 10 minutes until tender and crispy.

Mary Nell's Mushroom Casserole   Serves 8

Make this ahead and pop it in the oven while dinner is grilling.

¾ pound mushrooms, sliced
½ cup green pepper, chopped
½ cup celery, chopped
½ cup onion, chopped
4 tablespoons butter
⅓ cup mayonnaise
¼ teaspoon salt
¼ teaspoon pepper
12 slices white bread, lightly buttered, cut into 1-inch squares (use a good, firm quality bread)
2 eggs
1½ cups milk
1 can cream of mushroom soup
½ cup cheddar cheese, grated

1. Melt the butter in a large frying pan and add mushrooms, green peppers, celery and onions. Sauté for 5 minutes until tender-crisp. Stir in the mayonnaise, salt and pepper.

2. Place half of the bread cubes in a 2-quart casserole, cover with the sautéed vegetables. Then cover the vegetables with half the remaining bread cubes.

3. Beat the eggs with the milk in a small bowl until foamy. Pour mixture over casserole. Finish with remaining bread and spread the mushroom soup evenly over the top. Bake at 300° for 1 hour. Sprinkle cheese on top and increase heat to 325°. Bake for 30 more minutes until browned.

Onion and Blue Cheese Melt

Serves 6

A delicious choice with grilled fish kebobs and rice.

3 large Bermuda onions, sliced
6 ounces blue cheese, crumbled
6 tablespoons butter
2 teaspoons Worcestershire sauce
½ teaspoon dill
black pepper

1. Arrange sliced onions in a buttered 9x13x2-inch baking dish. Sprinkle with crumbled cheese and dot with butter.
2. Drizzle Worcestershire sauce overall and sprinkle with dill and pepper. Bake for 20 minutes at 425° and place under a hot broiler for a minute to crisp the top.

Onion Kuchen

Serves 4 to 6

Take this along to a picnic, and it is usually gone *before* dinner.

2 medium onions, peeled, sliced, and cut into rings
3 tablespoons butter
1 10 roll package refrigerated buttermilk or homestyle biscuits
1 egg
1 8-ounce package sour cream
½ teaspoon salt
pinch of black pepper
1 teaspoon poppy seeds

1. Melt the butter in a medium frying pan and sauté onions until just soft.
2. Separate the biscuits, place in a single layer in an ungreased 8-inch layer cake or square baking pan. Press together to cover bottom completely. Spoon the onion mixture over the biscuits.
3. Beat the egg in a small bowl and blend in the sour cream, salt and pepper. Pour over the onions and spread evenly. Sprinkle with poppy seeds and bake for 30 minutes in a 375° oven or until topping is set. Slice into wedges and serve warm or cold.

Basil Stuffed Sweet Peppers   Serves 6 to 8

**Alternate colors on the serving platter and garnish
with more fresh basil.**

2 large green peppers
2 large red peppers
3 cups cooked white or brown rice
½ cup scallions, finely chopped
½ cup basil leaves, finely chopped
4 tablespoons black olives, chopped
2 teaspoons lemon juice
½ cup olive oil
¼ cup pine nuts

1. Cut peppers in half lengthwise and discard the seeds.
2. Mix together the rice, scallions, basil, olives, lemon juice and olive oil. Fill the peppers with the mixture and place them in a shallow ovenproof casserole.
3. Pour a little olive oil over the rice and around each pepper. Sprinkle with pine nuts. Cover with aluminum foil and bake in a 350° oven for 30 minutes until peppers are soft.

Double Baked Potatoes Liederkrantz   Serves 10 to 12

**If serving a simple grilled fresh fish, the smoky flavor of this cheese
will liven up your taste buds.**

6 large Idaho potatoes, baked
4 tablespoons butter
½ cup light cream
½ cup scallions, chopped
1 teaspoon chives, chopped
1 teaspoon tarragon
1 4-ounce package Liederkrantz, softened
½ cup bread crumbs
melted butter

1. Cut potatoes in half lengthwise and scoop out the flesh into a mixing bowl. Mash with 4 tablespoons butter, cream and scallions.
2. Season with tarragon and chives. Do not be tempted to add salt, the cheese will add enough flavor.
3. Mash in the softened cheese and combine well. Refill the potato shells, sprinkle with crumbs and drizzle with butter. Bake at 425° for 15 minutes until crusty.

Zesty New Potatoes

Serves 6

1½ pounds new potatoes
½ cup butter
½ cup scallions, finely chopped
1 tablespoon prepared horseradish
½ teaspoon dried dill
⅛ teaspoon black pepper, freshly ground

1. Wash the potatoes and place in a large pot of water. Bring to a boil and cook for 20 to 25 minutes until tender but slightly firm.
2. While potatoes are cooking, melt the butter in a small saucepan. Add the scallions, horseradish, dill and pepper. Simmer for 1 minute.
3. Place the potatoes in a heated serving bowl and pour butter over the top. Toss gently to coat.

Hässelback Potatoes

Serves 6

These are a specialty of the Hässel Backen Restaurant in Stockholm, Sweden. Baked potatoes with a difference.

6 medium baking potatoes, peeled
6 tablespoons butter
salt and black pepper, freshly ground
½ cup seasoned bread crumbs or homemade
4 tablespoons Parmesan cheese, grated

1. Slice the potatoes in half lengthwise and then in thirds across, curved side up. With a very sharp knife cut each piece in thin slices, cutting almost through to the bottom. The pieces should look fan-like.
2. Place potato slices, curved side up in a buttered 8x10-inch baking pan. Drizzle with 3 tablespoons of the melted butter and with salt and pepper. Sprinkle crumbs on top and bake for 20 minutes at 425°.
3. Sprinkle potatoes with grated cheese and drizzle with remaining 3 tablespoons of butter. Bake for 10 to 15 minutes longer, until potatoes are crisp and tender. Remove from pan with a spatula and serve immediately.

There will never by any leftovers, guaranteed.

Horseradish Potato Salad

Serves 8

An excellent change from the standard mayonnaise variety of salad.

2 pounds small red new potatoes
2 teaspoons sugar
½ teaspoon salt
½ teaspoon dry mustard
4 teaspoons fresh horseradish
4 tablespoons vinegar
2 celery stalks with tops, chopped
I small red onion, chopped
2 cups sour cream
black pepper, freshly ground
2 tablespoons fresh dill or chives, snipped

Must be made ahead.

1. Boil potatoes in their skins for 20 to 25 minutes until tender but still firm when pierced with a fork. Cool and slice into a salad bowl.

2. In another bowl, mix the sugar, salt, dry mustard, horseradish and vinegar. Stir in the sour cream.

3. Add the celery and red onion to the salad bowl with the potatoes. Pour the dressing over the potatoes and gently toss until vegetables are coated. Grind black pepper overall and sprinkle with dill or chives. Chill and serve.

Scalloped Mushrooms and Potatoes

Serves 6

A family tradition with holiday salmon.

4 large potatoes
I pound mushrooms
½ teaspoon salt
¼ teaspoon black pepper, freshly ground
1½ tablespoons dried basil
¾ cup heavy cream
¼ cup Parmesan cheese, grated
4 tablespoons butter

1. Peel potatoes and slice them very thinly. Slice mushrooms ⅛-inch thick.

2. Line a 2½-quart buttered casserole with a layer of potatoes. Add a layer of mushrooms and sprinkle with some of the salt, pepper, basil and cream. Repeat layers until all of these ingredients have been used.

3. Sprinkle the top layer with Parmesan cheese and dot with butter. Cover dish with aluminum foil and bake at 350° for 30 minutes. Remove foil and bake for another I5 minutes until the potatoes are tender and the cheese is browned.

Salmon was once so plentiful in Ireland that the contract for indentured servants forbade the serving of salmon to them more than three times a week.

Island Rice

Serves 4

Toss with some cooked shrimp and voila, dinner!

1 small red pepper, chopped
1 carrot, chopped
½ medium onion, chopped
1 cup rice
1 tablespoon curry powder
1 teaspoon allspice
½ teaspoon salt
1¾ cups water
2 tablespoons butter

1. Place all ingredients in a 1½-quart casserole dish. Mix well and cover.
2. Bake at 375° for 30 minutes. Fluff with a fork and serve.

California Rice Casserole

Serves 10

A terra cotta casserole makes an attractive serving dish.

¼ cup butter
1 cup onion, chopped
4 cups white rice, freshly cooked
1 16-ounce container sour cream
1 cup cream-style cottage cheese
1 bay leaf, crumbled
½ teaspoon salt
⅛ teaspoon pepper
3 4-ounce cans medium green chilies, drained and cut into strips
2 cups sharp cheddar cheese, grated
fresh parsley, chopped

1. Melt the butter in a skillet and sauté the onion for 5 minutes until golden. Transfer to a large mixing bowl and add the hot rice, sour cream, cottage cheese, bay leaf, salt and pepper. Toss lightly to mix well.
2. Layer half the rice mixture in the bottom of a buttered 8x12x2-inch baking dish. Spread out half of the chilies and half the cheese. Repeat with another layer using remaining ingredients in the same order. Bake uncovered at 375° for 25 minutes until bubbly and hot. Sprinkle with parsley before serving.

Rice preparation (for 4 cups fluffy rice):
1. Bring 2½ cups water to a boil.
2. Add 1 cup converted rice and 1 teaspoon salt. Cover tightly and cook over low heat for 25 minutes until all water is absorbed.

Brown Rice with Two Cheeses   Serves 6

A nutty combination of flavors.

2 tablespoons butter
¼ cup oil
½ cups scallions, chopped
2¼ cups brown rice
6 cups chicken stock
½ teaspoon salt
½ teaspoon pepper, freshly cracked
¾ cup Swiss cheese, grated
¾ cup cheddar cheese, grated

1. Heat the butter and oil in a medium saucepan. Add the scallions and sauté for 3 minutes.
2. Wash and drain the rice. Add it to the pan and fry, stirring constantly for 5 minutes.
3. Add the stock, salt and pepper. Stir, cover and simmer for 45 minutes. When rice is cooked, stir in the Swiss cheese. Place in a buttered casserole and sprinkle with cheddar cheese. Bake in a hot 425° oven until cheese melts and turns golden brown.

Fire and Ice Tomatoes   Serves 8

Color, texture and flavor

6 medium tomatoes, peeled and quartered
1 large green pepper, sliced into thin rings
1 large red onion, sliced into thin rings
½ cup red wine vinegar
1 teaspoon celery salt
1½ teaspoons mustard seed
5 teaspoons sugar
⅛ teaspoon Cayenne pepper
⅛ teaspoon black pepper, freshly ground
¼ cup water
1 large cucumber, peeled and sliced
parsley, freshly chopped

Requires some advance preparation.

1. Layer tomatoes, green pepper and onion alternately in a bowl. Clear glass looks especially nice.
2. Make the dressing by mixing vinegar, seasonings and water in a saucepan. Bring mixture to a boil and cook for 1 minute. While hot, pour evenly over the vegetables. Let cool, cover tightly and refrigerate.
3. Just before serving add the cucumber to the bowl and spoon some of the dressing on top. Sprinkle generously with parsley. This will keep several days refrigerated, without adding the cucumbers.

233

Baked Tomatoes with Spinach   Serves 6 to 8

These go well with a casserole buffet-style dinner.

4 large tomatoes
salt and pepper
1 10-ounce package frozen chopped
    spinach, thawed and squeezed dry
8 tablespoons butter
1 garlic clove, minced
1 tablespoon shallot, minced
2 tablespoons parsley, chopped
½ cup Parmesan cheese, grated
¼ cup bread crumbs

1. Cut the tomatoes in half. With a teaspoon, scrape out the seeds and center core, leaving the shell. Sprinkle with salt and pepper. Fill each tomato half with chopped spinach.

2. In a small bowl, cream the butter, garlic, shallots and parsley until soft. Spread a tablespoon of the butter mixture on each tomato. Place in a shallow baking dish.

3. Combine Parmesan cheese with bread crumbs and sprinkle on top. Bake at 375° for 20 minutes until browned.

Chinese Tomatoes   Serves 4

These spicy tomatoes are addictive.

4 medium firm tomatoes
1 tablespoon sesame oil
1 tablespoon vegetable oil
1 tablespoon fresh ginger, minced
½ teaspoon sugar
pinch of salt
⅓ cup scallions, chopped

1. Set a wok or large frying pan over high heat. When hot, add the oils.

2. Add the ginger and sizzle for 5 seconds. Add the tomatoes and stir fry them gently but quickly until heated with oil and heated through.

3. Sprinkle tomatoes with sugar and salt. Mix well, toss with the scallions and serve.

Once you open a can of defrosted lobster or crabmeat, it essentially should be treated as fresh and used within 3 days of opening.

Zucchini Pancakes

Serves 6

Something different to do with "all of that August zucchini."

1 pound zucchini, shredded (4 cups)
½ cup cheddar cheese, grated
¾ cup packaged pancake mix
¼ teaspoon salt
¼ teaspoon black pepper
½ cup milk
1 egg, beaten
¼ cup onion, chopped
sour cream
paprika

1. Place shredded zucchini in a colander to drain off excess liquid.

2. In a medium bowl, combine cheese, pancake mix, salt, pepper, milk and beaten egg. Mix to moisten.

3. Stir in zucchini and onion, chopped. Drop by teaspoons onto a hot, lightly greased skillet. Cook over low heat until pancakes are browned and bubbles appear on the surface.

4. Turn and brown other side. Transfer to a platter and spoon a dollop of sour cream on each pancake and sprinkle with paprika.

Warm Walnut and Prosciutto Salad   Serves 6

Add a sliced apple or pear for a little more contrast.

½ cup walnut halves
1 head garden lettuce, bibb or red leaf
4 large Belgian endives, cut into 2-inch matchsticks
2 ounces prosciutto, thinly sliced and cut into strips
¼ cup red wine vinegar
½ cup vegetable oil
¼ cup olive oil
salt and pepper to taste

1. Place the walnuts on a small baking sheet and toast for 10 minutes in a 350° oven until browned. Check after 5 minutes and move them around in the pan to cook evenly.

2. Place the torn lettuce and endive in a salad bowl and sprinkle with the prosciutto and walnuts.

3. In a small saucepan, combine the vinegar, oils, salt and pepper. Over medium heat, bring to a boil. Pour the hot dressing over the salad and toss well.

This must be served immediately so gauge the rest of your meal accordingly.

Cheese Colcannon

Serves 6 to 8

Bake this right along with your haddock or scrod.

1 medium head green cabbage
4 large potatoes, peeled and cubed
½ cup cream
¼ cup butter
½ cup scallions, finely chopped
1 teaspoon salt
½ teaspoon black pepper, freshly ground
¼ teaspoon nutmeg
1 cup sharp cheddar cheese, grated
2 tablespoons butter

1. Finely shred the cabbage and place in a large pan with one cup of boiling water. Cover and cook for 10 minutes until tender-crisp. Drain.
2. Cook the potatoes in boiling water for 8 to 10 minutes until soft. Drain and place in a large bowl with the cooked cabbage.
3. Mash the mixture with the cream and butter adding more of each if needed. The mixture should be lumpy.
4. Add the scallions, salt, pepper, nutmeg and ¾ cup of the grated cheese and mix well. Turn into a buttered 2-quart casserole and sprinkle with remaining ¼ cup cheese. Dot with additional butter and bake at 450° for 15 minutes until golden.

Fiesta Bread

This can be cooked directly on a grill if you are picnicking.

1 large or 2 small loaves French or Italian bread
¼ cup butter, softened
1 cup cheddar cheese, grated
½ cup ketchup
⅓ cup ripe olives, chopped
½ cup green pepper, chopped
½ cup onion, chopped

1. Split the bread lengthwise in half. Mix all of the ingredients thoroughly and spread each half with the butter mixture.
2. Wrap each half in foil and bake for 15 to 20 minutes at 400°. Unwrap, cut into wedges and serve hot.

Golden Gate Snack Bread

Makes 2 large loaves

One pass around the table and a basket of this disappears like magic.

Dough:

2 packages active dry yeast
1 cup warm water
4 to 4½ cups flour, sifted
1 8-ounce jar Cheese Whiz
2 tablespoons sugar
2 tablespoons butter
1 teaspoon salt

1. Soften yeast in water in a large bowl. Add 2 cups of flour, Cheese Whiz, sugar, butter and salt. Beat with a mixer for 2 minutes at medium speed. By hand, add the remaining flour until dough is stiff.

2. Cover and let rise in a warm place until dough is light and doubled in size, about 30 minutes.

3. Roll out dough on a lightly floured workspace to 20x14-inches. Spread the filling (see below) evenly over the dough and roll up jelly roll fashion, starting with the 14-inch side. Seal edges and ends.

4. Using a sharp knife or scissors, make a lengthwise cut down the center to form two loaves. Place, cut side up, on a greased baking sheet. Cover, let rise in a warm place for about 45 minutes, until light. Bake at 350° for 25 to 30 minutes. Serve hot, cut into slices, or freeze and reheat, wrapped in foil.

Filling:

½ cup butter, softened
1 packet dry onion soup mix

Onion Filling preparation:

Combine ½ cup softened butter with 1 packet of dry onion soup mix, blend well.

Seaport Mom's Treasured Blueberry Pie

A perfect ending to a meal and our _Seaport Seafood Secrets_ . . . .

1 baked 9-inch pie crust
3 cups blueberries
¾ cup water, plus 2 tablespoons
3 tablespoons cornstarch
¾ cup Chambord or raspberry liqueur
⅓ cup raspberry jam
whipped cream
1½ cups sugar

Must be made ahead.

1. Place 1½ cups of the blueberries, sugar and ¾ cup of water in a saucepan, bring to a boil.
2. Mix the cornstarch with the 2 tablespoons of water and add to the blueberry mixture along with the Chambord. Cook over moderate heat, stirring gently for 2 to 3 minutes until thick and clear.
3. Remove pan from the heat and cool for 15 minutes. Fold in the remaining 1½ cups blueberries.
4. Spread the jam evenly over the crust and pour in the blueberry mixture. Chill for several hours before serving. Pass the whipped cream after slicing the pie.

INDEX

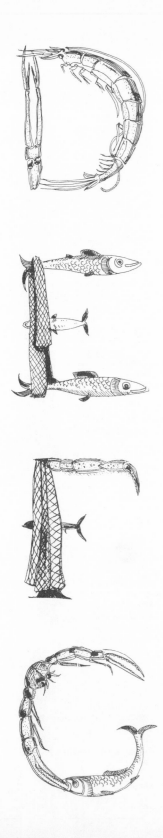

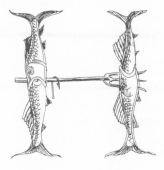

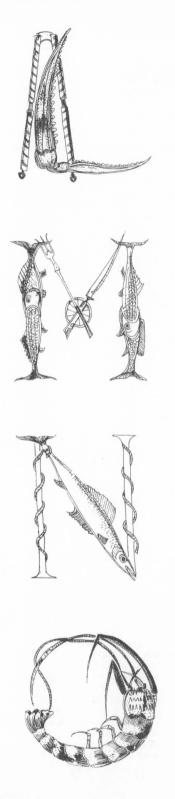

NOTES

Also Available:

Christmas Memories Cookbook

A collection of outstanding Holiday suggestions inspired by the private recipe files of the Members of the Mystic Seaport Museum. 350 refreshing ideas for festive year-round entertaining and personal gift giving. You will discover a rich array of imaginative variations on classic New England cooking; based on the lasting traditions of Victorian festivities. Delightfully illustrated by artist Lynn Anderson, with additional pages for recording your own memorable Family Recipes and Christmas Menus. The *Christmas Memories Cookbook* is an excellent resource for both the beginner and the adventurous cook.

In just 4 years of print, 50,000 copies have been sold.

It includes such distinctive fare as: • Block Island Turkey • Chocolate Mousse in Hazelnut Meringue • Gingerbread Muffins with Smoked Turkey • Cranberry Almond Coffee Cake

THE MYSTIC SEAPORT ALL SEASONS COOKBOOK

New Englanders have an old saying about their weather: if you don't like it, wait a minute! While the weather doesn't always change *quite* that fast, each of the four seasons puts its own distinctive stamp on New England's climate, lifestyle, and the availability of many foods. How do New England cooks plan around such radical changes? *The Mystic Seaport All Seasons Cookbook* gives an exciting glimpse into seasonal meal preparation adapted to the ever-changing weather patterns of the regional northeast. This outstanding collection of more than 400 recipes comes to you from the private recipe files of the Members of the Mystic Seaport Museum; creativity runs the gamut from the typical pack-and-go fare of the summer months, when many New Englanders take to the water, to the fortifying soups and stews savored by a winter's fire. Imaginatively illustrated by noted New England artist Sally Caldwell Fisher, the cookbook is filled with tips, culinary lore, and a treasury of recipes pertaining specifically to each season.

Inside you will find: • Asparagus with Orange Butter Sauce • Strawberry Watercress Salad • Beach Plum Jelly • Maine Black and Blue Pie • Johnnycakes • Pork Chops with Pumpkin Sauce • Rosemary Cream Chicken • Boursin Quiche Tartlets • and many more.

HOLIDAY COOKBOOK for Kids

We all know that "Holiday" really means "Food" and here for the first time, is a collection of holiday recipes kids can cook by themselves (or with a little help from a grown-up). Illustrated step-by-step instructions guide kids through the preparation of both gourmet and "homestyle" main dishes, desserts, snacks and salads. The origins of each of 14 major holidays and how each was celebrated in the "olden days" is presented in the delightful, living history manner for which Mystic Seaport is famous.

Kids of all ages will enjoy cooking and eating:

• Queen-of-Heart's Tarts • Hurry-Up Fruit Salad • 3rd of July Layered Salad • Chocolate Spiders • Holiday Potato Bake • Lazy Lasagna • *and much more!*

Credit Card Telephone Orders • Call Toll Free (800) 331·BOOK • in Conn. (203) 572-8551
Mail Orders: Mystic Seaport Museum Stores • Bookstore • Mystic, CT 06355

- -

ORDER BLANK
Mystic Seaport Museum Stores • Mystic, CT 06355

Please send me:

_____copies of *Mystic Seaport's Seafood Secrets*
        Cookbook   @ $14.95 ea._____
_____copies of *Mystic Seaport All Seasons*
        Cookbook   @ $14.95 ea._____
_____copies of *Christmas Memories Cookbook*
                    @ $14.95 ea._____
_____copies of *Holiday Cookbook for Kids*
                    @ $12.95 ea._____

           Packing and shipping: $4.00

                  Total: _____

Ordered by:

Name_____

Address_____

City _____ State _____ Zip _____

☐ Check ☐ VISA ☐ AMEX ☐ MC Exp. Date _____

Credit Card No. [ ][ ][ ][ ][ ][ ][ ][ ][ ][ ][ ][ ][ ][ ][ ][ ]

Signature _____